TERROR OF THE
AUTUMN SKIES

TERROR OF THE AUTUMN SKIES

BLAINE L. PARDOE

Skyhorse Publishing

Skyhorse Publishing books may be purchased in bulk at special discounts for sales promotion, corporate gifts, fund raising, or educational purposes. Special editions can also be created to specifications. For details, contact Special Sales Department, Skyhorse Publishing, 555 Eighth Avenue, Suite 903, New York, NY 10018 or info@ skyhorsepublishing.com.

www.skyhorsepublishing.com

10 9 8 7 6 5 4 3 2 1

ISBN-13: 978-1-60239-252-6

Library of Congress Cataloging-in-Publication Data

Pardoe, Blaine Lee, 1962–
    Terror of the autumn skies: the story of Frank Luke, America's rogue ace of World War I/Blaine Pardoe.
        p. cm.
    Includes bibliographical references.
    1. Luke, Frank, 1897–1918. 2. United States. Army. Air Service. Pursuit Group, 1st. 3. World War, 1914–1918—Aerial operations, American.
    4. World War, 1914–1918—Regimental histories—United States.
    5. World War, 1914–1918—Campaigns—Western Front. 6. Fighter pilots—United States—Biography. I. Title.

D606.L9P37 2008
940.4'4973092—dc22
[B]
                                                2007052426

Printed in the United States of America

"Luke lived and died in the spirit of fearlessness. He was the very embodiment of surging victory, a personality that stood aside and apart for all recognized army procedure or law—a creative individual whose very presence lifted his fellow men from the depths of despair to a confidence and forbearance that could not be denied."

—EDDIE RICKENBACKER

This book is dedicated to the memory of the following people that have flown off into the setting sun of the western horizon, where all pilots and their lovers go when they die:
Frank Luke, Jr., AEF
Marie Rapson-Jackson
Ivan A. Roberts, AEF
Joseph F. Wehner, AEF
Frederick Zinn, AEF
Donald Jackson, USN

And to:
My wife Cynthia, my son Alexander, and my daughter Victoria
Douglas Jackson and the extended Jackson family, descendants of
Marie Rapson
John Luke
And, of course, Jean Armstrong

Contents

Acknowledgments ix
Prologue xiii

1. First Blood 1
2. The Wild Boy 13
3. Fly with the Eagles 29
4. Into the Air 43
5. The American Expeditionary Force 53
6. The Front 71
7. Busting Balloons 87
8. Fire in the Sky 99
9. The Dynamic Duo 107
10. Roar in the Skies 117
11. Recognition 127
12. The Darkest of Times 133
13. In the Limelight 141
14. Ivan the Missing 151
15. Crescendo 161
16. "Watch for burning balloons ahead..." 165
17. Into the Setting Sun 173
18. When Time Stood Still 181
19. One Man, Many Lives 195
20. The Stuff of Legends 207

Afterword 225
Bibliography 247
Notes to Chapters 267
About the Author 301

Acknowledgments

An enlisted man who served with the 27th at that time had this to add: "Frank was a loner, you know. He didn't have much to do with the other pilots. But we got along. He was all right. Boy, could he shoot! I've seen him come down that road on a motorcycle with a Colt .45 in each hand, shooting at the trees. Hitting them too. All he ever wanted to do was shoot—pistols, rifles, anything. He never flew back with any shells left; he shot them all at something or other on the other side—'anything that moved' he used to say."

—LEN MORGAN AND R.P. SHANNON, *FAMOUS AIRCRAFT: THE PLANES THE ACES FLEW, VOL. I.*

This book took years of research and the contributions of dozens of people to pull together. The words you are going to read are those of the actual people, culled from letters and interviews. Their stories are as truthful as can be validated. I want you, the reader, to experience the life of this young man and the men and women around him. Any errors are unintentional.

This book would not have been possible without the efforts of a number of people. Those that deserve the greatest recognition include:

Jean Armstrong, who gave me a new perspective on research, digging through the genealogy tied to the people who were part of this story.

Tim King, keeper of the faith who is working on a Frank Luke documentary.

Walter Kloss, who is the steward of the Wehner family archives.

Andy Parks of the Lafayette Foundation, easily one of the greatest historic resources on WWI aviation.

Mitch Yockelson at the US National Archives Administration, who helped me wade through both the U.S. and German records.

Jon Guttman, a walking encyclopedia of WWI aviation and author of countless articles and books. Jon took it upon himself, on his own time, to help me with the technical editing of this book for which I am grateful. Any mistakes in here are purely the author's, not his.

Rick Duiven, whose work in the German records was invaluable.

Douglas L. Jackson, son of Marie Rapson-Jackson. His willingness to share his family's records and photographs was an important part of this book.

John Luke, the nephew of Frank Luke, Jr., for helping me keep Frank in perspective.

One source I came to know well was Charme Kirby. Charme was the wife of Lt. Commander Jackson, Marie's son. As a daughter in-law of Marie Rapson-Jackson, she was able to provide me with wonderful insights into Marie as a person.

Nancy Sawyer, Archivist at the Arizona State Library, Archives and Public Records. Nancy is one of those special archivists that goes above and beyond in helping you find material. Her assistance in the Arizona archives helped add quality to this book.

Other individuals who were of great assistance include:

Suzanne McNamara, a Senior Library Assistant at the Department of Archives and Special Collections at Arizona State University.

Ellen Thomasson, Missouri Historical Society.

Mrs. Lynn Gamma, HQ AFHRA/RSA.

George Livingston, Local and Family History Librarian, Willard Library, Battle Creek, Michigan.

Arthur W. Bergeron, Jr., Ph.D., U. S. Army Military History Institute.

James H. Kitchens, III, Ph.D., Archivist, Maxwell AFB.

Leslie Couture, Denton Public Library System, Emily Fowler Library, Genealogy/Special Collections.

Mary Elizabeth Ruwell, Ph.D. Academy Archivist and Chief, Special Collections, HQ USAF/DFLIB.

Jim Turner, Arizona Historical Society.

Michael F. Milewski, Senior Archives Assistant, University of Massachusetts, W. E. B. Du Bois Library. His unearthing of material on Ivan Roberts was timely and highly useful.

Cory Graff, Assistant Curator, Dahlberg Center for Military Aviation History, Museum of Flight, Seattle, Washington. Cory helped unearth some wonderful pieces of Joe Wehner material.

Georgia A. Massucco, Library Director, Lee Library Association.

Ed Desrochers, Archivist, Phillips Exeter Academy.

Dr. Hans-Christian Pust, Leiter der Bibliothek für Zeitgeschichte, Württembergische Landesbibliothek Stuttgart.

Alan Renga, Assistant Archivist, San Diego Aerospace Museum.

Stephen Twigge, Remote Enquiries Duty Officer, National Archives of the United Kingdom.

Colonel Leonid Kondratiuk, Massachusetts National Guard Museum Archives, WWI Records.

Scott Anderson, Assistant Archivist, Sharlot Hall Museum.

Alfred and Katrin Colombo, who assisted greatly with the translation of the Prussian 5th Army Records.

Ralph Edy, friend of the Luke family and aviation historian.

Ms. Beverly Lyall, Archives Technician, Department of the Navy, U.S. Naval Academy Special Collections and Archives Division.

Rell Francis, DUH Museum, for help on the engagement at Springville.

Ann-Marie Harris, Senior Technician, Berkshire Athenaeum.

Bob Blunt Burke.

My daughter Victoria and my son Alex, who retyped German documents to assist in the translation process.

Doris Dickinson, Archivist, Stone House Museum, Belchertown Historical Association, Belchertown, Massachusetts.

Sebastian Remus, a German historical researcher. Sebastian helped me find the copies of the Prussian Army, Air, and Ballonzug records in the most unusual of places—the U.S. National Archives. The U.S. Army War College decided in the 1920s to write an official U.S. Army account of the Great War. A small team of researchers went to Germany and got access to the archives where they retyped all of the orders and combat records for those units engaged against America in the war. In an age before copy machines, retyping the records was the only way to get a copy of them sent home. Maps were retraced by hand as well. During World War II, the records in Germany were destroyed, both the archives and the additional material that Göring had shipped to his estate in Potsdam. When I had contacted Sebastian for assistance, he told me that very little was left in Germany, but that I might be closer to the records than he was. As it was, he was right. Thanks to some assistance from Mitch Yockelson of the National Archives, for the first time, these records can be brought to bear on the stories of Frank Luke, Ivan Roberts, and Joseph Wehner.

Finally, my wife Cynthia, who stood by me throughout the writing of this book.

Prologue

"His career during the World War was short, but in the time he served he emblazoned his name upon the pages of our history with a trail of accomplishments. For a time he seemed to be immune from danger. It was as if an allotted time had been given to perform this great service for his country. With almost superhuman strength he fought against the enemy until even they looked in awe upon this youth who knew no fear. Brought to earth, he took his last stand, pistol in hand, and fought single-handed for his life which was lost against overwhelming odds."

—ARIZONA GOVERNOR JOHN CALHOUN PHILLIPS.[1]

His name was Frank Luke, Jr., and for a brief time he was the greatest fighter ace America had ever produced. His life was made of the same stuff as great Westerns. His death captivated people. He flew balls-to-the-wall, and took on the most dangerous air missions of the war: destroying heavily-armed observation balloons. He flew his planes through such punishing enemy fire that five of them were written off after his combat missions.

Frank flew at a time when the airplane was new, when they were still made of canvas and spruce and could literally be flown to pieces if they were dived too quickly or turned too sharply. Just flying a plane required an incredible amount of coordination and physical endurance. His gas tank was wedged under his armpit, and he had to pump it by hand while he handled the stick and foot pedals. He flew at mind-numbingly cold altitudes in an open cockpit with no oxygen.

The battles he fought were savage affairs of machine guns at point blank, flesh-ripping range. Airplane machine guns had to be fired in short bursts or they would jam, leaving a pilot defenseless. Ground-based anti-aircraft fire tore at the skies around Luke when he went after his balloon-targets. The fragile airplane wrapped around him had no armor, in fact, no protection at all. He wore no parachute. Any tiny fragment of hot shrapnel could turn his airplane into a roaring bundle of kindling or send it spiraling into the savage no-man's land of the front. The same piece of shell could rip through a pilot as well, leaving him to a cold and painful death. A bullet in the underarm gas tank would mean a brilliant ball of flames and a plummet to earth.

Nor was it a glamorous war for those on the ground. The war unleashed poison gas, flamethrowers, rapid-fire artillery, and countless other forms of death and destruction. In the American public psyche, it was a short little war, one that the United States arrived at near the end. The only images that were remembered fondly were those of the fighter pilots and aces. The brutal war fought in the trenches has largely faded from the memory of the American people.

The aviators of the Great War, World War I, stood out because they defined heroics. They became icons for a generation of our youth. Their planes bore the marks of their countries, their squadrons, their own coats of arms, and those of their brother knights of the air. And to be "the best of the best," "the Ace of Aces," was a new and rare distinction. It was a title that few had the honor to bear—a title that Frank Luke carried for a few short days in the early autumn of 1918. In that hot final fall of war the legend of American air power was born, bred out of the sweat and sheer determination of men like him fighting in the twilight skies.

Luke defined generations of fighter combat jocks. His style was overly aggressive and annoyed more conservative pilots. He approached his balloon busting battles with a bravado that today is still recognizable among fighter pilots.

Far too many people have tried to define Frank by how he died rather than by how he lived. The myth of his final mission is alluring, and it seems to personify Frank for many people. Having lost his wingman and best friend, he was grounded by direct order, but went up anyway, flying for the German line for a final, furious battle. Some have guessed that Frank was angry and bitter and was taking out his vengeance on the Germans. Others have surmised that it was his defiance of authority and his commanding officer, Alfred Grant, that drove him into the air that day.

Grant summed it up best when he took off in pursuit of Luke and was asked what he was going to do: "… I'm going to recommend him for the Distinguished Service Cross. Then, by God, I'm going to court martial him!"[2]

The image of the last of the men from the Old West pulling out his pistol and fighting it out with a horde of the enemy, just before succumbing to his own wounds, reminds one of the last stand of the defenders of the Alamo. It is an image that embodies what we all think of Westerners, the last cowboys. His last few minutes in Murvaux have been misrepresented, misunderstood, and exaggerated.

We want our heroes to be larger than life, and American heroes need to be larger still—they have to be symbols for the rest of the world to admire. While the myth of Frank's death is engaging, the true story is far more compelling. To examine his death and attempt to use that as a template for his life would be a mistake. The *real* story of who Frank Luke, Jr., was goes beyond the skies over the battlefields of France.

Ninety men received the Congressional Medal of Honor, many decades after the war as political favors or gestures. Only four of those men were pilots. The Medal of Honor is a distinction that is unique among the armed forces in the United States. Only the best of our men and women receive it. It is so prestigious that it is the only military decoration protected by federal law. It is so sacred that it is a federal felony to wear or sell a Medal of Honor if you were not the recipient. It is the highest award our country can bestow on a person for courage, honor, and bravery.

Lieutenant Frank Luke, Jr., was not *just* one of the four Army Air Service aviators to win the medal. He was the *first* pilot to receive that honor.[3] He received the Medal of Honor decades before the more widely known Captain Eddie Rickenbacker. Most people who know any American First World War pilots know one name: Eddie Rickenbacker, the top ranking American ace of the war. His was the name that history chose to etch in our collective consciousness as the pilot worthy of our memories. Rickenbacker knew Frank Luke personally. "Had he lived he would have put me out of business long ago as America's leading ace. I wouldn't have had a show against him."[4] Rickenbacker is remembered as America's "Ace of Aces". But there were a few days in the early autumn of 1918 when Frank Luke held that title. That September, Eddie Rickenbacker was number two to a young stallion, a maverick pilot who captivated a nation—if only for a few days. Rickenbacker merely inherited the title from Frank.

Frank was a celebrity nationwide; his face and story were front-page news. Men admired his daring. Women wanted to know this dashing blond-haired maverick who flew his airplane as if it were a wild mustang. He was a German-American with something to prove. The war cost Frank more than his life. He lost his best friend—and with the death of his wingman, he lost hope. He carried the burden of others believing he was a cursed wingman. He was a complex man whose flame burned hot and bright, but for a tragically short period of time.

His nicknames were numerous as newspapermen and writers attempted to capture his essence. He was "the Balloon Buster from Arizona," "the Arizona War Eagle," "the Sausage Buster" or "Cooker," and "the Lone Eagle," (in reference to both his fighting style and the symbol of the squadron he fought in). Some referred to him as a "cowboy." His peers sometimes called him the "Arizona Braggart," at least until his reputation was made and he surpassed his own boasts. One pilot simply referred to him as "the nut." All of these are true descriptions of Frank, and yet none of them alone paints the complete picture.

Chapter One

"Am waiting now to be sent to the front and am very anxious, for I feel that I am better than the average German and as good as the best."

—FRANK LUKE TO HIS MOTHER, JULY 9, 1918

First Blood
August 16, 1918
Near Coincy, France

The pilots flying into battle that day hated their new airplanes. Almost universally, they held the same flat opinion: "The thing flies like a bloody brick."[1]

The American 27th Aero Squadron (the Eagles, or Fighting Eagles as they were most commonly known) had recently received their new Spad XIII C.1s. The Spad XIII aircraft were temperamental and hard to maintain. These fussy planes would present new challenges and dangers during the combat patrol on the morning of August 16, 1918.

Major Harold Hartney took up fifteen of the new Spads with him in an escort mission. A dozen or so were with the 27th Squadron, the rest were from the 94th Squadron. They were to provide cover for a photographic mission over the trench lines led by the 88th Squadron and Major Kenneth Littauer.[2] It was supposed to be a simple mission, and after take-off the Major led his squadron in almost perfect formation. For the new replacement pilots, it was a chance to gain valuable flight experience.[3]

Four years of war had mauled the once lush green French landscape. There were still patches of green, grass that had not been blasted or burned, leaves that still clung to their trees; but these were exceptions from the air. The ground was mostly brown and black, the sod and mud of the war had ripped it up and turned France into a vision of hell. The trench lines of the Germans and the Allies ran parallel to each other like jagged scars across the burned and churned landscape. The space between the trench-lines was a deadly jumble of shell holes and barbed wire and death known as No-Man's Land. Smoke clung to the ground, smoke often mixed with the horrors of chemical gas shells. From the air, pilots could see the lands beyond the front. They could see what France had been before the war.

The afternoon of August 16 was clear, only a few clouds in the sky. The sun would have been welcomed, though once the aircraft got into the air, it would provide no warmth for them. It was perfect flying weather.[4]

* * * *

The universe of Spad XIII pilots was not the glorious one that is often associated with World War I aviators. The twin Vickers machine guns were mounted in front of the cockpit, in a narrow space between the top of the engine cowling and the bottom of the upper wing. It was a space only one foot by three feet to see though, shoot through, and live and die by. The freezing wind-tunnel was only protected by a tiny windshield and a menacing gun sight in their field of vision. Further out in front of the pilot was a nasty engine that belched choking smoke and Castor oil as it ran. Each breach they drew was ice cold air laced with smoke. It seared at their lungs and stung at any exposed portion of their flesh. The noise was loud enough to rise above the rush of the wind and the padding over the ears that they wore.

The pilot sat with only some thin wood and doped fabric between him and a potentially deadly bullet. To the sides of the pilot, there was nothing substantial—a thin layer of doped canvas. Dope was a varnish-like covering painted onto the canvas to make it more rigid and durable. He had a similar level of protection at his feet, and he sat on a thin seat of light brown leather stretched over a piece of plywood.[5] Pilots wore a lot of clothing, as the open cockpit made flight over a few thousand feet a bone-chilling experience. Fur lined goggles and a leather flying cap encased their heads, but that was not enough to keep anyone warm, not at 21,000 feet. The trademark scarves that most pilots wore were not just for the warmth, but to keep the light spray of Castor oil out of their mouths. While often times the lives of pilots were portrayed as glorious compared to the infantry, the truth was that if they took in even a small amount of oil they would be confined to their latrines. Pilot's gloves were really massive mittens, usually lined with fur or wool. The only part that was open was for the index finger, to allow the pilot to hit the gun trigger.

Parachutes had been around for years, but were reserved for members of the Signal Corps, who sat under observation balloons. Some pilots experimented with parachutes, but the thought was that they were not suitable for American pilots. The Germans provided their pilots with this "luxury" for survival, but the Americans did not. If your Spad was hit and forced down, you had no choice but to ride it all the way to the shell-scarred, trench-torn ground. If you were lucky, you might be able to guide what was left of your aircraft to make some sort of landing. If not, you would most likely flip over, or pancake, on the ground and be crushed in your cockpit.

Flying the temperamental new Spad XIIIs was not simply a matter of working the throttle, rudder pedals, and the flight control stick. Just keeping the aircraft in the air required constant concentration and was complicated even by today's standards. You had to watch your oil pressure, making sure that it stayed near the midline of 150 grams. A pilot had to monitor the temperature of the engine and try to maintain it at around 70°C. When you were performing combat maneuvers it was important to keep the engine above 500 RPM. Pilots had to make sure that near the end of a long flight they turned on their Nourrice fuel tank. If you dove vertically, you had to close the choke. There was a sediment cup on the fuel line that had to be cleaned prior to a mission or your line could clog and kill your engine mid-air. Managing and maintaining the Spad was summed up best by Major Hartney's number one tip for "General Maintenance of the Plane: *Live with your machine as much as possible.*"[6]

There was no armored protection whatsoever, not in this era. The standard .303 bullet fired at a cockpit had little to impede its trajectory other than the pilot himself. The cockpit controls were laid out in a semicircle and were more basic than a modern automobile's. Foot-pedals, a throttle, and a stick completed the controls. It was an icy world of chunks of wood, a handful of bolts, wire, flammable gasoline, hot oil, dope-painted canvas, and prayer.

Besides bullets from enemy planes, pilots had to contend with fire from anti-aircraft cannons (known as "Archie"), which was inaccurate but still deadly. Shrapnel could shred a fighter or the pilot. Machine guns on the ground, if you wandered too close, could pop through the tight canvas and mangle an engine or pilot. The aircraft themselves sometimes fell apart or were shaken apart from damage. Dive or bank too steeply and pull up, and the wing canvas could rip free from the wood framing and send you to your death.

The life expectancy of a new pilot in 1918 was less than three weeks.

* * * *

The fact that Major Harold Hartney flew with his men was a measure of the kind of officer he was. Some Aero officers did not fly aircraft but instead piloted a desk. Not Hartney. He had trained many of these new replacement pilots back in the states. He knew them, and trusted their skills and capabilities. The place for him was with his men, not on the ground filing paperwork. Besides, this was going to be an easy mission. With over a dozen aircraft, they would have local air superiority even if the new recruits were green at best. All they had to do was escort the reconnaissance planes in, let them take their pictures of the German troops and artillery positions, and get out.

Things went wrong almost immediately thanks to the temperamental Spads.

The flight took off at 5:05 that afternoon with Lieutenants Grant, Hoover, Vasconcells, Roberts, Dawson, Hill, Hudson, and Luke. They climbed to an altitude of 3,000 meters.[7] Luke got a late start, having struggled with engine problems. His intention was to link up with the rest of the squadron, but they had a large head start on him.[8]

The American formation began to lose Spads only a few short minutes into the mission courtesy of engine and reduction gear housing problems. The pilots with faulty engines signaled by hand to the Major and peeled off for the nearest airfields, hoping to get on the ground safely before the engines quit altogether. One by one, the Spad XIIIs descended and departed, downed not by enemy aircraft, but by their own mechanical deficiencies.

Lieutenant Frank Luke, Jr., a relatively new replacement pilot in the 27th Squadron arrived. Now, looking back, the major was pleased to see the young Luke had rejoined his dwindling number of planes. At 18,000 feet, the major and only a pair of other airplanes from his command hovered, providing cover.

Major Hartney had begun the turn back toward his lines when suddenly he heard the rattle-click of a machine gun. He had been in combat before and knew that this was not ground fire but another plane. One bullet snapped through the canvas fuselage of his Spad with a cracking sound. The canvas had been covered with dope, which tightened it to a drum-like tension and strength. The canvas was more like thin wood when finished. The .303 bullet popped through it with a loud cracking sound, a noise that experienced combat pilots knew all too well.

Hartney dodged as he saw the German dive in on him. Rather than fight, he dove the Spad at top speed to get away from the pursuing aircraft toward his own airfield. At one point he glanced back and no longer saw his pursuer.

Frank Luke had seen the pursuer. It was the last of four German aircraft that had cut across the flight path of his fragmented squadron. Frank remembered his training and moved his Spad so that the sun was behind him when he would dive on the German. If the German glanced back he would be blinded by the sun and might not see the Spad diving in at him. From 18,000 feet, Frank entered his first combat of the war, diving down at the last airplane in the enemy formation. As he started his dive, he cut his engine. He was not going to give his intended target any reaction time to his initial attack.

The first three enemy biplanes saw him and broke formation, fleeing the scene of the battle. Only his intended target seemed unaware of his diving approach. When he came within 100 feet, Frank pulled up slightly and kicked the Spad's engine back to life. Less than a heartbeat later he opened fire with the Vickers machine guns in short controlled bursts, the guns had a tendency to jam if fired in long continuous blasts.

While 100 feet from the enemy sounds like deadly close range, it was a maddeningly long distance with no aids to aim at a dodging and weaving opponent other than a static sight mounted on the engine cowling. A hundred feet could feel like a mile when you were fighting to stay aloft, not get shot yourself, and still trying to hit a moving target in the air in front of you.

Every fifth round of Luke's machine gun ammunition was a tracer bullet. It was a treated phosphorous round that burned when firing, giving a glowing beam as it flew down its flight path. Although the tracers gave pilots a chance to see the approximate path of their bullets in flight, the tracer rounds had somewhat different flight characteristics than normal bullets. While they provided a rough guide, they were also not perfectly accurate.

Luke's shots were slamming into the German aircraft. The acrid smell of gunpowder from the Vickers mixed with the oil and gasoline smoke from the German's engine and would have left a bitter, metallic taste on the back of Frank's tongue. The German machine and pilot reacted to the hits. Luke could tell that that his foe had been hit—not just the aircraft, but the pilot. The German jerk-flipped over in a sideslip maneuver and Frank pulled up the Spad, revving its engine in a climb to turn and dive again. Hundreds of thoughts had to be dancing in Frank's head, yet somehow this excitable young man stayed focused. He had hit the enemy aircraft, and he wanted to finish it off. There were other enemy aircraft in the area, he had seen that in his dive down. Taking down the first aircraft would help even the odds for the Americans. He would have to be aware of the other enemies and not let himself become a victim. All the while, his weeks of training were about to pay off. Each important tip and bit of advice he had ever heard came to focus on these few minutes of battle.

It took a few moments, but when Frank did come about, he saw the aircraft, still flipped over on its back. He dove again and fired. The German aircraft slid down to 1,500 feet and began to turn and drop.

Frank knew the maneuver. The German was going to try a half-loop diving down. It wasn't possible, not at this altitude. The enemy angled downward to almost 200 feet and never even attempted to right itself. As he roared past, he saw the German plane dip down and knew that it couldn't possibly pull out at such a low altitude. It slowly descended towards the ground, upside down, flying to certain death.

Banking around, Frank scanned the air looking for the companions of the man he had just downed. They had shot off for their lines. He rose slightly, just enough to draw the attention of the German anti-aircraft guns for a few minutes as he sought his bearings. Having memorized the map of the area, he recognized the French villages of Jouy and Vailly and, from their positions, was able to determine where he was. He was prepared to fly back to his squadron base, but his own Spad finally began to succumb to engine problems. Frank made his way to a small airdrome near Coincy and landed.[9]

The mechanics there worked on his Spad, refueling it and adding oil. Frank had learned that his own squadron was still in the air. He set out after them but did not find them. Somewhere in the air he had missed them and they had landed. By the time the daily report had been filed, Frank's status had been noted with uncertainty: "Lt. Luke has not returned." A further grim note said, "Lt. R. Nevius killed in action."[10]

Upon landing Frank gunned his engine, something that his superiors had told the rookie pilots to not do. It was a way to get the attention of everyone at the airdrome and it worked. Frank's excitement only seemed to fuel the controversy of his first kill. What Frank faced was stern skepticism on the part of his peers. Most scoffed at his claim of shooting down an enemy airplane in combat for two reasons. First, Frank Luke was a rookie pilot. Second, Frank had been bragging about his untested skills against the enemy, something that didn't settle well with the seasoned veterans. His bragging had been seen as overanxious, but at the same time it insulted the men who had already gone up and risked their lives—many of them without taking down an enemy aircraft. The prevailing thought among most of the other pilots was that Frank had not flown off alone, but had been afraid and used excuses to flee from battle.

There was a third reason, mostly unspoken among the pilots in the 27th Aero because it was slightly embarrassing to admit. Frank was from a German family, the *Boche* were the enemy, and many had suspicious about German-Americans. A bragging German-American pilot was destined to be the brunt of scorn and suspicion. None of his fellow fliers were known to have ever mentioned it to his face … and with good reason.

Major Hartney was more concerned that he had lost track of the inexperienced pilot and Luke had been long overdue. One of the other pilots stopped him. "There's your boyfriend," he said to the major. "He said he was going to get his first Boche today or never come back. Let's see what the blowhard's got to say for himself. Bet he claims one."[11]

Hartney stowed his flight gear and was greeted by a follow-up report from his pilots who had reached Frank. "What did I tell you? He says he shot one off your tail!"

The major reached Frank who excitedly told him the events as they unfolded. Using his hands, he gestured for himself and his victim, showing how he dove in and how the German had flipped over and dropped. The other pilots of the 27th Squadron, with few exceptions, jeered at his rendition.

Hartney did not. He had been there. He knew he was being pursued at one point and something had forced the German airplane off of its pursuit. And there was something in the way that Frank told the story that convinced him that it was not a fabrication or a hollow boast.

He attempted to get confirmation of the kill. This process usually involved finding a friendly unit that witnessed the dogfight and the destruction and could confirm, in writing, that the events had happened and that a German plane had been downed. The need for confirmations had been proven early in the war as commanders discovered that there were many more claims than kills.

Several frustrating phone calls later, the matter was left up in the air, as it were. No one had witnessed the kill or reported new airplane wreckage. It was Frank's word against almost everyone else's in the squadron—none of whom had been there. Officially, without confirmation, he would not be credited with the kill in his records. Unlike for the United States Army Air Service, for Frank what went in the record and what was reality were two different things.

A few believed him. Major Hartney did—informally crediting him for one kill in combat, albeit unconfirmed. Two other pilots in the 27th Squadron, Joe Wehner and Ivan Roberts, both believed Frank's rendition of events, as did Norman Archibald, one of the pilots in the 95th Squadron that had been up with them on that mission. Everyone else viewed Frank as a braggart and a punk, claiming a victory that simply existed in his head.[12] The fact that his peers didn't believe him made him resentful.

Frank explained the engagement in striking detail to Hartney, though. "I never pulled [the trigger] until I had my gun right in that baby's cockpit and

I didn't leave him until he hit the ground and rolled over on his back, with me not more than two hundred feet in the air." Hartney himself believed it. "He was not lying and I know it."[13] "I am firmly convinced the boy got the plane. His verbal account of the battle contained those little differences that give such a report the touch of verisimilitude. But the squadron didn't believe him and that made Luke bitter."[14]

The German records show that twenty-two pilots and observers were killed in France on August 16, 1918. One pilot was taken as a prisoner of war. Three were wounded and two more were injured in the crash of their aircraft. Of these casualties, there are two that died in the general region where Frank claims that his kill took place. It is difficult if not impossible to marry together the German casualties and the Allied claims of kills since the Germans listed either where the pilot was confirmed killed, was last seen, or was listed as dead by the forces that recovered the body. In some cases the location of death is where the body of the warrior was buried. In this non-digital war it was difficult to draw conclusions as to which downed aircraft was brought down by whom. The only plane even in the region was one flown by Leutnant Hildebrandt. That plane was engaged by the enemy and skulked back to the air field with Hildebradt's observer, Leutnant Alex Jagenberg, dead in the rear seat.[15] If it was this aircraft, then Frank's estimate of the battle location was off more than he thought.

After the war, this first kill would be controversial in several regards. For a time there would be claims by the Army that it was indeed an official kill for Frank.[16] The author Laurence La Tourette Driggs would claim that after Frank's death he had read Frank's journal and that in it, Frank had admitted that he had lied about the kill.[17] Driggs was one of a handful of writers who spent time at the 27th Squadron during Luke's tenure there. Given the propensity for Driggs to exaggerate in his writings, to embellish material, and a lack of this journal as physical evidence, Drigg's account must be called into question. Adding to this the fact that Hartney's version of events meshes well with Luke's even though it would have been impossible for Frank to have known some of these details, such as Hartney's account of the German aircraft lagging behind the squadron, it is safe to assume that his first combat report was true.[18]

Frank had learned an important lesson: confirmed kills were all that mattered. He would make sure that he could prove his future victories beyond a shadow of a doubt. He typed up a series of black confirmation forms to carry with him. All future kills would be validated.[19]

Chapter Two

"Too happy-go-lucky to realize his own talents."

—ENTRY FOR FRANK LUKE, JR., 1917 *PHOENICIAN* YEARBOOK,
PHOENIX UNION HIGH SCHOOL

The Wild Boy
1861–1917
The Arizona Territory

The arrival of the Luke family in the western United States mirrors many stories of immigrants who migrated to the West after arriving in America. The first of the family to arrive was the Prussian-born miner Charles Augustus Luke (originally spelled as Luecke, changed later to Luke), the older of two sons of Carl and Justina Luecke.

Charlie arrived in California in time for the Civil War and enlisted in the Second California Volunteer Cavalry in the town of Yreka, outside of San Francisco, on October 3, 1861, at the age of 29. Charles was a member of the Third Military Regiment, Brandenburg Preussen.

The majority of the Second California Volunteer Cavalry did not serve in the Civil War but instead was put on patrol and garrison duty in the West, protecting settlers from Indians. Charlie was part of Company M, which was assigned to an upstart officer seeking to make a name for himself, Colonel Patrick Edward Connor. Connor wanted an assignment in the Civil War engulfing the country but was being kept out on the frontier. To gain the attention of his superiors, he conducted a military campaign against the

Indians. For Charlie Luke, the result of Connor's martial drive was that he was embroiled in the first of several Indian massacres he would encounter in his life.

Charlie and his company were at the time attached to the Third California Volunteer Infantry Regiment. There had been reports that the Shoshoni Indians had been raiding the nearby Mormon settlers and Colonel Connor sought to punish them. At a small icy creek called Bear River on January 29, 1863, the army units enveloped the Shoshoni encampment. The fighting was brutal. Many men suffered frostbite in the march and they found the Indians dug in along the creek bed. Connor pressed his men forward into the fray. The warriors were driven back and many were gunned down as they tried to escape across the river. The infantry and cavalry rushed into the camp with no discipline or restraint, amid innocent women and children caught in the melee. There were instances of rape. Many of the children were killed, by some accounts, stoned to death by the infantry. When the fighting ended against the background of softly falling snow, there were 27 soldiers and 5 officers dead, along with 200 to 400 Indian warriors and 90 women and children.

Later that year he was involved in another army massacre in Springville, Utah, on a river called Spanish Forks.[1] Three years later he was working at a mining operation in Mohave County in the Arizona Territory when the local Hualapai Indians staged a raid. Charlie escaped the massacre of the miners with the loss of most of his material goods. A year later he was working as a guide, leading easterners to the Arizona territory when he was ambushed by the Wallapais Indians. They rushed his camp and Charlie fled, so panicked that he cut loose his saddle and lost a young boy that was part of his party. His party was wiped out in what was known in the papers as "the Luke Party Massacre." Forty years after the affair a journalist recalled the event: " … his act stands out as the one single act of abject cowardice in all the history of the pioneer days of Mohave county."[2]

* * * *

Charlie's younger brother, Lorenzo Luecke, came to the United States after Charlie had arrived. Lorenzo shortened his name to Lorenz and took the more Anglo name of Luke. Lorenz's wife, Regina, and their children, John, Therese, Franz, and Joseph, followed him to the new country after he established himself.

Lorenz, like his older brother, opted for a military career. He was five feet, ten inches tall with light blond hair and blue-gray eyes. He initially enlisted in the 14th New York Cavalry Regiment in 1862 under the assumed name of Frederick Russell. According to affidavits filed when he applied for his pension, he had enlisted under a seemingly non-German name so as to not to attract the attention of his former fellow countrymen. Such name changes were not uncommon with recent immigrants who still spoke with accents from their home countries.

Lorenz, Frank's grandfather, did not accomplish much in the way of military glory. His only combat injuries came from being struck on his head during training in New York by an officer who used the flat of his sword on Lorenz, presumably to get his attention. The other came when he fell from his horse in Louisiana.

When his enlistment came up, Lorenz reenlisted under his given name, allowing him to collect a bounty again. This time his military career was even less glamorous. Attached to the Seventh New York Infantry Regiment in 1864, he spent his entire career with them stricken with diarrhea. Frank's grandfather, quite literally, sat out the remainder of the Civil War, never distinguishing himself in battle.[3]

* * * *

Lorenz settled in New York City working as a basket maker while his brother Charlie was out West struggling with the Indians. Lorenz became a U.S. citizen and had two boys, Frank and John, and two daughters, Regina and Marie. Charlie's first marriage didn't last, and he remarried Emma Liebenow from Brooklyn. Emma had two children from a previous marriage, Tillie and

Adolph Liebenow. Early in 1873, Charles visited his brother Lorenz in New York, and the fourteen-year-old Frank and his brother John went with their uncle to live in the West. The trip was long, through California into Arizona. Frank settled for a while in Prescott, then moved on to Globe, and eventually settled in Phoenix. He was introduced to his cousin, Tillie Liebenow, who would one day be his wife.

There was a point in his life, at the age of sixteen, that Frank Luke considered returning east to a different career—that of the military. Frank enrolled at the U.S. Military Academy at West Point but failed the eyesight test. He became smitten with his Uncle Charlie's stepdaughter, Otilla Liebenow. They were married on New Year's Eve, 1884, and had nine children: Eva, Anna Marie, Edwin Lawrence, Charles, Otilla Cecillia, Regina Josephine, John Allen, William Joseph, and Frank Luke, Jr.

Phoenix was a city that was growing out of the middle of nothing. The Southern Pacific railroad helped spur some of the growth, but the nearby silver and copper mines made the area a hotbed for the kind of rough-and-tumble miners coming out West hoping to strike it rich. Even by the turn of the century, Phoenix was mostly populated by Mexican nationals and a large American Indian community. It was one of the last bastions of the old West.

Frank Luke, Sr., took a number of jobs to make a living. He worked in copper and silver mines and speculated on property in the territory. In the hot summer of 1893, Frank and one of his business partners, Frank Czanowski, along with some other investors, cashed in on some of the water rights they owned, selling some locations along the Lower Gila River to the South Gila Canal Company. The made $20,000 in an age when incomes were measured in hundreds of dollars a year.[4] He went into business with R.E. Kirkland in 1893, investing in a highly profitable silver mine.[5] Frank Senior became a pillar in the community, and though his family was better off than most, the strict Catholic family he and Otilla were rearing did not flaunt their status.

Frank became a tax assessor, which gave him unique access to potential business dealings in young, burgeoning Phoenix. He was elected to the

Phoenix board of supervisors, only to step down after his first term. Frank got a role on an executive committee to seek statehood for Arizona in 1891. Once more he ran for the board of supervisors and, "after a struggle lasting nearly all afternoon two votes were cast by the board of supervisors for Frank Luke." His election to office was far from uncontested and Frank was the only person elected without formal endorsement.[6]

* * * *

Frank Luke, Jr., was born on May 19, 1897, and from the time of his birth his father Frank would bear the title of *Senior* to distinguish himself from his son. Like many fathers, Frank, Sr., was not present when Frank was born, but he was elated at the news.

His children would all do well in their lives. One would be a lawman, another a nurse, but it was the son that bore Frank's name that would make him, and all of Arizona, the proudest.[7] His father would later tell interviewers that this middle son stood out from the other Luke family children even as a baby. He yelled a little louder, kicked a little harder, and ate with a little more gusto than his other children. It was hard to stand out in the Luke household, but Frank found ways to do just that. Today, Frank might be diagnosed with ADHD, but in his era he was simply a wild boy. By most accounts he was a nervous talker, always energetic and on the move.

He was close to his brothers and sisters, especially his sister Otilla, known to the family as "Tilla." As a young boy, Frank was a compulsive collector and, together with his ever faithful companion Tilla, he gathered a variety of birds' eggs, bugs, and other items from nature. For Frank, Jr., the collections were simply exercises in goal-setting. He set benchmarks for himself and met them. The collections themselves were not important, but meeting the goal was.

One summer evening, Frank, Sr., decided to go fishing. He wanted a tin can to put his worms in and went to the barn to find one. In the rafters, he found an impressive collection of cans, most likely put on the crossbeams by the children. They were lined up on the beam and within reach. He grabbed the first one pulled it down. The lid was still hanging on and covered the top. Pulling it back he saw movement inside the can and he did what anyone would do—he dropped it. A tarantula spider spilled out onto the barn floor. Startled by the discovery, Frank, Sr., grabbed a shovel and killed the spider.

He glanced back up at the other cans and wondered what they were doing up there. This time he was more cautious. Frank, Sr., reached up and pulled own a second can. Like the first, its lid covered the top. Wary, he cautiously opened it and again, found another live tarantula. Startled again, he dropped it and again slapped down the spade onto the spider. Once would have been a fluke. For two cans, it had to be deliberate. Cursing, he pulled down each can and dropped it to floor. Each and every one had a large tarantula in it. Each one met its fate and the crack-smack of the shovel. Eventually he had dumped fifteen cans down, each one holding the same sort of prisoner.

The sounds of Frank, Sr., pounding the spiders drew the attention of the entire family. They gathered at the open barn door as he finished his work. A young voice, that of Frank, Jr., spoke up before the family patriarch could demand to know who was behind the devilish task. "Tilla," young Frank, Jr., said, "dad's killed our bugs."

"*You* put those dangerous things up there?" his father demanded.

"Uh-huh," the boy replied. "Tilla and me was collecting them to get a hundred."

"Why in heavens name did you want with a hundred tarantulas?"

"Aw, just to get a hundred."[8]

* * * *

The world was changing around Frank Luke, Jr., as it was for all of the people in Arizona. This last bastion of the Wild West was finding itself sucked into the twentieth century an inch at a time. In 1900, the dusty, dirty streets of Phoenix were being paved. The paving, while not new in the East, was an event in Phoenix. The newspapers covered it and the locals came out to watch the process. The teams of mules that came down from the mines bringing ore were still a common sight, but word of a new contraption—the automobile, would one day spell their end. By 1908, there were ten car dealerships in Phoenix, where four years before there had been none. By 1910, lawmen used an automobile for the first time in state history to lead a posse in pursuit of a robber.

A massive construction project was taking place on the Salt River—the construction of the Roosevelt Dam. This project would help control the flooding that occurred in Phoenix and provide electrical power to the city. Electric lights would eventually drive out the kerosene lamps. Well-to-do families like the Lukes had telephones installed.

In 1912, Arizona and New Mexico became states of the United States. Arizona became the forty-eighth star on the flag, the last of the contiguous states to be added to the nation. Frank was raised in a world that was changing all around him, but to a teenager, it's doubtful that he fully appreciated how the changing world—or events in Europe—might reach him.[9]

* * * *

Frank was popular in high school. His dirty-blond hair, tightly drawn face, thin smile, and gray eyes made him popular with the young women, and his prowess in athletics ensured he was admired by the rest of the school.

The tight circle of kids that he ran with included William "Bill" Gilbert Elder. Bill stood out in contrast to his friend. Bill was a short boy with a stumpy neck, and certainly not as popular.[10] Frank and Bill were an unlikely pair at first glance. There is no doubt that the smaller Elder was taunted by the taller, stronger boys, but Frank did not tolerate such teasing of his friend; Bill became his personal responsibility. They were friends, and in many respects, Frank became Bill's personal coach.

They didn't play out in the backyard, or in the street—they camped out together. At the age of twelve Frank's father bought him a rifle, and Frank and Bill would go into the wild and shoot, unsupervised. Riding ponies and taking along a pair of pack burros to haul supplies, they would set off for the Superstition Mountains or Indian reservations to camp out. It was a different era. Today one cannot imagine parents allowing their very young teenager to leave for days at a time to camp on his own with no adult supervision and a gun. Arizona was still one of the last bits of frontier in North America, though, and Frank was a boy that could not be constrained by the streets of Phoenix.

On one such trip, Frank and Bill set off for the White River Indian Agency, over 125 miles from Phoenix. The melting snows in the mountains had transformed the stream that ran across their path into a raging torrent jammed with logs, debris, and twisted and mangled mesquite stumps. It should have been clear water, but it had churned into a light brown soup, frothing and deadly.

They rode up to the usual ford and found it to be a mass of debris and white water. Bill suggested riding further upstream to find another place to cross, but Frank didn't want to. Adding to the tension of the situation, a small band of Navajo Indian boys from the reservation took up a place on the far bank. It was obvious that they had come to watch the two boys attempt to cross. One of the Indians waded into the water up to his chest, dodging logs and other debris. Having tested the water he returned to the far embankment with his peers. His verdict seemed to be that the white boys would never make it.

Frank was undeterred. He told Bill he would cross with the burros and then would help coach him across. Frank led his pony into the water and struggled, fighting the raging water to get across. The Indian youth on the embankment began to chant.

Slowly, sluggardly, Frank led his pony and the burros across the ford and onto dry land. He poured the water out of his boots and looked back at Bill on the far bank. The time had come for his friend to try.

Bill struggled to get his pony to enter the raging water. Each step the pony took was labored against the crushing rush of the stream-turned-river. The Indians called out an alert, and Frank snapped his head around to see the threat. A mesquite stump came tumbling down the river, straight at Bill.

There was nothing that could be done.

The gnarled stump plowed into Bill Elder. His pony bolted and the boy lost his grip. The twisted roots of the stump seemed to entangle him, and he lost his grip on his saddle. Suddenly, he was underwater, heading downstream, the stump acting like a tentacled creature bent on his destruction. Sounds were distorted as he lost his breath under the surge of the river.

He called out Frank's name.

Bill Elder should have died. But a pair of hands grabbed him in the brown darkness of the water, fighting back the pull of the stump. Bill broke the surface and saw Frank holding onto him, pulling him to the far shore. The slogged their way into a shallow pool out of the current, both gasping for air.

Bill all but collapsed. Frank was more optimistic, as if the event were nothing. "You're all right, Bill. Take it easy now and get your wind." In the distance, a strange cheering and whooping filled the air as Bill's ears drained of the water in them. Frank rose with a broad grin on his face. "Listen to them Indians holler!"[11]

* * * *

Every year at Halloween, there was a covert series of competitions between the classes at Union High School to raise class pennants on the school flagpole. The competition really consisted of an organized brawl, a free-for-all of the students, mostly the males, attempting to reach the pole and hoist their pennant. In 1916, Frank was a junior and despite his prowess on the football field, he alone could not carry the day. The senior class won the honors and hoisted their flag to the top of the pole.

The police were called that night to the sound of pistol fire near the school. When they arrived the shooter had disappeared. The only evidence left behind was that the large brass ball atop the flagpole had been mutilated by bullets. Frank had been trying to shoot the senior class pennant down.

The police left the area after a search for the shooter. What they couldn't have known was the determination of the young man. Frustrated at his attempt on the flag with pistols, Frank upped the ante. The police received a call later in the evening reporting two large blasts—shotgun blasts—having been fired in the same vicinity. When they arrived, the flagpole had been stripped of its pennant and had suffered further damage from shotgun pellets. Frank had taken the flag.[12]

Pranks and public stunts were part of Frank's life. In an age before radio and television, they were simply a form of entertainment for young boys. In his senior year, Frank was remembered for another stunt that he orchestrated. A group of freshmen students were rounded up by Frank and his friends to be the brunt of a practical joke that would be remembered years later. The freshmen students had done nothing wrong other than being captured by the seniors students led by Frank.

Frank's intention was malicious and devious. "People that were living here at the time and were not yet beyond middle age will remember some two or three years ago when a lot of freshmen of the high school emerged with their heads shaven. Lieutenant Luke was said to be identified with that tonsorial feat and it was urged on his behalf, as an upper class boy, that that was the only way these youngsters could be taught that the road to learning was not a royal one in no other way could be made to understand that Latin motto, a famous one among scholars, and the English, which is something like this: It's a rough and dusty going to the stars."[13]

But his stunts and practical jokes were not only at the expense of others. Frank and a handful of his friends pulled together one stunt simply for the sake of doing it. The thought was that they would parachute off of Union High School's roof using nothing more than a huge wagon parasol. Word was spread among the 300 students of the school so that there would be a large crowd gathered for what the boys considered to be a harmless prank. While not all of the pranksters are known, some of Frank's known accomplices on this venture were his friends Albert "Pidge" Pinney, Bill Elder, and Perry Casey.

At noon one day, the boys gathered on the roof of the school and were surprised that the crowd gathered below numbered in the thousands. Given the height of the roof, four stories over the hard ground, the risks of jumping off with a large umbrella were quite real. The boys gathered on the edge of the roof but were eventually persuaded to avoid the jump. In the end, they had to suffice with dropping a dummy made of out bundles of clothing which careened into the ground below.

The students below were disappointed. As one of them said, "Frank coulda done it if they had let him."[14]

Frank was very active in sports and school activities for the Union High School Coyotes. Two years before his graduation he earned a reputation in football as a great "plunger," with the capability to rush the the opponents' line. Frank was considered one of the best plungers at the twenty-four high schools that existed in Arizona.[15] During one football game in 1915 he broke his collarbone. Rather than sit rest of the game out Frank continued to play.

In track, Frank ran the hurdles. His close friend "Pidge" Pinney ran with him. Luke again demonstrated his rebellious streak during his last year on the team—when he was kicked off for breaking training.[16]

In baseball, he played right field on the same team as his friend Bill Elder. Frank was an all-around athlete and played on the tennis team as well. In an age where athletics was a primary form of entertainment, Frank also managed to squeeze in roles in the school drama department productions. He was even a member of the agriculture club. But mostly, Frank found ways to remain in the spotlight in sports, where he could measure his success and where his winning was noticed.

Like his father, Frank was no stranger to hard work, and if you wanted to make money in Arizona as a young man, that often meant back-breaking work in a silver or copper mine. Frank spent the summers of 1915 through

1917 in Ajo, Arizona.[17] His older brother Charles (who went by Charlie, like his uncle) and his wife had settled in the mining town of Ajo and his sister Anna went there often to sing in the opera house. The city of Ajo, in 1915, looked as if it were a set from a Hollywood Western, with an unpaved road down the middle, wide streets, clapboard buildings with broad fronts, and hitching posts for horses on the main street. It was the kind of rough-and-tumble town where miners, and those who made money off of miners, came to strike it rich or to eek out a living in the mines or nearby. Charlie ran the Palace Hardware Store in town, selling supplies to anyone who was hoping to strike it rich in copper or silver. Frank worked a variety of jobs, from Thayer's Hardware Store to his brother's own store.[18]

Frank also worked at the New Corleia copper mine. The pay was fair for miners, but the work was hard and long. The men that he worked with were a rough and hardy bunch. Miners lived outside of the mines in tent cities, and they drank, fought, and found numerous ways to spend the pay they earned. For a young man, it was the kind of environment where he toughened himself up quickly. While working in the mines, he crossed paths with a tough miner named James Joseph Breen, known more commonly as "Irishman Breen."[19] While Luke was carrying a heavy load of drill bits, Breen allegedly stepped in front of him forcing Luke to bump into him and spill his load of bits. For whatever reason, perhaps pure orneriness, he was out looking for a fight with the younger man. Frank was more than happy to oblige. Frank and Breen squared off in the mine, in dim light, in space filled with tools, rocks, and other implements that could cause injury or death. The other miners huddled around them, enjoying the break. The "Irishman's" hope of a quick victory was vain. Frank dodged, weaved, and struck at him with pure fury. James Breen dropped under the onslaught. The foreman came up and demanded to know what was happening. Frank's response was short and to the point. "He asked for it; and I gave it to him."[20]

Frank became friends and eventually a business partner with a man named Floyd Craver. Floyd was born in Kansas and had worked throughout the West in a variety of jobs. He was a skilled cartoonist and he provided artwork for everything from his high school yearbook to newspaper ads. He hauled goods as a trucker, worked as a miner, and, like so many others in old Arizona, he sought to make his life better. Together in the summer of 1916, Craver and Frank borrowed money and opened a dance hall in Ajo.[21]

There was a paradox in opening a dance hall. Ajo was a rough-and-tumble mining town, populated mostly by men, rugged miners. A Western dance hall conjures up a variety of illicit images, but the likely reality was that Frank and Floyd wanted to pry the miners' hard-earned money from them. This was an era before radio, when people made their own entertainment, and dance halls were a popular form of that entertainment, for both men and women. This dance hall provided dance lessons for the miners, who hoped that their ballroom skills might help them secure either wives or "friendship" with the opposite sex.

Frank embraced his role as a dance instructor. He would put on a dress to help the miners learn their basic moves. The pay was not great, and Frank took to a common mining camp pastime to earn additional money: boxing. The boxing matches in the mining towns like Ajo were not formal, highly publicized events. They usually consisted of the contestants and a circle of viewers who bet on the match. For a young man who taught dancing in such a town, the boxing matches were probably a good way to keep ruffians from assuming that he had a more feminine motivation for putting on the dresses. For the miners, it was a chance to bet their money, and gambling was one of a very few mining town pastimes. His fight with Irishman Breen earned him a reputation as a pugilist, and he managed to make a little money off of his efforts, though many accounts of his bouts were blown out of proportion over the years.

The dance hall venture ended when Frank returned to high school in Phoenix. Floyd remained in Ajo working in the mines as a diamond drill miner. On December 16, 1916, he was attempting to load a truck and lost his footing while the truck was moving. His skull was crushed under the loaded wheel of the truck and his body was badly mangled. Frank took the death hard. For him, it was the first of many other tragic deaths to come, this time on the battlefields of France.[22] Frank tried again in the summer of 1917 to reopen the dance hall, but he met with disappointment. As he wrote his mother, "They are giving free dances over at the other town so there is no use starting up the Dance hall."[23]

The summer of 1917 would leave Frank with no solid job prospects at a time when the U.S. was entering the war in Europe. His first exposure to the military in his life was probably through stories that his relatives relayed to him about his uncle Charlie and grandfather Lorenz dating back to the Civil War. Arizona was a place where military operations were not entirely old news. The pursuit of Geronimo was something that had occurred only a few decades earlier and many men had been pressed into informal military service to pursue the Indians.[24]

After that came the infamous raids of Pancho Villa across the border from Mexico. The U.S. Army, under General Pershing, led a punitive expedition to hunt down this outlaw to little avail. Many Arizona settlers resolved themselves to the possibility of military action.

The First Arizona Infantry (volunteer), in 1917, was stationed outside of Ajo. When a Villistas raid came across the border, they traveled to Quitobaquito in pursuit of the bandits. "The Villistas escaped but in their place they caught and jailed one Frank Luke on suspicion of being of draft age. Frank's brother, Charles Luke, had to confirm his age to get him released."[25] For Frank, this was a rough start to a promising military career.

America's declaration of war on Germany in April 1917 was primarily motivated by the Zimmermann Telegram, which implicated Germany in a plot to encourage Mexico to attack the United States. There were other factors, such as Germany's return to the use of unrestricted submarine warfare—but the key factor was a direct threat to the sovereignty of the U.S., the prodding by Germany to get Mexico to strike at America. Per the telegram, when the war was won, Mexico could reclaim its former holdings from Texas to California if Mexico could keep the U.S. Army busy repelling border incursions. While the vast majority of people in America were stunned by such thoughts, the people that lived in these relatively new states that bordered Mexico found such plans to be a direct threat to their homes and lifestyles.

Arizona was eager to contribute to the war effort. Rallies were held in most cities encouraging young men to enlist. Frank and Bill Elder were in Globe, Arizona, when Congress declared a state of war. The whole town was out celebrating the declaration. Men lined up to enlist. Even the brothels flew the American flag. It was a wave of patriotic fervor that swept the new state.

The Luke family was doing its part. Frank's older brother, Edwin, had joined the Army and headed off to the East for basic training. His sister, Eva, had applied to join the Red Cross and was awaiting her acceptance and assignment. Frank ultimately decided that he, too, should enlist, but what Frank wanted to do was something different, something daring.

He rode to Tucson with Bill Elder; their intent was that both of them would enlist. The recruiting officer took Frank and let him fill out his draft card but passed on Bill.

Chapter Three

"… although flying schools have been established throughout the length and breadth of the continental United States in the past two years, none of them have had so romantic and thrilling a history as Kelly."

—LIEUTENANT H.D. KROLL, 1919

Fly with the Eagles
April 1917–February 1918

America was not prepared to go to war when it came in April of 1917. The Great War had been something far away, across the seas. The Wilson administration had done everything possible to keep the United States from being dragged into the quagmire of war in Europe. Though America's peacetime military had not managed to stay current, the U.S. didn't shy away from the fight. Factories stepped up for wartime production, prewar draft registrations took place, and programs were put in place to fund the war effort. But, for all of her bluster, the United States was simply not ready to jump into the fight with Germany and her allies … not yet.

Perhaps America's deficiency was in her air power. General Pershing had taken an airplane with him on the punitive raid into Mexico to track down Pancho Villa, but beyond that tiny effort there was little that had been done leveraging this new weapon. The use of the airplane had not helped catch Villa. He successfully evaded American efforts to capture him and since then, America had not invested sufficiently in its air service. Part of the problem was naïve hope that the war would end before the U.S. had to get involved; part of it was the speed with which the war was changing aviation. "On 6 April 1917 not a single air unit had been trained for warfare. The two flying fields operated by the Army had only 55 trainers, of which, General John J. Pershing said, '51 were obsolete and the other 4 were obsolescent.'"[1]

The Great War was evolving the use of aircraft at a lightning pace in terms of technology and tactics. When the war had begun, the airplane had been used initially for observation, reporting on enemy troop movements and artillery emplacements. The air service mounted guns on the airplanes for defensive purposes, then the pilots dropped grenades and bombs. Pilots took shots at each other when the chance presented itself. That situation changed when Anthony Fokker invented the interrupter gear for a forward-firing machine gun.

Until that time, firing a cockpit mounted machine gun meant risking shooting your propeller apart. The French invented a temporary work-around, mounting steel triangles of metal on the propeller to deflect bullets that hit them. This helped reduce some of the risk, but it also meant that a pilot could be hit by his own ricocheting bullet or that a wooden propeller would eventually fail from the impact of numerous shots. Fokker's system stopped the firing of the machine guns when a propeller was in front of them. Finally, a pilot could fly at another airplane, line up his shot, and both fire and fly at the same time (without killing himself). The age of the pursuit fighter aircraft was born.

It was only a matter of time before the Allies captured the technology that Fokker had created and integrated similar systems into their own airplanes. Suddenly observation and bombing missions had aircraft escorting them designed with one purpose in mind—shooting down enemy aircraft.

Back in the United States the entire Aviation Section consisted of only 131 officers, mainly pilots and student pilots, and 1,087 enlisted men. Just over two dozen officers were fully trained with the rating of Junior Military Aviator. Congress had simply not appropriated funding for increasing military aviation. At the same time, the Army was not sure where aviation should reside, whether as a stand-alone entity in the Army or part of another branch such as the Signal Corps. Commissions were formed and sent to Europe to study the war and attempt to arrive at a decision, but on the short-term the control of the aviators and their machines was bogged down in a quagmire of politics. Simply put, no one was in charge of military aviation.

That was not to say that American pilots had not been in battle. While America was not at war, some of her brave men had already gone to Europe and had enlisted with the French. They had been formed into their own squadron, or escadrille, the Lafayette Escadrille. The core of this unit was formed in 1916 around forty pilots, many being Americans that had been serving in the French Foreign Legion or other French infantry units that no longer wanted to fight in the horrific ground war. They were volunteers, one and all, and had their own unit, under French leadership, fighting the Germans. Those early volunteers had been in the unit from the darkest days of the war and had seen the evolution of military aviation. They were Americans that were fighting, killing, and dying for a cause long before their own country had acknowledged that fighting in the Great War was necessary.

The Lafayette Escadrille, while technically a French unit, was inadvertently doing something that the fledgling American Army Air Service was going to need—providing combat trained pilots. These men were flying the state-of-the-art Nieuport and Spad VII airplanes up against the Germans. They were learning the strengths and weaknesses of the German aircraft while at the same time honing their combat skills.

The Lafayette Flying Corps was a logical extension of the Lafayette Escadrille, seeding volunteer pilots and observers with French squadrons. It helped handle the excess of American volunteers who wanted to learn to fly. As the United States entered the war, the Flying Corps would serve as a clearing house to migrate the members of the escadrille into the newly forming Army Air Service. That was not going to be enough. As America entered the war, it was acknowledged that help was going to have to be drawn from a wide range of allied sources.

The long painful process of building that new air service from the ground up was slowly beginning. And through that growth there were officers that were going to emerge that were going to have an impact on Frank Luke. While he was still in Ajo earning a living, people who would play important roles in his life were assembling from all over the globe. Each was going to be instrumental in the life of the young man from Arizona.

None would come farther or have greater influence than Harold Hartney, who was exactly the kind of officer that the Army Air Service needed even before they realized that need. The problem was that Hartney was not American, but Canadian, moreover a Canadian in the service of the British. He had a typical English look about him. Thin, almost to the point of being wiry, Hartney wore a finely trimmed mustache. He was rigid in posture but had an explosive laugh. Even covered in mud or the heavy padding of a flying suit, Hartney had a look of distinction and an air of propriety about him.

The young Hartney graduated from the University of Toronto in June of 1911 with a two-year degree in engineering. Like many young men of his generation he enlisted in military service in Canada, joining the infantry—the Saskatoon 105th Fusiliers, a militia unit roughly equivalent to a National Guard division. He became a first lieutenant in the Fusiliers, and when war broke out in Europe he quickly determined that he wanted to get into the flying war. By May of 1915, the Saskatoon 105th Fusiliers were on their way via steamship to England—then to war.

It was not long after his arrival in England that Lieutenant Hartney was working hard to get himself transferred into the newly-formed Royal Flying Corps (RFC). The 105th Fusiliers became folded into the 28th Canadian Infantry Battalion. His unit was just about to be sent into the meat grinder of the ground war of the Western Front when word came down—Harold Hartney was going to be transferred to the RFC to become a pilot.

The first aircraft that he flew in the Great War were little more than massive box kites, sticks frames of wood propelled by primitive engines that often stalled or outright died. He started out in already outdated Farman

Longhorns and worked his way up to F.E.2bs, pusher aircraft. Eventually, he worked his way up to more sophisticated Avros. Hartney made the right choice for a military career as he learned a few months later. Word reached him that only twelve men from his former platoon were still alive. At least in the skies, Hartney stood a chance at survival.[2]

Hartney served in No. 20 Squadron and on June 12, 1916, was finally sent to France. Like most aviators, his first taste of combat was a mix of sheer terror and pure luck. Anti-aircraft shells burst all around him, a reminder that all that stood between him and a piece of hot shrapnel was the thin doped canvas of his aircraft and the thick clothing he wore.

His front seat gunner downed his first victim—a Fokker Eindecker, or single-winged aircraft. It was a dance of death in the air as Hartney did what he could to maneuver his airplane so that his observer-gunner could line up the shot. The Fokker Eindeckers were considered part of "the Fokker scourge." At that time, they held the advantage of using the interrupter gear to deadly advantage. British and French pilots did not have that luxury. Hartney was criticized for not following orders and dropping out of formation, despite the victory.

Hartney was a typical pilot but an atypical leader. He took part in bombing and photography missions. He piloted interception missions. Like many men, he crashed his share of aircraft and had the luxury to walk or crawl away from those wrecks. Hartney was not afraid of fighting, but, at the same time, he had no desire to die.

* * * *

Pilots on both sides of the front became well known. Sometimes it was the paint schemes on their aircraft. Sometimes it was their personal logos adorned near the cockpit. Some pilots were known by reputation. On February 14, 1917, while assigned to the 20th Squadron, now-Captain Harold Hartney was shot down. Hartney thought he recognized the pilot that downed him as the infamous "Red Baron."

The affair unfolded when he was on a mission to the area near Passchendaele to photograph some of the region. He was accompanied by one wingman, Lieutenant F. J. Taylor. Both were flying F.E.2ds. Hartney's observer was Second Lieutenant W. T. Jourdan. They flew through the bone-rattling anti-aircraft barrage near the front and knew that as long as the Germans on the ground were shooting at them, there were no German pursuit aircraft in the area. They looked around the German rear area for signs of aircraft but didn't see any. Then they spotted them, not from the German lines but coming at them from their own lines—seven Albatrosses.

Grabbing his Very pistol, a type of flare gun used to signal friendly aircraft, he fired a red flare to warn Taylor. Almost the moment he fired he heard the click-snap of bullets raining down on him, cracking the air near his cockpit and snapping through the fabric of his wings and fuselage. The battle was on!

Hartney dove his airplane downward to gain speed and then pulled back hard on the stick, nosing upward. The plane almost reached a full stall when he rolled to the right in a half-spin. It duped the German fighters, if only for a moment as they roared on past him.

The air battle was fought at tight, deadly ranges as the two British planes hurried for home. Hartney's rear gunner sprayed one of the fighters, sending it careening into the ground below. The other six chased after them, filling the air with glowing tracer rounds as Hartney and his wingman tried to work their way back to the British lines.

Two more of the German fighters were caught in a hail of fire and dropped, at least from Hartney's perspective. His wingman was caught by one of the Germans. He watched in terror as he saw his wingman's propeller fly apart.

Hartney always claimed that it was the notorious "Red Baron," Manfred von Richthofen, who had engaged them in that fight. That was probably due to the color of the aircraft that was pursuing him—an Albatross with bright red trim. At a glance, with its guns blazing at his wingman, he didn't take the time to make a positive identification. He dove for the British lines. The reputation of the Red Baron was enough alone to send a chill of fear into any aviator.

Hartney was probably fortunate that the plane was not Richthofen's but was rather Leutnant P. Strähle of the Jasta (short for Jagdstaffel, or fighter squadron) 18.[3] As Strähle's Albatross closed with him, Captain Hartney tried his old trick of a fake stall. This time his pursuer was not falling for it, spraying his airplane with more bullets dangerously close to the cockpit. His plane suddenly started to violently vibrate. He pulled out flat and tried to throttle back, but it only seemed to make it worse. Hartney tried to kill the ignition but it didn't work. In desperation, he reached down and killed the fuel feed.

The propeller finally stopped but their glide continued on. "I'll stretch this glide out as far as I can. We'll probably crash into a shell hole. But we're going down on our side, anyway, Jock, old thing. Just watch me."

According to Hartney, Lieutenant Jourdan simply grinned. They hit the ground near the front hard. The soft soil, while more cushiony than hard ground, did little more than rip their landing gear apart and send the plane into a crumpled mess in the mud. Jourdan had been tossed clear of the wreckage like a rag doll. Hartney was pinned in the fuselage by a 775 lb. motor resting on his lower back. An Australian infantry platoon found them and helped extract him. Both men were badly injured, but somehow had survived. Hartney was convinced that Richthofen had been the one that downed him. His wingman, Lieutenant Taylor, had been injured when his plane had landed, and Taylor's observer had been killed in their crash.

After his recovery, Hartney trained on the new DH.5 aircraft and fully expected to be assigned back to his squadron for combat duty. At that time, September 21, 1917, he received an order that was destined to change his life. "Captain Hartney will report to Colonel Roscoe at Toronto, Canada, to command 27th American Aero Squadron with Rank from this date of Major, Signal Corps, United States Army."[4]

There were restrictions placed on U.S. Army troops such that they could not be commanded by non-American officers. This problem was quickly alleviated with a formality. By the order of President Woodrow Wilson, Majors Geoffrey Bonnell and Harold Hartney were made U.S. citizens. Bonnell would initially be put in command of the 147th Squadron. Hartney would take over the still untested 27th Squadron.[5] The arrival of this experienced combat leadership would be a boost to the young Army Air Service.

* * * *

The Army struggled with the fledgling Air Service, not just trying to build it, but trying to determine where it should belong. Men like William "Billy" Mitchell traveled to Europe to take in the air war firsthand. The Bolling Commission came together to specify what the new Air Service should look like. At the same time, the U.S. struggled to even build serviceable aircraft. It would be June of 1917 before the first Curtiss JN-4s, or Jennies, the training aircraft that the new airmen would use, would finally start entering service.

This period of time was a form of structured chaos. Air Service planners speculated that an amazing 120 combat squadrons would be needed by 1919.[6] Eventually, the Air Service found its "home" for the duration of the war, in the Army Signal Corps. There was still a thought, already outdated by events and technology changes in Europe, that the airplane's primary role was in observation. Observation was the role of the Signal Corps, so on paper at least, it seemed to be a good home for the Air Service. At the same time, Billy Mitchell was navigating the political waters of the Army to attempt to seize control of the Army Air Service. Already a visionary, he knew that the airplane was going to be pivotal in the battles that the Army would be facing in France.

Having aircraft to train with was one problem; having the schools to train pilots in was another. There were two primary fields used for military training when the U.S. entered the war. The need was going to be far greater as the Army lumbered toward the conflict. The service created a curriculum with three phases of pilot training: ground, primary, and advanced.[7] Pilots would spend time in the classroom mastering theory. Those that passed this phase went on to actual piloting of aircraft—learning the basics. Advanced training would be done under the supervision of combat experts and would deal with taking pilots and turning them into trained killers, masters of gunnery and combat maneuvers.

One of the early additions to the training cadre of the Army Air Service was a flat piece of land in Texas. Kelly Field was a dusty isolated cotton field on the prairie before the war, a treeless landscape of depleted soil and hot Texas sun. Almost overnight, hundreds of quickly assembled clapboard buildings sprouted up on streets marked off by carefully piled stones. The roads themselves were macadamized rocks that would chew up even the hardest leather boot soles. Row upon row of tents housed the enlisted men. An endless caravan of Army trucks came into this small, self-contained city, depositing the hardware and gear of war. Airplanes eventually arrived, as did pilots, and countless ground crew members. The blistering sun baked the red tin roofs.

This was the birthplace of the 27th Squadron, the squadron where Frank Luke would soon find himself assigned. The field was named for named for Lieutenant G.E.M. Kelly of the 36th Infantry Division. A budding young pilot, he lost his life on May 10, 1911, over the site of Kelly Field. His plane was forced into making a crash landing. Kelly sacrificed his own life to avoid his airplane slicing and smashing into a tent filled with civilian women and children. It was a constant reminder to the pilots there of the risks that they faced.

It was here amidst the dust and rippling heat of the Texas prairie that Company K was formed into the fledgling 21st Squadron of the Signal Corps in May and June of 1917. After discovering that a clerical error had created two 21st squadrons, the Army renamed one the 27th Squadron under the command of Major Michael Davis, who took the unit north by train to Leaside, Ontario, Canada, for additional training.

Leaside was run by the British Army, and the 27th Squadron was drilled according to the British Army standards. Major Davis was replaced by another officer, one who understood the rigors of both the British Army and the nature of the combat conditions on the Western Front: Major Harold Hartney.

Four days after assuming command, Major Hartney took his new command back to the United States. The squadron arrived at Camp Hicks, Texas, for flight training on October 29, 1917. Their training field and temporary home was Talliferro Field Number One.

Many officers in the new 27th Squadron were destined to stay with the unit throughout the war. Jerry Vasconcells of Denver, Colorado, was one of the officers assigned to the unit who would see the unit fight in battle in France. Another pilot who learned to fly at Camp Hicks was Lieutenant Alfred Grant. Grant had a different path in the unit, one destined to collide with an extraordinary young cadet—Frank Luke, Jr.

* * * *

Alfred Grant, born February 5, 1895, was the son of Scottish immigrants and was raised in the small town of Denton, Texas—only a short distance from Camp Hicks and Talliferro Field. Alfred was a lanky young man with a bulldog expression. He had five living brothers and sisters and his father owned a flour mill in Denton. He graduated from North Texas Normal High School and went to college for a year at Kansas State University. When war broke out, Grant wanted to be a pilot and left college to enlist in the Army Air Service.

Grant was a rigid man, even by the earliest accounts. The word circulating with his fellow pilots was that Alfred was so stiff because he was a West Point Graduate. Apparently, this was a rumor that either Grant himself started or did little to suppress. Grant was a relatively well-known figure in a small, dusty Texas town. He now had a chance in his life to truly stand out, to be recognized as a skilled aviator. During training, he began a practice of flying out to his parents' farmhouse and landing, usually in time for dinner. He brought with him a number of other officers, including Jerry Vasconcells. Sunday dinner with the Grant family was a treat, a break from the camp fare.

When the planes would arrive, they would put on a short show, acrobatics, mock dogfights with their lumbering Curtiss Jennies, then land and enjoy a home-cooked meal.

Grant's family welcomed the visits, and his younger brother Silas, who wanted to be an aviator himself, enjoyed having all the aircraft and pilots around the house. He had applied himself to be a pilot in the Army, but his application had been rejected. In his youth, Silas had been caught in a building fire and collapse and had been injured enough that the Army did not want him as a recruit. His older brother and some of the other pilots would occasionally take Silas up with them, letting him get some air time. Silas hoped that if he had enough time in the air, he could reapply with the Army, and perhaps this time he would be accepted. For the time being, he stayed as a student at Iowa State College.[8] Silas went home as often as possible and never gave up his dream of being a pilot. It was a dream that had dire consequences for the young man.

Another budding officer destined for the 27th Squadron was Jerry Cox Vasconcells. Born in Lyons, Kansas, Jerry moved to Colorado where he was raised by his uncle. An athlete and quick thinker, Jerry attended Dartmouth and Denver University where he obtained a Bachelor of Laws degree in 1916. Jerry turned his back on a promising law career with the firm of Owen & Clark, where he was a legal consultant, to fulfill his patriotic ambitions with the Army, and after a mere sixty-five hours of flight time, Jerry became qualified as an Army Air Service pilot.

The structure and staffing of the squadron was recommended by Alfred Grant to their new commanding officer, Major Hartney. Vasconcells was one of the aviators that Grant chose. Others were Fred Ordway, Fred Norton, Robert "Bugs" Raymond, Alden Davison, Harlan Sumner, and LeRoy Prinz. This group of pilots formed the nucleus of the 27th Squadron.

While the young men had not officially received their commissions, they were confident that they were coming. Vasconcells and Grant both decided to have some fun on their trips into Denton. They took one-inch-wide red ribbons and tied them onto their epaulets as if they were some form of piping. Marching through the streets with authority they demanded salutes and convinced other soldiers in the town that they were "third lieutenants." It was a stunt that worked for only a few of their visits before someone posted a flyer warning soldiers of the unidentified pranksters.

The risks for pilots in 1917, especially those in training, was constant. One of the original pilots, Alden Davison, died in a crash when his engine failed. Alden attempted to glide back to the field but fell short. It was a painful lesson for them all: death was a matter of a single bad judgment call, in this case merely misjudging distance.

On January 11, 1918, the pilots of the 27th Squadron received their commissions as first lieutenants, and they celebrated with a trip to Fort Worth on Saturday and the traditional flight to Denton the next day for dinner with the Grants. The celebration was short-lived. The squadron transferred to Garden City, New York. Jerry and Alfred said goodbye to the Grant family and headed for the East Coast by train on January 22. It was the first step of their journey to Europe and the war. The young men were excited to take part in the adventure of it all.[9]

* * * *

The pilots of Camp Hicks had grown accustomed to flying to Denton for dinner with the Grant family and Alfred's father did not turn them away. Despite the fact that the 27th had moved on, some of them, friends of Alfred, still came flying in to visit the family. The temptation of a home-cooked meal and time away from the post had infinite appeal. And as always, Silas Grant was there, starry-eyed about the planes and the men who flew them.

On Monday, February 4, 1918, some pilots dropped in on Denton. One of them, a cadet, named Robert M. Foote, of the 182nd Squadron offered to take Silas up in his Jenny. It was not an unusual gesture for the visiting pilots to offer their hosts. Silas climbed aboard and Foote gunned the engine. The Jenny rose into the air, climbing to an altitude of 200 to 300 feet to the northwest of the city. Then, suddenly, the plane careened off to one side, stalling and diving straight at the ground. Foote tried to pull the plane up but he didn't have enough skill or altitude to recover the airplane's descent. When it hit the ground, the airplane flipped over onto its top wing.

Witnesses to the crash rushed to the scene. Cadet Foote was badly injured, but Silas was far worse, crushed in the cockpit. His legs were mangled in what was left of the wreckage. A metal bar had smashed his jaw as the plane had crumbled around him. After being pulled from the crumbled heap of spruce, wire, and canvas, Silas only lived for a few more agonizing minutes. Gasping for breath, he died next to the aircraft. Cadet Foote had been tossed from the cockpit and thrown clear. He was badly injured, having suffered a skull fracture and several broken bones, but he was destined to recover.

Silas's death was a blow to the Grant family. Word was sent to Alfred in New York. The choice he faced was difficult: return home for the funeral of his younger brother and miss joining his unit overseas, or stay with his unit and miss his brother's funeral. Grant opted to stay in New York.

Silas was laid to rest three days after he died. His father, torn up by the death of his son, decried that it was the Kaiser that had killed his son. If the Germans had not brought war on the United States, then his son never would have been in the cockpit and died. "My wife and I have toiled and struggled for twenty-five years to raise and educate this boy and give Texas a good and useful citizen. And all the while we were doing this, the Kaiser across the ocean was building up a great war machine to rule the world or, by destroying my boy and thousands and thousands of other boys like him, to wreck civilization."[10]

* * * *

Another officer who was going to play an indirect role in Frank's life, and more importantly, his death, had been fighting in Europe since the start of the war. His name was Frederick Zinn. He was a skinny young man with a dry sense of humor and wit who had been born in the sleepy little hamlet of Galesburg, Michigan, outside Battle Creek. Zinn had graduated from the

University of Michigan and had been touring Europe when war had broken out in 1914. He enlisted in the French Foreign Legion with such comrades as Norman Prince, Kiffin Rockwall, Bert Hall, and James Bach.

Zinn had enlisted at a time when Europe's governments had expected that the war would only last a few months, but it turned out to be a meat grinder that almost took Zinn's life. He was wounded with the Foreign Legion and convalesced with his family for several months in Battle Creek. When he returned to Europe he transferred to the Air Service and became one of those young men that flew for France until America joined the war effort.

Zinn was an observer and one of the very first combat photographers, pioneering techniques that would last decades. Photography was a passion with him. War correspondents often were not allowed to take photographs of the action, but Zinn was a passionate photographer himself. He took photographs and sold them to magazines back in the United States—offering many readers their first glimpses of the war in Europe.

When the United States first entered the war, Frederick Zinn was one of the first officers transferred into the Lafayette Flying Corps. As a true American air service emerged into existence, the value of an officer who had seen the war from its inception was noted. Zinn was the first officer assigned to the command staff of the U.S. Army Air Service under Billy Mitchell.[11]

One of his many responsibilities in those early days was the assignment of pilots to squadrons. It would be his role *after* the war that would distinguish him even more.

Chapter Four

"Do not trust any altitude instrument. Learn to judge altitude, especially in landings. Barometric conditions may change in a cross-country flight so that even a barometer that is functioning properly may read an inaccurate altitude. The altitude of the landing place may be different from that of the starting place."

—FROM *RULES FOR PILOTS AND CREWS*, 1917, RULE #23

Into the Air
1917–1918

Frank Luke, Jr., wanted to join the Air Service much more than it wanted him to join. He applied to the Army Signal Corps on August 2, 1917, to become an aviator. The forms were short then. What little the U.S. Army knew about Frank was boiled down to hard statistics—he weighed 155 lbs and was five feet, ten inches tall, had blue eyes, and he had graduated from Phoenix Union High School.

The Army didn't reply right away. With America's entry into the war, the service branches were still reeling from the sheer number of volunteers. Frank demonstrated his renowned impatience by writing the Adjutant's Office on September 10 requesting a reporting date. It was an arrogant demand from a young man but typified his single-mindedness. Frank demonstrated a high degree of focus, bordering on obsession, when it came to milestones in his life. Entering the Army as an aviator was one of those instances.

In this instance the Army caved in. If Frank wanted to be a pilot, he had to pass aviation training. He was to report to duty on September 29, 1917, at the University of Texas in Austin. It was a year from this date that Frank would meet his fate in France.

The aviation training program was nine weeks long and Frank completed it in seven. This was because the Army was condensing the training, doing everything it could to get servicemen ready for active duty—though many authors point to this speed of study as evidence of Frank's determination. Both elements probably played a factor in his rapid completion.

During the training, Frank did not generate much mail. He wrote his sisters and mother and father. His parents received separate letters, an indication of the different relationship he had with each of them. The days were long and hard, and for Frank, a middle-of-the-road student, it was grueling work, tackling the basics of aviation mixed in with a boot-camp for the Army. He found himself chafing at the authority that the Army represented, as well. "If the least little thing was out of place, your shoes not shined, any button unbuttoned, your bed not made perfect, you were taken down on a slip and a certain percent of your coming money and grade was taken. Made no difference if you were new."[1]

Frank had never been an outstanding student in high school, though he was no slouch either. He was going to school with professional students, "95% [were] college men." For Frank, it was merely another form of competition, and he loved to compete. He was told that three-quarters of the men in the program would flunk out and he was determined to not be in that number.[2]

He learned to field strip a Lewis machine gun and to work on aircraft engines—engines that would not even resemble those of the planes he was destined to fly in France. It didn't matter; it was all necessary and Frank waded into it. On top of the classes, there was drilling, and Frank learned that while the Army provided his meals, he was responsible for purchasing his own uniforms. He was forced to borrow money from his father and was very careful to ensure that he would be paying him back as soon as he started earning pay from the Army. "This is sure hard on me. Saturday afternoon and Sundays we have off and can go downtown if we want to. But you must have certain quality of clothes and have a full uniform before you can go. So it's been like a prison to me, for I have nothing to wear. We thought at first we were going to be issued uniforms but not so."[3]

Frank was in the twentieth graduating class at the University of Texas and, as was his knack in life, Frank made friends with his peers. In this case, he became close with Granville "Woody" Woodard.[4] "Our bunks were side by side, after graduation we were assigned to Rockwell Field, San Diego California for flying training. We completed our R.M.A. tests and received our commissions on the same date."

Woodard was from Wisconsin and was born in 1895. Like Frank, he was excited about the Air Service and couldn't wait to get over to Europe. How he gravitated to Frank is unknown, but the two remained friends throughout their lives. Upon his graduation, Frank treated himself to a break from camp life. He stayed at a hotel in Austin, the Driskill, along with several other graduates.

He was anxious to get to France and into the war and was not looking forward to his new assignment.[5] Going to San Diego meant assignment to Rockwell Field. It was in San Diego that Frank would take to the air for the first time and develop some of the basic flying skills that would make him an aviation legend. Rockwell Field had been established before the war as a military aviation center.

The training at Rockwell Field was not on the theory of flight, but actually flying. America was still working on developing its own fighter aircraft. For the time being, that meant flying Curtiss Jennies. Compared to combat aircraft being flown in Europe, these aircraft were two years behind the times. They had gravity fed engines which somewhat limited their capability to maneuver. If you flew too long upside down, your engine would simply cut off and you would be forced to restart it in-flight, a harrowing experience at best with the unreliable engines of the time. Jennies had massive wingspans and limited speed. If they were armed with machine guns, they would have been easy prey for almost any aircraft currently fighting in the war. While they were not fighters, they were good training equipment.

Some of their training was in mock cockpits, or "penguins," that were manually moved as the student pilot adjusted the controls. After some time in these, they went up in the two-seater Jennies to practice the basics in the air. Theory was one thing, but real flying in real airplanes was danger-ous work. There was no room for mistakes or errors. The U.S. Army did not employ parachutes for pilots for fear that they would bail out and cost the Army the price of an aircraft.

Flights started out simple—landings and takeoffs only, barely a few feet in the air. Then came limited turns, just enough for the airplane to turn around and return to the field. These were baby steps for the new aviators. Each step along the way the pilots gained valuable experience. Downtime between flights was filled with study and drilling. The Army believed that good marching skills made good aviators.

At initial glance, Frank stood out. "When he became excited he talked exceedingly fast, and he was the sort who is never still. In all the camp esca-pades, Luke was sure to be found playing an active part."[6] Frank, at least in this stage of his career, was not a loner but was well accepted by his fellow pilots at Rockwell Field.

Frank was encountering some problems—namely that the Army was not paying him in December of 1917. With America stepping up to a war footing, some pieces of the infrastructure necessary to run a large army were not up to snuff. He was pressed again into borrowing money from his father and other members of the family, including his sister Anna.[7]

Frank quickly became very skilled at flying, but all of the time, he was pushing the limits of both himself and his aircraft. He took risks that were probably unnecessary, but ultimately gave him the skills to handle a combat aircraft. In one letter to his father, he provided details of some of his training, painting a grim possible picture of what fate some pilots faced: "Yesterday flew on a triangle trip from North Island to La Jolla then to Mt. Cowles and back to the Island. Today we went to Buena Vista and made a landing. After a little stop we were sent back to the Island by a different route. I told Anna in my last letter that I was going to pull off a few stunts. Well I did everything I ever heard of or saw. Pulled eight loop the loops a number of wing overs, stalls, side slips! On my back and everything else. To tell you the truth I didn't mean to fly on my back but in making one of the loops I did not have enough speed so went over and turned on my back. I thought my last day had come. My motor which is a gravity feed of course, when I was up side down failed to get gas and stopped. I fell over a thousand feet in that position before I was able straighten it out. I was traveling about five hundred per. At least it seemed that fast.

"One of the new fellows yesterday side slipped and went into a tail spin then came out upside down. Luck was with him for he managed to get out o.k. But today he pulled the same one and fell nose down. Luck was with him again for he landed in a real soft spot and the mud broke the fall. The machine was half-buried in the mud and he received only two broken ribs and cut face. If he had struck a hard piece of ground though would have had to pick him up with a sponge. There have been dozens of smash ups since I have been here but this is the first injured. All the other accidents have been on the ground or very close to it. Most of them caused by bad landings."[8]

While in San Diego, Frank's life took an unexpected turn. The young man who was so excited about going to France and flying for the U.S. was going to meet a girl in California that was going to stir his passion.

* * * *

Frank had enjoyed girlfriends before joining the Army Air Service. As a star athlete in high school, he was known to have had several girlfriends, but none of them serious. This is not surprising given his participation in sports and the position his family held in Phoenix. People in general were drawn to Frank, and he was a good looking, athletic young man—he was bound to attract the attention of young women. Frank's previous girlfriends had been more impulsive teenage relationships. At the end of 1917, that changed when he met Marie Rapson.

Marie came from a broken family, the daughter of Cora Wells and Frank Rapson. Her mother was a tough matriarch. She owned a boarding house and a great deal of property in what is present-day downtown San Diego. Cora was a shrewd investor and managed her affairs closely, turning her holdings into a sizeable financial stake. She had more than one daughter, but Marie was the center of her life.

Marie had olive skin and dark hair. Her smile was infectious. At first glimpse, she probably appeared as Hispanic or Indian. She was medium height and of buxom build. Marie was a very skilled pianist; in fact, her mother one day hoped that she would go to Europe to learn classical music and play in the great music halls. The Great War dashed those hopes. In December of 1917, Marie was sixteen years old and was about to meet the love of her life.

Frank was a good Roman Catholic boy but on December 24, 1917, he was attending mass at All Saint's Episcopal Church. How he ended up in that church is unknown, but chances are he was simply accompanying another pilot. Marie was there, playing the organ. Frank tended to approach everything in his life by jumping in—and falling in love was no exception. He was smitten with the young girl playing the organ almost instantly.

Cora was not about to let her daughter go out with this pilot from Arizona alone. She escorted Marie's first dates with Frank. She took them on a ride through the hills around San Diego for picnics in the first days of the New Year.[9] Frank fell for Marie, and fell hard—as did she for him. An early January letter to his mother revealed only a hint of his feelings for Marie. Frank always soft-pedaled the state of his life with his mother, most likely to prevent her from worrying. "Mother, I have met some little girl here. She sure is nice. She and her mother have been taking me to all of the parks, beaches, etc. There are some awfully pretty places here. I am invited to take supper with them next Saturday evening and a long drive on Sunday. They treat me very nicely. If things continue like they have been, I will hate to leave them here."[10]

Marie occupied all of his spare time. "Sure will be glade [sic] to get home again ... This little friend and her mother are treating me great."[11] His impish nature found a new audience in his new love. Frank would let Marie know when he was going to be flying at Rockwell Field. He would wait until Marie came down to the edge of the field to watch him fly at the fence-line. He would soar straight up over her until the gravity fed engine failed. In a full stall he would dive the airplane down where she could see him, thinking that he was going to crash. At the last moment he would turn the engine over and pull up, sending a ripple of fear into his girlfriend.

In their private moments, Frank shared with her his stories of Arizona, even of his stunt to jump off of the high school with a parasol.[12] He and Marie became entwined in a romance that was destined to have a tragic outcome. Marie loved Frank, as well, as she commented in later life, "I was *madly* in love with him." As was Frank's impulsive nature, he asked Marie to marry him on February 1, 1918. They had only known each other for just over a month. Frank's all-or-nothing approach to life excited this young woman, and Marie accepted.[13]

Their dates were far too infrequent for either of them. They went to dances, and on one occasion went to the beach to go swimming together. Frank gave Marie a set of his pilot's wings. At one point Frank's parents traveled out and met with Marie. There was probably nervousness on both sides. Cora Rapson was not sure if the Lukes were in pursuit of her financial holdings. At the same time the Lukes were suspicious of their son being so taken so quickly with a younger woman.

Despite some parental misgivings, Frank and Marie made plans together for their future.

* * * *

At one point, Frank was faced with the choice of being a pursuit or fighter pilot, or being a bomber-observer. It was something that he contemplated seriously because the choice of assignments would be based on his specialty.

It is hard to picture this energetic young man not taking up a career as a pursuit pilot, but apparently Frank had given it a great deal of thought, as he expressed to his sister Anna: "I was informed today that the board had decided to send me to pursuit school rather than bombing. I only hope everything goes o.k. and the change is made."[14] Despite his decision, the bureaucracy of the Army Signal Corps made the mistake of assigning Frank to bomber duty. He was so irate that he sent his complaint out by telegram to ensure that the issue was cleared up.

Frank received his commission on January 12, 1918, and received written orders to report to the Third Aviation Center for "flying instruction" at Issoudun, France.[15] For Frank, it was a big hurdle he had finally crossed.

He had been granted one final leave at home—just a few days before he would be traveling off to France. Frank saw his family at home in Phoenix, not realizing that it would be the last time they gathered. At one point, he was planning on going off with his friends to play football when his mother asked him to help on one more chore—planting some lilies in the front yard. Frank didn't complain. He planted the bulbs in the flower bed and covered them over, then left to spend time with his friends.[16] Lilies usually took a year to fully bloom in the arid Arizona climate. The flowers were a parting gesture from a loving son to his mother, and Frank took the time to add a personal touch to the effort, one that would not be evident for months to come.

Frank's departure from Marie was not easy on his young fiancée. "My little girl sure cried when I left here. She sure is the sweetest girl I ever met."[17] Frank, along with Granville Woodard, traveled to New York by train, stopping off in Chicago along the way. Frank drank in the countryside and let his mind turn to Marie. In a hastily scribbled note, he sent her a few words recalling their last walk along the beach and swim in the warm California surf.[18]

Frank's mind was not on the risks that he would be facing, but on the future that he and Marie were planning. Frank and Marie's future had not been decided by fate at this point. His thoughts were of the handful of romantic moments they had shared together.

The pair of pilots arrived with some time to kill in New York. Frank used the opportunity to visit his uncle Joseph, who still lived in the city. Frank also managed to get in a visit to the Aero Club of Manhattan, an elite establishment for this copper miner from Arizona. Frank was fascinated with the elevated trains and subways. His biggest concerns were for the future of his brother Ed, who was in artillery basic training, and that his mother send photographs of him on to Marie.[19]

Frank and Woody were assigned to the troopship *Leviathan* for their trip to France. The *Leviathan* had been a German ocean liner named the *Vaterland* before the U.S. declared war on Germany. Captured as a spoil of war, she had been renamed and pressed into service to carry troops across the Atlantic.

* * * *

The 27th Squadron was trained in England before being shipped off to France. They were put in one of the many holding camps where American troops were staged prior to deployment. Their camp was near Winchester. It was an idle time for the unit as it lacked equipment and its pilots had not yet gone through their final stage of combat training. Major Hartney provided lectures to the men based on his experiences over the front, but beyond that the men of the 27th sat and waited.

A darker side of Alfred Grant was beginning to emerge. Sergeant "Wobbly" Saunders was an enlisted man in the 27th Squadron and related a story regarding Grant's style as an officer: "One morning Grant took the squadron out to drill. We were hungry and cold and dirty. As there was no bathing facilities and no hot water for shaving. So we did not do very snappy drilling. Grant lined us up and bawled us out collectively. And finally he said if any one did not like what he said, he would meet outside the camp and take off his coat and it would be man to man. That disgusted most of us. For if he had been stark naked, he still would be an officer and me an enlisted man. For I would have chosen to be the guy. From then on Grant went down with about all the enlisted men. No one never neglected their duty because they did not like Grant."

Saunder's recollection of Grant continued: "Grant had this cook locked up in and [sic] old stone house. The other cooks were afraid to feed him. Grant had gave him 5 days on bread & water. I got a chicken and some more grub and sliped [sic] it to this man in the dark from the back while one of my good buddys [sic] engaged the guards in frount [sic] of the building." All of this over a man sneaking off to a YMCA fight without permission.[20]

The bully-like attitude of Lieutenant Grant is difficult to understand. Was he coming to grips with some guilt over the loss of his brother Silas, or was Grant simply an abusive man? Major Hartney apparently had no idea of Grant's attitudes or approach to leading the men.

On March 17, St. Patrick's Day, the word finally came to the 27th Squadron—they were to report in April to the Third Aviation Instruction Center at Issoudun in France.[21] The thought Frank revealed to his sister upon getting to France seemed to reassure his family that his commitment to Marie was not wavering: "I don't think there is going to be any change in girls for me. For Marie is a wonderful girl and I am growing stronger for her all of the time."[22]

The Luke family, his sisters and sister-in-law especially, reached out to Marie in the form of letters. It was obvious that they were doing what they could to welcome her into the family.

Marie however was facing difficulties of her own. She dropped out of school shortly after Frank left for France, and would remain out of school for just over eight months.[23] On top of this, her mother, Cora, had fallen sick, and Marie, as the only child in San Diego, was left to take care of her. For Marie, only her music would provide her solace while her true love was flying and fighting half a world away.

Chapter Five

"Mothers here seem but to bear their sons to make them soldiers and then sacrifice them to the cruel jaws of the greed of nations. How unlike modern 20th century policy it sounds too. The condition of the world today is no different than it was in the barbarous times in the 2nd and 3rd centuries that we read about. Such being the case, what real good has civilization done? You can answer that yourself."

—JOSEPH WEHNER AUGUST 29, 1916

The American Expeditionary Force
April–July 1918

There were forces at work in the late spring and early summer of 1918 that were bringing elements of the war together and in Frank's life. America was about to fully engage in a war that had torn Europe asunder for the last four years. It was a time of whirlwind friendships and a clash of cultures. Frank Luke flew into this mix blissfully ignorant.

The 27th Squadron went through advanced combat training at Issoudun. The facility was spread out over miles of ground and consisted of eight flying fields. When pilots were not training, studying, or in the air, they were working on simply building Issoudun, everything from digging foundations, to building barracks, to laying the rail line. They didn't like the duty at all but it was necessary. Even their command staff didn't enjoy it. General Pershing himself referred to Issoudun as "the worst mudhole in France."[1]

Pilots started at Field One and, as a group tested and "graduated," they moved on to the next field for training. Field One used the penguin (non-flying) simulators to teach combat techniques. Field Two was flying with the 23-meter Nieuport aircraft. Field Four was where pilots learned how to spiral aircraft, doing their flying there with the 18-meter Nieuports. Advanced acrobatics were taught to classes on Field Five, this time flying the more agile 15-meter Nieuport airplanes. Pilots then moved on to Field Six, where they were trained in formation flying, important for patrol missions. Field Seven was where pilots learned cross-country flying techniques and navigation.

The last two fields at Issoudun were the most important. Field Eight was where combat training and tactics were taught. The skills learned on Field Eight determined who won air battles. There was gunnery training, where proficiency with real machine guns was tested, and dogfights were simulated with cameras mounted in lieu of guns on the airplanes. Pilots would bring back their films for developing and would be evaluated on whether the "shots" they took were close enough to the targets to be considered hits.

At Issoudun, you either graduated the eight fields and moved on, or you ended up at the last field, Field Thirteen. No flying took place at Field Thirteen. It was the graveyard for those pilots that failed to master the skills. White crosses marked where their failures rested. Crashes were not uncommon at Issoudun and activities occurred with eerie regularity and grim solace at Field Thirteen.[2]

In its day, Issoudun was spoken of with the same recognition as the Navy's Top Gun or the Air Force's Red Flag programs. By the end of the war, 776 American men graduated from Issoudun. Completion of the course was a mark of excellence, and Issoudun provided the skills to keep a pilot alive and deadly in the air.[3]

Major Hartney's 27th Squadron made its way through the training field at Issoudun, but it paid for that training with its own dear blood. The U.S. Army Air Service was so new that there was no list of standard equipment to outfit it with. Quite literally, they were counting on combat veterans like Hartney to help flesh out these kinds of details. It was painstaking work, ordering every little tool, spare part, and item needed to put a squadron at the front and keep it operational.

While in Paris ordering the necessary gear, Hartney got word that two of his most promising pilots had died in two separate crashes: Pat Ingersoll and James Marquardt. "They were buried in Field 13 before I ever heard of it."[4] The major had rushed back to perform a duty he never cherished, letting the parents know that their sons were not coming back from the war.

One of the biggest concerns that Hartney had was over what kind of aircraft his squadron would use. America did not have its own aircraft comparable to the fighting pursuit planes being used at the front and there was a persistent fear that they would receive aircraft that were obsolete or previously used. Major Hartney was pleasantly surprised when they were assigned Nieuport 28s. These were well-established fighters, not old, obsolete aircraft. For a while, they would serve as the core of the 27th Squadron. They were graceful aircraft, easy to fly, perfect for the newly-minted American aviators.

On May 1, 1918, Hartney had orders to take the 27th to the front. The time had come for his eagles to show what they could do. Back at Issoudun, one of Hartney's best future pilots had no idea that the squadron he was going to serve in was on its way to the front.

* * * *

One of the first things Frank did after he arrived was to let his parents know via telegram that he had gotten there safely, and he followed the telegram with a letter to his father to confirm that he had a $10,000 life insurance policy in place. "I know that nothing is going to happen but I am telling you just the same."[5]

Frank found Issoudun to be a place where he could test his mettle. He demonstrated his aggressive techniques when Harry Starkey Aldrich, destined to be a flight commander in the 1st Aero Squadron, went up against him at Issoudun on Field Eight. "Well do I remember the day when Luke's name and mine were listed together and we flew up over our appointed section of the sounding country to do battle. That we in the class realized that Luke was a bit reckless is putting in mildly. I was still peacefully climbing for altitude when this fact was abruptly recalled. Luke was heading straight for me. Just as I pulled up to avoid colliding, he executed a perfect renversement to get in position behind me. My plane passed under him as he dropped to straighten out. His right wing nipped my left ever so slightly. Another inch, and we would have flown our last flight. My ship was still wobbling from the effects of his propeller wash when he made another terrific dive at me. For the reminder of that period I contented myself with avoiding what I considered a series of collisions. That in itself was 'battle' practice.

"He landed just before me and approached my ship as I was wrathfully climbing out."

"'You aren't peeved at me are you?' he asked innocently enough."

"'Well, I can get over it,' I answered. 'If you can remember that I earnestly desire to live long enough to get to the front in case we have to fly together tomorrow.' Which was mind enough considering the jangled state of my nerves. His films, when developed, showed that he had scored several deadly shots on vital parts of my anatomy."

"I never did fly with him again, but several others who did made no effort to conceal the fact that they were on the verge of nervous prostration when they landed. I knew just how they felt!"[6]

Whatever mad exploits lay ahead of Frank over the fields of France, he was a conscientious young man. On Mother's Day, he wrote his future mother-in-law, the iron-willed Cora Rapson, as well as his own mother. Frank's mother was beginning to warm up to the fact that she was going to have a new daughter-in-law. "I am glad there is no other girl, but Marie. I am getting to love her more every day so don't you dare to love anyone else."[7] Frank spent some time boxing other aviators and settling in with the good food offered pilots.

Frank was wide-eyed at France and what he was learning. Only a few months earlier, he was learning how to fly, now he was across the world in a strange country, struggling with the language, preparing for battle. His letters home were a mix of attempting to explain tactics and formations to his mother and expressing the things that gave him fun: "I went down and did some contour flying. That's flying near the earth, skimming trees, farms, etc. It is also great sport to chase French farmers."[8]

For a young man from Arizona, France was a totally different world. Frank's letters home speak of the differences, "Everything is so old and the buildings are made of stone and most of them have great stone fences about them."[9] Coming from Arizona, even the most subtle things seemed to impress him. Frank wrote his family and told them that he was struggling to learn French. "Am having a hard time with my French. Pick up a word now and then. Start taking lessons and YMCA this evening. Think they will help me a great deal."[10] He wrote Bill Elder at home of some of the horrors of war that he was beginning to witness: "I just passed a double-seater motorcycle. One of the fellows was carrying a pilot who had run into a tree and smashed his head. Gee, it was a tough sight! His eyes were bulged out and his head was one mass of blood. He died a short while after reaching the hospital. The trouble was a bad fog came up just after he left the ground. He tried to land before it reached him but was too late, lost his way, and hit the tree."[11]

His thoughts were never far from his fiancé. In letters to his family, he pressed for them to get to know his future wife: "Sure hope you get to go to San Diego and see Marie."[12] In most of Frank's writing, he spared his family from the dangers and risks he faced as a pilot. With Marie, Frank was able to open up a little. During Frank's cross-country flying, he ran into some problems and was forced down. In an almost cavalier tone, Frank relayed the story of a crash he was involved in in a letter to his beloved Marie:

April 5, 1918
Dearest Sweetheart
Have just come back from a two day leave. Had a forced landing on one of my cross country trips and was out for two days. Broke

the machine up quite bad. Had dinner with a French farmer and was treated real fine. Staid [sic] in a small hotel that night.

Will try and answer two real nice long letters I received from you. Say, what do you think I gave those wings to you for? Why of course I want you to wear them. And tell whoever you want who they represent. When I was there I said something about you not wearing them when you were out with me. For I did not want anyone to think that they were someone else's. I think that's the way they would have taken it if we were both wearing wings. It was very sweet of you to say you would get down on your knees and scrub floor all day long for me. But let's hope that you never have to scrub floors, etc.

Am going over to the commanding officer tomorrow and see if I can get permission to ask for my sox and pictures from you. Very sorry that order came out. For would have liked, very much to have a nice box from you and your mother. Hope I receive some mail tomorrow.

Sweet Kisses,

FRANK[13]

On May 30, Frank was sent for some additional training in gunnery skills at Cazaux, near the Pyrenees. For a young man that had been raised around guns and shooting, he excelled at his work there. Frank received letters from Marie and from her mother as well as members of his family. From his bed in France, he did what he could to ensure that his family maintained contact with his fiancée. His thoughts were still on their future together: "No mother you don't need to be afraid of me changing my mind about Marie. I know I am very changeable, but not this time. Am saving money to buy her a ring."[14]

Frank wanted a change of pace. He was chafing for an opportunity to put his skills to the test in a real dogfight. The war was only a few short miles away, and for some reason, he was not in it yet. The one person that he opened up to, Marie, was a long way away. He was in need of a friend … and one was not far away. He was in need of action, and it, too, was closer than he realized.

* * * *

Germany realized that once the United States declared war in April of 1917, the clock was ticking. The ground war in Europe had been a deadly slugfest with little lost or gained in even the large-scale battles. Germany was slowly being starved on the war front and at home. With America siding against her, Germany realized that if she did not win the war decisively before the fresh troops from the U.S. arrived, it would be too late. If a German victory was going to be a reality, it was going to have to come swiftly, before America could muster her strength with the Allies. With the defeat of the Russians, Germany was able to shift nearly the full weight of her military onto the Western Front.

The resulting German Spring Offensive rocked the British and French lines in early 1918. Using storm troops and modified tactics, the Germans had pulverized a gap in the front lines that had been stalled for so long. They successfully drove to within 25 miles of Paris before their momentum was lost. Slowly, stubbornly, they gave ground back as British, French, and the fresh American troops, tanks, and planes were tossed in front of them. From a German perspective the chance to win the Great War had passed.

The stalemate of the trench fighting on the Western Front was on the verge of returning as the Allies pressed a counterattack. By July of 1918, the Germans had massed forces in Château-Thierry. The key to fighting in that sector was the Fère-en-Tardenois railway. For the Germans, it was a lifeline to their troops and allowed them to quickly move their resources to respond to Allied attack. The Americans reached Fère-en-Tardenois, but the Germans mounted a counterattack that turned the battle into a see-saw of give and take.

This set the stage for the three major campaigns that defined the American military mission in Europe. *Château-Thierry* was the first, though it was not a highly planned engagement; American forces were tossed in as stop-gaps where needed. The second was the *St. Mihiel campaign*. And the third was the *Meuse-Argonne offensive*. Château-Thierry would be the first true test of the American army in fighting on European terms. The St. Mihiel offensive would be the first truly planned operational use of the American Air Service. For the new U.S. Army Air Service, it was to be a deadly first start. The Meuse-Argonne operation was to come later in 1918, ringing the funeral dirge of the German fighting forces on the Western Front.

The bulge, or salient, in the line at St. Mihiel had been there since the early days of the war. Located near Verdun, it had proven to be a sore spot for years, and the Allies feared that the Germans would use the bulge as a launching point for an offensive to encircle Verdun or even drive on past the fortress there to Paris.

The St. Mihiel salient was approximately 25 miles long and 15 miles deep. The terrain had been chewed up by artillery and bombing and the gouging trench-lines that zigzagged across the rolling hills. The western edge of the bulge was the Meuse River and this was far enough back from the devastation of the artillery that thick woods still covered the hills and ridgelines. The southern edge of the line had the independent heights of Montsec and Loupmount. From these rises the Germans could observe any movement against them on the flat plains.

The trench lines were not simply challenging, they were deadly. The salient was part of the infamous Hindenburg Line of defense. Sections of the trench line were concrete reinforced with staging bunkers for troops to protect them from the rolling and box artillery barrages that were necessary to advance into the pocket. Machine gun emplacements were reinforced as well. There were areas of independent secondary works to the rear of the front lines so that if retreat was necessary, the German forces would have prepared positions to fall back on. If anyone was going to try to take the bulge it was going to be a tough operation.

At the same time, St. Mihiel presented an opportunity. It was not an all-out offensive aimed at penetrating the rear of the German lines, but was simply the reduction of a risk area on the map. It was a relatively small area, perfect for testing the battle skills of the new American soldiers that were arriving. There was some skepticism among the French and British as to how the Americans would hold up in their first real campaign.

For the U.S. Army Air Service, there had been some minor actions during the German offensive drive on Paris—but the final reduction of the St. Mihiel salient would represent their first true test.

* * * *

After his training at Cazaux, Frank found himself placed in the pool of available pilots. The pool was replacements for losses that the squadrons already fighting at the front were destined to need. The good news was that his friend Woody Woodard was at Cazaux with him. They managed to get some time away from training to go down to the French coastal beach and relax.

Soon, Frank and the other aviators were given duties at Orly, outside Paris, as ferry pilots. The losses that squadrons felt were not just pilots and observers, but aircraft as well. Planes were sometimes repaired, re-patched or simply delivered to the field at Orly. A ferry pilot like Frank would then fly that plane to the front-line squadron, and obtain ground travel back to Orly. Most pilots found this duty frustrating, and Frank was no exception. He wanted to get to the front and fight, not deliver airplanes for other pilots. Despite the fact that ferry duty would give him invaluable experience in the air, what mattered to him was getting into the real war.

Frank found out that his brother-in-law, John Sherry (married to his sister Eva), was in Europe, as well. He contacted him with several letters. He took the time to go out and visit many of the famous sites in Paris. On July 5, he made his way to American University Union Hotel in Paris, treating himself to a room there.[15] During his time at Orly, Frank did the majority of the writing he did during his wartime career. Most of his letters dealt with the mundane, describing France, writing of the thrills of flying, asking the family to continue to write him, and about Marie. Frank did not express the concerns he must have had—of war or his own possible death. Some of his silence on this score was probably to shelter the family from concern, while some was probably because of his confidence in himself and his skills.[16]

While Frank didn't believe that being a ferry pilot was a test of his skills, he did see the true intentions of the program. Every hour a pilot spent in the air was experience that would prove invaluable in combat, even if that duty was nothing more than shuttling airplanes. Frank flew a wide range of airplanes and logged time in the air. He learned the subtleties of each plane, how each handled and responded. This would give him some appreciation for the variety of aircraft that the Germans would fly against him.

* * * *

The 27th Squadron under Major Hartney had been at the front for a few short weeks but was already making the transition from a group of green pilots to seasoned veterans. But the men of the squadron were still wet behind the ears. As if to emphasize this, on June 23 a French airplane landed at the 27th's field. The pilot got out and in fluent French, asked to be refueled. The Fighting Eagles were planning a celebratory party that evening, commemorating their one-year anniversary and felt obliged to invite their visitor to join them in the festivities. In broken English, the pilot welcomed the 27th to the front lines. He took out a camera and pictures were taken of the pilot with his new American friends. After the party he took off, waving thanks to them.

They discovered after the war, when that pilot's photos were shared with the Americans, that he was a German flying a captured French aircraft. The pilot, dressed in a captured French flight suit, had managed to play a practical joke on the new American squadron.[17]

The incident was a colorful example of the type of camaraderie that pilots exhibited during the Great War. It was also proof that the Fighting Eagles were still a young unit, still attempting to make that transformation to veteran combat unit. Unfortunately, that transition was coming with a high cost—in terms of human lives.

The squadron was moved around like a fire brigade as command attempted to figure out the best place for it to operate. Hartney's boys had been sent to Toul and to Touquin to help blunt the German offensive operation, splitting the squadron up. Toul proved hot and dusty for the unit, but not at the forefront of the fighting. Touquin had been almost like a vacation for the officers—their billet was the 900-year-old Château de la Fortelle and its surrounding farm houses. On July 8, the squadron was reassembled and was relocated to Saints. The majority of the officers billeted in the Hotel de Marie, which had doubled as a hospital earlier in the war. Some of the officers and most of the enlisted personnel made use of a large nearby farm house. Because of the stifling heat, many simply pitched tents in open fields.[18]

Jerry Vasconcells was declared dead on June 10, 1918 when the engine on his Nieuport cut out and he glided down just in front of the American lines. Caught in a massive trench mortar bombardment he was rescued by some doughboys just before the mortar blew up his crashed airplane. In their rescue, they bumped his head on a gun breech and knocked Jerry out. Word had gotten back to the 27th that he was dead, and his parents were informed that their son had died. It took Jerry three days to make his way back to the mess of the 27th, and when he arrived, half-stumbling in at dinner time, the mess hall erupted with cheers. Some of the men even pinched him to make sure he was really there.[19]

On July 20, a five-plane patrol went up and slammed headlong into seven German Albatrosses. The battle was lopsided at best. One man, Zenos "Red" Miller, was shot down but managed to land what was left of his Nieuport. He came down on the other side of the battle lines and became a POW.

Lieutenant Fred Norton made his way back, crippled with a chest wound. From his bed, before he died, he scribbled a note to Major Hartney: "Twenty-seventh, more power to you."[20] Lieutenant John MacArthur's death was quick. He was one of the first aces of the 27th and had been a rising star.

His passing was a grim reminder to everyone of just how dangerous their profession could be, regardless of skill.

Two pilots made it back from the mission relatively unscathed—physically at least: Lieutenants Leo H. Dawson and Ivan Roberts, Roberts's machine had taken a total of twenty-six bullet holes and had to be declared as salvage—not airworthy.[21] The losses had gutted the 27th's combat capabilities and had dealt a blow to their morale. There had been a few losses of pilots up to this point, but the events on July 20, 1918, hit the unit hard.

The time had come for the unit to call up some new pilots, replacements from the pool of aviators. The call went out from Hartney to the officer in charge of determining who went on these flights, the personnel officer. Captain Frederick Zinn, the young officer from Galesburg, Michigan, took that call, and, going over the log books, determined that the time had come for Luke and Wehner.[22]

* * * *

For Frank this was the opportunity that he had been waiting for. He packed his gear and his flight log, and set off with his bunkmates for assignment. Granville Woodard received his word from Zinn's office, as well, that he was destined for combat duty at last, as did two other pilots, Oliver Beauchamp and Norman Archibald. In later years, in his serialized story *Heaven High, Hell Deep*, Archibald conveyed his recollection of their trip.

> With plenty of room and many seats unoccupied the trip was a contrast to previous ones in France. Two other men, also ordered to the First Pursuit Group, were aboard—Grandville [sic] Woodard and Frank Luke. We four sat together. Four men in the same uniforms, four men with the same goal, four men with the same thoughts … the First Pursuit Group … Chasse pilots … the Front!
>
> The slow train stopped frequently. Every five minutes of waiting was unbearably long. About four-thirty in the afternoon we

jerked into Coulommiers, a peaceful village about thirty kilometers southwest to Château Thierry. A truck from the Group met us. Twenty minutes later we drew up before headquarters tent and reported for duty.

An officer, seated behind a desk in the corner, looked up and, smiling, greeted us. We handed him our orders and received a questionnaire. We must fill in the blanks: our parents' names ... home address, and whom to notify in case of death ...

Fully a dozen times I had answered these same questions, filled in these same blank spaces and it always seemed a useless, red-taped procedure. But now—WHO SHALL BE NOTIFIED IN CASE OF DEATH stood out. It was, after all, necessary and important. For the first time the question seemed sane and logical.

Quickly and with little conversation, we were assigned to our squadrons. Beauchamp and Luke to the 27th, Woodard and I to the 95th.[23]

For Frank, this was his first meeting with Harold Hartney, a man who would help him channel his energy to purpose of action. He was about to meet his new family, his squadron-mates of the 27th. It was going to be a time when egos, ambitions, and skill would form a crucible that would produce one of the greatest aviators in American history.

* * * *

Joseph Fritz Wehner was born on September 20, 1895, in Boston, Massachusetts. His father owned a tailor shop where he also performed repairs as a makeshift cobbler. In the same little shop his mother worked as seamstress. Joseph was the child of Prussian immigrants who came from a small town less than 50 miles from where Frank Luke's family was from. Joe's father had served as a marine in the German navy for a few years before he migrated to America.

Joe was a quiet man who kept his words to a minimum when he did speak. He had chestnut hair and deep brown eyes. Compared to many early aviators, Joe was tall, just an inch shy of six feet. His entire life he had been a skilled athlete, playing baseball and football. His last year at Everett High School in 1914 he was the top football player and the president of the senior class.

In the summer of 1914, Joe hitchhiked out to Kansas to get a glimpse of the Wild West. Joe gained an appreciation for horsemanship and for the first time in his life, saw a great deal of the United States. He rode a cattle drive in South Dakota, further testing his endurance. When he did return to school, he did so at the prestigious Phillips Exeter Academy in New Hampshire on a scholarship. At Exeter he was on the crew team and was center on their pennant-winning football team, the illustrious "Academy Eleven," as they were known. The oddly quiet Wehner was in the Assembly Club, responsible for organizing dances, and was a June Ball Officer. He was a member of the Bay State Club for boys that came from Massachusetts at the school.

The years between 1915 and 1916 were a period of change for Joe. His grades at Exeter dropped markedly, performance that placed his scholarship at risk. He excelled at sports but that was not enough. In Europe, the war was grinding on. All of these factors contributed to Joe seeking some sort of change in the direction of his life.[24]

Joe left Exeter and took a secretarial job in London with the Citizens' Relief Committee. This group's primary mission was to help neutral Americans stranded in London when the war broke out. Joe came back but his feelings about the war were mixed, because of his German heritage and his English experience. The impact of the war ate at him and he wanted to seek out another way to get involved with the crisis in Europe. Joe wanted to help his countrymen in Germany and with the United States being neutral at the time, such efforts were possible.

He traveled with the YMCA to Berlin to help distribute food to war refugees. It gave the young man a unique perspective on the war that his fellow Americans could not appreciate. In a letter to his sister Hazel, Joe painted a gloomy picture of the war that most people in the U.S. had not been exposed to: "It really is impossible for you people in America, not being able to witness the conditions here, to conceive of the tense, unspoken, un-murmured suffering here endured. These thousands of legless, armless, eyeless, jawless, and otherwise crippled soldiers of Europe live on to tell a sad, mournful, painful and altogether horrible story of their share in this greatest of all world's struggles."[25]

At the age of twenty-one, Joe had witnessed more of the effects of the Great War than almost any other American at the time.

When the U.S. declared war on Germany in April of 1917, Joe was evacuated back to America with the staff of the embassy. Joe's loyalties were clear to him—by July he was enlisted in the U.S. Army Air Service.

He was sent to the University of Texas at Austin to take the same training that Frank had a few months earlier. Joe hitchhiked there as he had two years earlier when going to Kansas, saving his parents and himself the cost of travel. He was sent on for his flight training at Kelly Field in Texas and was assigned to the 186th Aero Squadron as a bomber pilot. He went for additional training to Scott Field in Belleville, Illinois. He received his commission as a second lieutenant on January 9, 1918.[26]

Not all of his time training went smoothly. Another cadet, Walter Whalen of Dorchester, Massachusetts, was involved in a discussion when Joe had commented on how easy it was to secure a U.S. passport and talked of his time in Germany before the American declaration of war. Whalen contacted Captain Thomas McConnell and related his suspicions regarding Wehner's true loyalties. Given Joe's German origins, his comments seemed to indicated that he might have pro-German leanings. The hint was there—Wehner might be a spy. Captain McConnell contacted the Justice Department, who immediately dispatched two agents to look into the young tailor's son.

It is important to note that the Secret Service (authorized by President Wilson to investigate espionage) was being taxed to its limits by patriotic-minded Americans who saw potential spies everywhere. Thousands of letters were sent to the federal government, from Wilson on down, each asking that a neighbor, co-worker, union, or even bar be investigated as a potential spy or a hiding spot for enemy saboteurs. The German-sanctioned sabotage at the Kingsland and Black Tom munitions facilities only added to the tensions regarding families with deep German connections.

Agent Louis Loebl arrived at the Scott Field Aviation School where Joe was training. He interviewed Joe's classmates and what he found was not a spy but a "very studious and ambitious young man," who "does not associate with anyone in particular and spends most of his spare time reading and writing."[27] Wehner was considered "a most efficient candidate for a commissioned officer."

Joe did not try to hide his background. In conversation, he freely offered up that he had been to Sweden and Germany before the U.S. had entered the war. Another cadet, Irwin Stone, in his interview indicated that Joe had stated that he had a bitter attitude towards England and believed that the British were the main cause of the European conflict.

Lobel did not interview Joe himself but instead waited until Joe went to church, then tossed his bunk searching for some evidence of Wehner's collaboration with the Germans. The commanding officer, Major Wheeler, was present to ensure that Lobel did not do anything inappropriate. Aside from Joe's diary and address book, the most subversive material he found were copies of the *Christian Science Monitor* and some books Joe had checked out of the Belleville Public Library.

The entire investigation was deemed as "unproductive," and suspicion of Joe Wehner as a German spy was dropped.

Joe went to the Third Aviation Instruction Center at Issoudun at the same time that Frank was there. He had been attached to the 186th Squadron until he, too, received orders to report to the front with the 27th Squadron.

The two young aviators became quick friends, though in many respects they were opposites. While Frank was a nervous, fast talker, Joe Wehner was quiet, and when he did speak he used as few words as possible. Frank was excited and energetic, whereas Joe tended to always operate on an even keel. Where Frank was gregarious, Joe was introspective and thoughtful. At first glance, it would appear that they were not going to get along, but the reality was that they would be a dynamic pair of fighter pilots.

Wehner's letters home offer a glimpse of their first times together:

> About a week and a half after I first joined the 27th Aero Squadron which is located directly behind the Chateau Thierry district, where the big fighting is going on. The aviation camp is, of course, located a little distance behind the lines and consequently the only real taste of war that I get is in my daily trips over the lines, or in an occasional bombing raid. As the camps are not permanent, all the flying officers are billeted in different homes in a little village near the camp. There are always autos handy to convey us to and from the aerodrome.
>
> I happen to be sharing a room with another lieutenant by the name of Luke, in a little farm house on the outskirts of the town. The farm is very peaceful and quiet and an ideal place to rest up during the evening. The French people treat us fine and give us practically anything we want. The weather is hot and sultry, typical of New England, hot and sultry during the day time and pleasantly cool during the night.
>
> I don't mind the heat much because I spent a great deal of the day in the air. When I am not on the front I take trial trips with my ship and combat with Frank Luke up in the air, which is very good fighting practice. During my spare time on the farm I play with my mandolin, running through everything from the "Twelfth Street Rag" to "Pour Soir d'Amour." [sic]

Joe did find some romance in France. He met a young French woman named Charlotte. Joe made an effort to fly out to meet her whenever he got the chance. His experiences in his first actual combat were nothing more than a footnote: " P.S. Flew over the lines this morning and had beaucoup excitement. Two big battles with a lot of Huns. I had a new sensation today. Bullets, when they fly past your ear don't whistle but they whine like a high note drawn out on a violin."[28]

For Frank, in the evenings, hearing of Joe's first brush with real air combat had to be exciting and frustrating. Like other pilots in the pool, he was forced to wait until the right moment when destiny would intervene and allow him to show everyone what he was capable of.

* * * *

Frank made a conscious decision around this time; he was not going to write the family regarding his stationing at the front. With only a few exceptions did he give any hint that he was at the front lines. Most of his letters were filled with the details of his life that did *not* deal with combat and the risks he was facing. He knew his mother was just going to worry. Instead, his mail to family and friends began to diminish. Whereas Frank was writing a letter or two a day for many days when he was behind the lines, during his time at the front the volume dropped dramatically.

He made the same decision to keep Marie in the dark. As far as she would know, Frank was still ferrying airplanes, waiting for his chance to go to the front and prove himself.

Chapter Six

"If a man can be brave, he was the bravest man I ever saw. He'd burn a balloon then turn around and chase the gunners away from the guns on the ground just for the hell of it. If the rest of us got a good crack at a balloon, it was in and then gone because the bullets were kind of thick. I could never get one."

—LIEUTENANT CHARLES R. D'OLIVE, 93RD AERO SQUADRON

The Front
July 31–August 15, 1918

Frank Luke was joining a squadron that was at a low point in its morale. The original pool of pilots had suffered losses from their time at Issoudun and recently in combat. The shocking losses of the young men hardened some and embittered others. Frank, Oliver Beauchamp, and Joe Wehner were untested, and to the experienced pilots of the 27th Squadron, these new pilots were wet behind the ears. Some, they knew by now, were simply going to end up dead.

Frank's arrival at the 27th was less than glamorous. He along with the other replacements stood at attention in front of Major Hartney, whom they knew from his reputation, if not personally. "You men stand in front of me today [but] within two weeks each of every one of you will be dead—cold dead—unless you weigh what I say. You are going to be surprised in the first, second, or third trip over the line and, despite all I can say right now, you will never know there is an enemy ship near you until you notice your windshield disintegrating or until a sharp sting interrupts your breathing. School is all over. You have a man's job. You hold a commission. You are the right hand of the President of the United States himself. If when you get up there over the lines you find you want to come back that means you're yellow. I do not ask you to be brave enough to go over, I only ask you to have enough guts to come back and tell me so and get to hell out of this outfit.

"Remember, we are about two hundred officers up here all told. You are now members of the 27th Squadron in the First Pursuit Group, the finest flying outfit on this front. Back home there are 50,000 young men learning to fly and eager to be where you are. But you are in the 27th in name only. When you have shown your buddies out there that you have the guts and can play the game honestly and courageously, they'll probably let you stay. You'll know without my telling you when you are actually members of this gang. It's up to you."[1] His words carried weight. The word with the other pilots was that Major Hartney had gone up against Manfield von Richthofen, the infamous Red Baron ... and lived.

What most people would have done is kept quiet, gotten to know the now-veteran pilots, and attempted to blend in. That wasn't Frank's style or personality. He almost seemed to go out of his way to not endear himself to the pilots of the squadron.

Much has been made of Frank's boastfulness and bragging when he arrived at the 27th Squadron. Frank *did* boast to his new squadron-mates as to what he was going to do, and it *did* rub them the wrong way. He was cocky, self-confident, and far from shy. Sergeant George Jordan was speaking with Frank once after his arrival, and the two of them saw a German aircraft fly near their field. Frank's comment to the sergeant was blunt: "Gee, that plane would be a cinch for me."[2] Comments like that were misconstrued as bragging when in reality Frank was simply stating the facts as he saw them. Enlisted men in the 27th noted his behavior too. "Luke was sort of a braggart when he arrived but he was no mixer. He was remarking, 'I'll get them Germans.'"[3] What made the boasts more irritating is the fact that Frank would live up to his words. He was not bragging, he was simply stating facts. Like a savant, he knew events that would come to pass.

Hartney put them on a rigorous training program. They did formation flying with seasoned flight leaders. No solo flights. Hartney even took up flights himself to see how the pilots performed. They would gradually be exposed to the risks of battle, and hopefully would do so under his supervision. Major Hartney cared for his men as if they were his own sons.

On August 1, a series of routine training flights ended up as a bloody round of battle. At 7:05 A.M., Frank and Joe Wehner were in a flight of aircraft assigned to protect a pair of Salmson reconnaissance aircraft. Frank broke formation with that flight when they entered the clouds and used the opportunity to take off on his own. For a green pilot, this was daring to the point of recklessness. While he did not score any victories, he was setting the tone for how he planned to fight the air war. Frank claimed that engine problems had forced him to break with the formation—a legitimate reason if it were true. It was an excuse that he would overuse many times in the coming days.

In retrospect, the pilots realized that Frank was running off to engage the enemy and using the mechanical (and other) excuses as his cover. At the time, the thought was quite the opposite. Word circulated that Frank was yellow—that he was afraid to face the enemy and was faking engine problems to flee from potential battles. Coupled with his bravado and bragging, it only served to make his relationships with the other pilots more tense.

Lieutenant Don Hudson's flight had taken off at 8:10 and it was attacked east of Fère-en-Tardenois by eight Fokker D. VIIs from Richthofen's Jagdgeschwader Nr. I. Though the Red Baron was now dead, his flying circus under the command of Hermann Göring was still a potent threat. The estimated eight German fighters came from high and in front of the Americans, heading straight at them. The fight was a whirling tornado of aircraft all diving, looping, and swirling to get each other in their sights. It was pandemonium and confusion painted with the red hand of death. The 27th Squadron managed to disengage and claimed five victories, but the cost was high—six of their pilots dead or captured.[4]

* * * *

Major Hartney saw something in the young man from Arizona. Only a few days after Frank's arrival in the 27th, the unit had suffered its most devastating losses in battle. Six pilots had been injured or killed. The flight leader, Don Hudson, had downed two German Rumpler C observation aircraft in the fight, securing his fourth and fifth victories and making him an ace. On August 3, Hartney had received word from a newspaper reporter that the aircraft that Hudson had downed had been located, and that the two pilots and observers had been left unattended to in the wrecks. Hartney wanted to check it out for himself. One of his officers, Frank Luke, asked if he could come along. Together they took a train, then a Packard automobile, setting out to find the downed aircraft.

Frank opened up with Hartney during the trip. He spoke about his experiences in training, his assignments at Orly, his desire to be an outstanding fighter pilot. Hartney was impressed with the young man, despite the rumors he had heard. When they arrived at the crash site, they found the two Rumpler Cs actually crunched together, a jumbled mess of wood, canvas, and engine blocks. The heat of the sun had turned the faces of the dead men black and the air stank of gasoline and death.[5]

On the next ridge they spotted other dead bodies: infantry. Frank and the major walked over to them. They too were showing the initial signs of decay. They had attempted a rush against a German machine gun nest, and failed. Frank checked one of them and found a number of un-mailed postcards to the victim's mother in Iowa.

"Leave them there. That American padre over there is busy picking up such things to send back to the next of kin," Hartney replied.

Frank slowly and carefully put them back. "Boy," he said back to his commanding officer, "I'm glad I'm not in the infantry. They haven't a chance, have they, Major?"

They left the area in the Packard but were stopped by an American lieutenant who warned them that if they continued on, they would be in enemy territory. The last car that had gone before them had been captured. It was so quiet that the small party had not realized that they had drifted this close to the front lines. Hartney asked if there were any other downed aircraft in the vicinity and the officer told him where several downed French airplanes were.

When they arrived they found two British Sopwith Camels and the wrecks of two German aircraft. They were lying in a torn-up field of shattered stumps and the occasional crater from artillery. Major Hartney called Luke over to one of the aircraft and asked him to look at it in order to determine what had taken it down. Frank crawled over the wreck, looking at the bullet holes and their angles.

"These men were all diving away when they were hit, weren't they, Major?" Hartney replied. "Yes. It's what I've told you and the other boys a dozen times. That's about the only time you get hit."

Frank surveyed the crashed aircraft one more time. "By God, they'll never catch me that way."[6]

* * * *

There is a tendency for people to portray Frank Luke as a man that did not fit in at all with the pilots of his squadron. That is simply not true. He was simply different from many of them. Frank was not afraid to be himself. His nervous energy, excitable attitude, and sheer confidence allowed him to stand out. He was not a loner: he ate and drank with his fellow pilots. When gambling was done after hours, Frank took part just like everyone else. Frank seemed to have a knack at gambling and often won. His strong Roman Catholic upbringing held true while in France, and he regularly attended mass while the squadron was at Saints. When he went to mass with Joe Bronz from the unit, Bronz took his winnings from the night before and dumped them into the collection plate. When Frank saw him do that, he did the same. The next Sunday the sexton, having been so gleefully rewarded by the soldiers, had a larger water basin he was passing to collect their craps winnings. Frank took his blessings with a clean conscience.[7]

* * * *

As Norman Archibald recalled after the war:

> "Frank's missions were varied, mostly at getting his commanding officers comfortable with him and his style. He flew on several missions, mostly training exercises. These were short patrols. Again, he developed a knack for dropping away from his formation and heading off on his own. There were no official reports, but his flight commanders sent Frank over to have his plane checked out each time."

This "lone wolf" approach wore thin with many of his peers. On top of his apparent bragging, Luke was not seen as a team player. This did not entirely make sense given Frank's participation in so many team sports when he was in high school. Frank demonstrated that he played well on a team—but at the same time showed that he was a young man that loved the limelight.

Frank would wander over to see his friend Granville Woodard in the 94th Squadron. Archibald Norman recounted how Frank's going solo to engage the Germans rubbed other pilots the wrong way. Not so much that he did it, but that he talked about it.

> "His own squadron almost ignored him. So he would come over to see us, Woody and me, for he had known Woody in the States and I was an amused listener.
>
> "Luke. Light haired, stocky and just twenty years old. The tales he told!
>
> "'Well, got another Boche,' he boasted and thereby began a recital of such flying and fighting as none could imagine.
>
> "'Did you get confirmation?' we parried.
>
> "Well, no, he hadn't but, hastily switching to the details of another victory, he so graphically described his personal triumphs, always against such terrific odds, that we would smile, insultingly.
>
> "But Luke was undaunted.

"He insisted he always left the formation. So, flying off somewhere all alone, how could anyone see what happened? He was a good flyer and a natural pilot. We knew that. He was fearless, too. But his commander, Hartney, had told him not to leave the formation so nothing hung together.

"One evening in front of the operation test, Luke again was narrating about his prowess. He said he left the formation, saw a German plane about a mile over the lines, had a terrible fight and his opponent went down in flames.

"Another flyer was standing near by. '*Those* kinds of victories are easy,' he said with dry sarcasm. 'You better go back and get confirmation.'

"Luke looked a bit hurt. But, launching afresh into another yarn, he novelized a hair-raising air battle in which, as always, he was the hero.

"No one believed him. No one ever saw his conquests. Luke still came over. His stories, more self-trumpeting as time went on would have paled the 'Penny-Dreadfuls.'

"Again and again after Hartney assumed command of the group and 'Ack' Grant became his commanding officer, Grant called him to account for deserting the formation. Always an excuse. He saw a German across the lines. He got lost in the clouds. He had motor trouble. Luke always had an alibi.

"'I want to *do* things,' he explained. 'I just can't help going off alone. I'm a different person once I get into the air.'

"The conceited jackass, we thought. His self-heroism sickened us. His cocky assurance made us fume. He had been too much for his own squadron, now we, too, were through. We would not tolerate such talk. We would not listen.

"Luke, the towheaded kid from Arizona, was an outcast."[8]

* * * *

After their tough losses, a big chance came for the squadron when the Nieuports that they flew were replaced with new model Spad XIII. This was not the morale-boosting event that one might imagine. Yes, these were newer model fighters and in many ways were superior to the Nieuports. But the Spads carried with them a terrible reputation in terms of reliability and maintenance issues. It had been rushed into production and many of the problems with it had to be worked out by the units at the front. For someone like Frank, who sought excuses to cover for leaving formation, the Spad XIII was a godsend.

The Nieuport was a slightly bigger aircraft, had more grace in the air. With a small engine, it wasn't very responsive, handling like a massive glider with a kick to it. Flying the Spad XIII was like riding a bucking bronco in comparison. Yes, it was faster, and it had a better climb rate and maximum altitude, but the controls seemed to fight against the pilot. Gone was the sweeping grace of the Nieuport 28s that the pilots had loved. What remained was an aircraft that required a pilot's constant attention and focus.

Their Hispano-Suiza (referred to as Hisso) engines required four *days* to dismantle, service, and reassemble. The reduction gear housing in the Spad was not secure and was prone to slipping out of alignment. The Spads would develop a slight vibration in their engines. While this may not sound too terrible, one must remember that the Spad was a plane built of thin strips of wood covered with stretched linen canvas for covering and a maze of crude plumbing around the engine. Vibration of any sort was bad. A small vibration, after a few minutes, would start shaking loose fuel, water coolant, and oil lines, and could even damage the propeller mount. Even a brand-new Spad could shake itself apart in the air if the engine mountings were not properly anchored. Ironing out these problems in the first few months of their deployment took time and added frustration to the fledgling American forces' tasks.[9]

Frank still was keeping most of his family in Arizona and Marie in San Diego in the dark regarding his assignment to the front. The only person in his family that he told the truth to was his brother-in-law, John Sherry.

John was in France as well and Frank had obtained his address and sent him a few letters during his time at the front. He felt comfortable sharing with John where he was, but maintained keeping the rest of the family in the dark. "Don't tell the folks anything about me being on the front."[10]

Frank's tone changed on August 16 when he filed his first request for confirmation of a combat kill, as recounted in Chapter One. Up until this point, he had been deemed a boaster; now he picked up a new title—liar. Frank was not dissuaded by the comments and jeers of his fellow officers. If confirmations were what was necessary, he was determined to provide them. Frank sat at a typewriter and created a blank form for his confirmations. The next time he downed an aircraft, he would land and make sure that it was confirmed.

The afternoon of his first combat victory, Frank was up again. He took off at 5:05 P.M. but did not immediately return from the mission. This is the first documented time that Frank chose to land at a different airfield, again with just a hint of rebellion.

Only three men believed Frank the day he claimed he shot down his first kill: Harold Hartney, Joseph Wehner, and Ivan Roberts. They would remain the most important men in his life.

* * * *

There was one officer in the chain of command who had the same rebellious nature as the young pilot: Army Colonel William "Billy" Mitchell. Mitchell was, as much as any one man, the father of the modern air force, even before it had been created. He understood the value of aircraft not just as observers but as part of an air dominance strategy. Mitchell managed to get appointed to the commissions that spent time in Europe earlier in the war to learn all that he could from the British and French about air power, tactics, and logistics. Colonel Mitchell was a special kind of officer. On his own time off-hours, he had learned to fly himself so that he could fully understand the complexities and capabilities of aircraft.

Mitchell lacked political savvy but made up for it with understanding. He comprehended the best way to use airpower in warfare—not as merely an attachment to the ground forces but as a means to cripple an enemy. Mitchell, like Luke, was right—but his critics did not always see it that way at the time. He locked horns with Brigadier general Benjamin Foulois, the chief of the Air Service. Mitchell believed that officers in charge of airmen should be pilots themselves, so that they could understand the nature of this new beast called the Air Service, and he dragged General Pershing into the squabble. For a time, it appeared that Mitchell might end up being sent back to the United States. But Pershing kept the fiery colonel around and moved in Major General Mason Patrick to assume leadership over the Air Service. The hope was that the level-headed Patrick would be able to soothe the situation that Mitchell kept brewing in terms of how the Air Service should be managed.

Billy Mitchell had two things going for him. First, he was right. Second, he was a man who could get things done. He cut through the bureaucracy and proved to Patrick how capable he was. He knew people well and manipulated Foulois to overplay his hand with General Pershing. Having stepped on Foulois's toes many times Foulois asked Pershing to relieve Mitchell. It didn't work. The Army needed men like Mitchell and General Pershing knew that. By the end of the Chateau Thierry campaign, Mitchell ended up as the top air combat commander in the Army.

Mitchell shook things up from the very top to the front lines as he prepared for the St. Mihiel Campaign—the first true test of his air service. Bert Atkinson, who commanded the First Pursuit Group, was bumped up to a new command. The man Billy Mitchell tagged to replace him as the commanding office of the entire First Pursuit Group was not a natural American at all, but the wily Canadian Harold Hartney, now promoted to Colonel. Hartney's old command, the 27th Squadron, would go to First Lieutenant Alfred Grant. These changes came down on August 21. There were no cheers for Grant taking command, but the men of the 27th arranged a formation fly-over for Hartney in tribute to their commanding officer.[11] Word also came down that the 27th would be moving again.

For Frank, this change of command was going to have some implications in his life. Lieutenant Grant was a stiff officer, more by-the-book. Hartney seemed to take the young Luke under his wing and understood how to get the best out of him. Grant did not have those kind of relationships in the unit. Frank was a rebel who defied authority. For Grant, authority was everything.

The twenty-six aircraft of the squadron were broken into three flights, A, B, and C. Frank was now part of C flight. Each of these flights consisted of six aircraft flown by second lieutenants and a lead plane flown by a first lieutenant, who was to serve as a flight leader. In the air, the flight leader was in charge. Using hand signals, gestures, and by his own actions, he guided a flight into battle or away from it.

That left a handful of aircraft and pilots not assigned. Simply put, these were replacements for losses. And there were losses. The aircraft were temperamental, some downright stubborn. While the mechanics could repair bullet damage quickly, the damage to engines was often a bit more complicated.

Hartney's new command, the First Pursuit Group, consisted of four squadrons, the 27th, 94th, 95th, and 147th. Each squadron was, on paper, to consist of twenty-six aircraft and a pilot for each aircraft. Three mechanics were assigned to each aircraft—testimony to how temperamental the machines were. The First Pursuit Group reported up with the III and IV Observation Groups, and the Army Observation Group to the First Pursuit Wing under Major Bert Atkinson. This reported to the Corps Observation Wing, which in turn was under the First Army of the American Expeditionary Force (AEF).

With Hartney assuming command of the First Pursuit, it was bound to mean closer interaction with the other squadrons. One of the 27th's most cherished rivalries was with the 94th Squadron. The 94th was called the "Hat-in-the-Ring" squadron because their aircraft were adorned with a distinctive Uncle Sam Top Hat, complete with stars and stripes, surrounded by a red halo. It was the most well known unit of the First Pursuit Group because of some of its members—especially Eddie Rickenbacker. Eddie was considered by some as one of the best of the American fighter pilots. Rickenbacker had been a celebrity before the war as an auto racer. Because of their combat records, the 27th and 94th squadrons were constantly competing for the most kills, the top slot, or any other honors that they could secure.

* * * *

Life at Saints had been somewhat carefree under Major Hartney. The squadron members held "Liberty Parties" where they would load up in a truck and drive to a local town or village within a 60-kilometer range, party, then come back. This practice had begun when the squadron was stationed at Tours and had continued on at Saints. Along with the Knights of Columbus Canteen, complete with piano, the down-time for the pilots and crews was aimed at being as relaxing as possible.

Things began to change when Grant took over command of the squadron. Grant was not as understanding as Hartney had been. He began implementing true military protocol, starting with reveille at 5:00 A.M. This did not endear Grant to the enlisted personnel (not that he cared about being endearing), and it was a mark of order that Frank was likely to chaff at.[12]

Grant wasted no time in cracking down on Frank for his lone wolf stunts. While there is no official record of his punishment available, Luke documented it in a letter to a former flying mate from Rockwell Field, Nelson A. Cliff, who was also stationed in France at the time. "Was over the lines alone the other day. Ran into a German formation, they did not see me so got into the sun and shot down the last man and then made a grand retreat for home with the whole bunch after me. Have not received it official yet but hope to real soon. We patrol nearly every day but nothing much doing. Was put on the ground for three days for going over the lines alone. My time was up today so guess I will take a ride tonight. That three days has cured me for a while anyway of going over the lines alone. Please don't say anything about my getting a Hun to those in San Diego. I don't want to say anything until I get some official or that official."[13]

Frank, having learned his lesson, was in the air again on August 22 flying a formation patrol at 9:00 A.M. The next day, Frank went up on a patrol over the lines in the afternoon, flying under Grant's command. The Spads were still proving troublesome for the squadron: Lieutenant Clapp had to land to have his aircraft fixed. Frank got a chance to fly with his bunkmate Joe Wehner.

On August 25, Frank again was up in the air at 6:30 P.M. for a dusk flight. While Frank did not have mechanical issues, Joe Wehner had to perform a risky forced landing at Montreuil-aux-Lions and Lieutenant Hoover had similar issues forcing him to land at Coincy.

Grant had his new pilots honing their skills on gunnery target practice and testing their flying skills, usually with the morning flights. The pilots would go up with experienced pilots for evaluation. August 26 was cloudy and Frank had late morning target practice. In the afternoon he went on a trial flight with Grant and Vasconcells.

On the 28th, Frank went up for a trial formation flight in the morning. Each time the squadron went up, the problems with the Spads seemed rarer and rarer. On the 29th, Frank went up on a target practice flight in the morning with Joe Wehner. In the afternoon Frank broke out of formation, claiming to have engine problems. He did a landing at Touquin with a dead engine that was fixed in just a few minutes, allowing him to take off alone. For Frank, this was another chance to fly solo, looking for potential victims.

At one point during this series of training flights, Frank's engine died mid-flight. He dived for the field and glided to an almost perfect landing. Joe Wehner who was flying at the same time saw Frank's dive and knew his engine had cut out. He assumed that Frank had pulled off the maneuver as a stunt, so Joe opted to do the same. He killed his own engine, dived for the field, and came to a landing next to Frank's plane. The ground crew who had witnessed the pair gave them a rousing cheer. Only after Joe was on the ground did he learn that Frank was not performing a flying stunt, he was saving his own skin.[14]

On the 30th of August, he was in the air again, this time alone for target practice. This would be the last time flying out of Saints for him. The 27th was ordered to pack up and relocate to Rembercourt. There it would join some of the other squadrons of the First Pursuit Group—and it would rejoin Colonel Hartney. Concentrating the First Pursuit there was preparatory for the St. Mihiel operation.

Rembercourt did not have housing, at least not for all of the squadrons that were assembled there. Tents went up. The grounds around the airfield turned into a mire of mud during the rains on the first two days of September as the 27th settled in. Some of the pilots, like Frank and Joe, managed to find accommodations in an abandoned farm house. The unification of the First Pursuit Group told everyone that something was coming, something big. Joining with the other squadrons was a hint that they were going to be involved in a large scale operation.

Frank went up again on September 3 as the weather cleared. Joe Wehner flew with Ivan Roberts to attempt to strafe an observation balloon. This was one of the deadliest missions pilots could undertake. They did not succeed. Frank went up with Lieutenants Vasconcells and Donaldson on an alert patrol. There were no encounters with the enemy.[15]

The arrival of the 27th Squadron at Rembercourt was not ignored by German intelligence. On September 5, a German plane swooped down over the field and dropped a note. It was a welcome greeting from the Germans, specifically addressed to the 27th Squadron. Hartney tried to suppress word of the note but it leaked out. While chivalrous, it was an ominous warning to the 27th that their enemies were aware who they were and where they were posted.[16]

In the afternoon Frank was up again, this time with eleven airplanes on patrol. On September 6, Frank went up again on a late morning patrol under Lieutenant Vasconcells and had a chance encounter with an old acquaintance. Harry Aldrich of the 1st Observation Squadron recounted in later years a meeting with Frank: "We met unexpectedly on the aerodrome between Rocourt and Coincy north of Chateau-Thierry. Until recently this field had been in the hands of the Germans and was reputed to have been occupied by Richthofen and his flying circus.

"That day a very important photographic mission six or seven miles into Hun territory had been assigned to an observer in my squadron and myself. We left the field rather late in the afternoon, accompanied by several protecting planes—six I believe from the First Pursuit Group stationed there with the 1st Observation Group, to which my squadron belonged.

"Once over the objective, forgetting to signal our intention, we dived through some low-hanging clouds in order to get the best possible photographs. The pursuit planes lost sight of us, for which I alone was to blame. Almost at once several gaudily painted Fokkers attacked us. By the skin of our teeth and the timely aid of our protecting planes, who were by that time diving to the rescue, we escaped from the rain of bullets limping home with a badly damaged motor and controls. As I was walking towards headquarters to turn in my report, a pursuit plane landed near by. The pilot jumped out, and, funning up, called out, 'We sure owe you an apology for falling down that way on our protection, old man!' I replied that it was entirely my own fault. Then I saw that the other flier was Frank Luke. And that is a good illustration of the sort of chap he was."[17]

The next day Luke flew again on a patrol from St. Mihiel to Watrenville with no encounters. On the 8th, he went up on a small patrol with Joe Wehner and Henry Nicholson. The 8th of September was a busy day with the squadron, exposing Frank to some of Grant's fury—this time not directed at him. Grant had the squadron adjutant "break" acting Sergeant Major Kruger. Kruger was dressed down in the headquarters tent and was deeply disturbed.

This time Alfred Grant had gone too far, pushing the enlisted man to the brink. Kruger disappeared near supper time and another soldier had found his diary. In red ink, he had penned in that he considered himself a failure and was "about to go out and blow his brains out." Kruger had penned his will.

Grant only partially believed that he was going to commit suicide but he ordered the entire squadron to turn out and attempt to track down Kruger. "The search [was] made more exciting by the fact that the 95th was having target practice and every shot, one thought, might be Kruger. He was eventually found, however, quite alive and unhurt, having evidently changed his mind."[18]

For Frank, it demonstrated that he was not alone in summoning Grant's ire and wrath. It had to be a chilling reminder of the stresses that these men faced so near to the front. Heavy rains moved in for a few days, grounding aircraft. Frank took some time to write his mother, still concealing from her and the majority of his family that he was up at the front. Rather than tell her what he was doing, he let her know that once winter came he was worried about how cold he was going to be.[19] Soon, however, he would not be able to hide from her where he was or what he was accomplishing.

It was during this period of time that Frank developed the habit of visiting a nearby French unit, Les Cigognes (the Storks) of Escadrille N.3. What drew Frank to this squadron was probably the fact that the unit was something of an ace factory. Led by Captain Georges Guynemer, the unit had a long and illustrious reputation on the front. For Frank, the Arizonian who struggled with French, it was a place he could go and tell his stories of combat and not be judged. Just communicating would have been a strain for the parties. Yet these were pilots like him, and some of them were outright legends. It was sad that one of the best pilots in the U.S. Army Air Service probably was more welcome among this non-American escadrille than in his own squadron.[20]

On September 12, 1918, the muddied fields of Rembercourt would quake and groan with the firing of American artillery. The start of the St. Mihiel offensive would rattle more than just the German trench positions—it would alter the fate of Frank and everyone associated with him.

Chapter Seven

"From the day Lieut. Luke first sailed over enemy lines until that fateful day in September when he did not come back to us, he played his game alone. A venerable lone wolf, he was forever snarling and snapping at the enemy, darting out of the darkness in the very midst of death with flashing fangs of white steel, wrecking havoc and consternation within the German lines—building morale in ours."

—EDDIE RICKENBACKER, MARCH 20, 1927

Busting Balloons
September 11, 1918

Before a large military operation, men experience a number of different emotions and anxieties; and the weather in the early fall of 1918 didn't help soothe anyone's feelings. A chill rain poured down on September 11, 1918, dampening the moods of the troops braced for the offensive. The squadron was grounded the entire day. Crews worked in makeshift tent hangars and buildings getting the aircraft as ready as possible. When the rain lifted, the American army was going to plunge into battle to retake the St. Mihiel salient. The nineteen pilots were waiting for the orders to come down for their assignments, of the twenty-five airplanes assigned to the squadron, twenty were in flying condition.

The pilots congregated at the Knights of Columbus Canteen along with the ground crews after dinner. The talk amid the drinks and music was about the big push that was coming.

Frank sat in on a conversation with Jerry Vasconcells as he reflected on the risks of combat. The lieutenant had been passed up for command of the 27th in lieu of Grant, but everyone recognized his skills and expertise as a pilot. Jerry had been one of the original members of the Fighting Eagles, and to the newer pilots, his insights and words could spell the difference between life and death.

While talking about flying, Vasconcells commented in front of Frank his opinion of going after observation balloons. "I think they're the toughest proposition a pilot has to meet. Any man who gets a balloon has my respect because he's got to be good or he doesn't get it."[1]

Vasconcells added, "I would never order a man down on a balloon. I'd go down myself before I'd do that, but I'd rather that the issue never came up."[2]

Frank must have hung on those words, not just because they came from someone that he respected, but because they defined a different goal and glory. It was like being the star player on a football team. Frank understood that kind of thinking. Jerry Vasconcells had defined for Frank what it was going to take to be accepted and honored in the 27th Squadron.

With these seemingly innocent comments, Frank was set on a path to becoming the greatest American balloon buster.

* * * *

The concept of using observation balloons to map enemy movements or spot for artillery was not new, even for the technologically struggling Army Air Service. Even in the Civil War, balloons had been used by the Army of the Potomac to observe the movements and troop placements of the Confederate Army. But the observation balloon had undergone a series of changes in the Great War. Gone were the days of round fair balloons on tethers. Balloons had changed and were referred to by infantry troopers as

"Sausages," due to their distinct shape. The lozenge-like shape was designed to allow the balloon to remain stable—like a kite. They were also referred to as "kite balloons." The Germans called them *Drachen* ("Dragons"), a nickname bestowed upon them for their explosive qualities and the roaring noise when filled. They were hydrogen bags that held a small gondola. They had an inflated air rudder that allowed limited turning with the wind, but by most accounts, the rudder caused more problems than it ever solved. Observation balloons were tethered to a truck or horse-drawn mobile bed with a winch. In the gondola, an observer with field glasses, or a large camera, would use a telephone or flags to transmit to the ground enemy troop activity or movements. An observer with a telephone line also could be used to correct artillery fire.

Correcting artillery fire was important. Trench warfare was defensive in nature, and trenches and bunkers provided excellent cover for infantry. These ugly, deep muddy scars on the earth were where soldiers huddled until ordered up and into the mire of no-man's-land between the trenches, or waited to repel an enemy assault. Trenches also concealed movement from ground level. Artillery and machine guns made movement treacherous and deadly. Observers in balloons could watch where an artillery battery's shells were landing and could signal down, adjusting fire, getting the shells to drop right on the targeted bunkers or trenches. They usually would be floated to around 5,000 feet for optimum viewing. Winching them down took time, but when under fire, a crew could do it in a matter of a few terror-filled minutes.

Balloons were made of rubberized silk and filled with hydrogen and suspended thousands of feet in the air. One might think that observation balloons were easy targets for aircraft to destroy given the explosive qualities of hydrogen; in fact, the opposite was true. The ground crew, winch truck, hydrogen pumps, and storage tanks were called a nest. Each nest was one of the most heavily defended targets on a battlefield. Out of range of artillery, their real threat was from aircraft, and anti-aircraft weapons were at the core of their defense. Going after a balloon, or Drachen, was deadly business.

It was a relatively stationary target until it was winched down and could be defended. But to destroy the balloon, first you had to get to it. Sausage balloons were not on the front lines, they were held to the rear. This meant you had to fly over the front risking encounters with enemy aircraft or anti-aircraft fire just to reach them. Getting to the balloon was simply the start of your difficulties. All of them knew what your target was and made it as difficult as possible to go after a balloon.

The German army's chief anti-aircraft cannon came in three sizes: 4.2 cm, 8.8 cm and 7.7 cm. Their maximum altitude range was between 12,000 and 14,000 feet, allowing them to easily strike at any approaching aircraft.[3] If pressed, they could fire upwards of ten rounds per minute each. The fusing of the shells could have them go off at variable altitudes so that the guns were effective at a wide number of ranges. The explosions formed a killing zone, a shield of protection and destruction for any aircraft that dared to try to penetrate the area.

Exploding shells alone were not the only defensive threat surrounding a Drachen. The Germans also employed a type of anti-aircraft round fired by 37 mm cannons called "flaming onions." These shells were segmented phosphorus rounds. When they rose in the air they burned brilliant white, usually two or three in a string, like bright burning onions. Given that the aircraft they targeted were built of wood covered with highly flammable canvas, a hit from a flaming onion could set a plane on fire and roast its pilot before it could land.

A typical balloon position would have at least one battery of anti-aircraft guns dedicated to it, typically consisting of four to six anti-aircraft cannons poised to take out any hostile aircraft that approached. Many Drachen positions had much more in the way of defense. When a "sausage" was aloft, these crews were armed and constantly scanning the skies for potential targets. The guns were positioned to provide an umbrella of deadly shrapnel to shield the balloon, shrapnel that could obliterate fragile canvas and wood aircraft.

The anti-aircraft cannons were not the only defense. Several machine guns on pivot mounts were poised around the balloon nest so they could add their close fire support. While their ranges were less than that of the anti-aircraft cannon, attacks made on balloons were most effective if you were close—within around 1,000 feet. For German balloons, this would most likely mean Maschinengewehr 08s, an older but common model of machine gun. Oftentimes the older weapons were relegated to anti-aircraft duty. Able to fire upwards of 400 rounds per minute, it was able to fire faster than it could be loaded. Getting at a low hovering balloon meant that you had to position your aircraft to avoid crossfire from multiple stationary machine guns. These, too, formed a ring of death and carnage at lower altitudes, all aimed at protecting the balloon on its thin tether.

The defense of an observation balloon placed the anti-aircraft cannons at a distance away. They could fire far above the 5,000 foot altitude of the balloon and their extended range allowed them to offer a high-altitude cover for the balloon as well as be able to attack an approaching aircraft at distance. The machine guns would be placed closer in and could, below 1,000 feet, cross their fire above the balloon—forming an umbrella of deadly lead. Coming in below 1,000 feet for a pilot was a flirt with death against the combined machine guns and the entrenched infantry shooting their rifles upward.

A platoon of infantry was usually posted to a "typical" German balloon nest. Their Mauser rifles were the last line of defense for a balloon observer. Against unarmored aircraft, a single well-placed bullet could kill a pilot or knock out an engine. When you think of the firepower that a balloon observation post could muster to protect itself, the numbers are staggering. Over 1,600 machine gun bullets, hundreds of infantry rifle shots, and upwards of 840 plus pounds of explosive air-burst shells—*in a minute!* Such firepower could turn the air around a balloon into a maelstrom of hot lead, exploding iron, and death. To get to the balloon you would have to fly through this tornado where your only ally was fate herself.

If that was not bad enough, it was rare to blow up a sausage on your first pass. This meant you had to fly through the ring of fire, attack the balloon, swing through the archie fire and start the process all over again.

To go after such a target was seen as near-madness by experienced aviators. You had to cross over to the enemy's side of the trench-lines. You had to dive on the target balloon, firing, attempting to ignore the fact that a shield of shrapnel and bullets was between you and your target. The balloon crew would winch the balloon down as soon as the attack started, and when they did, they forced you to fly lower and lower, into more and more fire. The lower the target balloon got, the more accurate the fire and the more machine guns and rifles could be called into play.

An aircraft attempting to blow up an observation balloon had other challenges to contend with. Normal bullets or even shrapnel fired at a balloon could not take a balloon down unless the observer was injured. They would simply puncture one of the sacks of hydrogen and release the gas. Shooting normal bullets at a balloon usually resulted in it slowly settling to the ground semi-deflated.

However, if an attacking pilot switched to incendiary bullets, the tears and small bullet holes in the hydrogen sacks would ignite. The balloon would erupt into a ball of orange and red flames, and a sickening black cloud of smoke. Rather than settle to the ground, its flaming remnants would rain down on the nest and ground crew. The only hope for the observer was that he might be one of the few men to be wearing a parachute. Observers in balloon gondolas did wear parachutes. Most observers were under orders that if their balloon was attacked, they were to bail out as quickly as possible and parachute to safety. Most also carried pistols, or even rifles, with them in their gondolas, taking pot shots at any pilot crazy enough to come at their sausage.

Equipping your fighter with incendiary bullets (or, as they were sometimes called, "Buckingham bullets") was a tricky prospect. They fired out of an 11mm machine gun which was incompatible with the guns typically mounted on Spads S.XIIIs. This meant swapping out one or both of your machine guns. A typical fighter had one out of every five or ten bullets switched out with a tracer bullet. These lit up when fired, allowing the pilot to see the path that his bullets were following and adjust his fire accordingly. A pilot could have incendiary or explosive bullets added into the mix of bullets that he carried, but that added another problem. Incendiary rounds could be used against enemy aircraft but were not very effective.

The bullets presented another issue. The Germans considered the incendiary rounds a vicious weapon of war. In an age before the treaties dealing with the treatment of prisoners of war, they spread the word that pilots who fought with incendiary rounds against other pilots would be shot if captured. If the rounds were used against balloons, under orders, the lives of captured aviators would be spared. Pilots were ordered to carry with them copies of their orders specifying that they were only using the explosive rounds against balloons.[4]

The French experimented with rockets to attempt to blow up balloons. Mounted at the ends of the wings of a Nieuport 16, these 1.5 inch Le Prieur rockets were highly inaccurate and stubborn to launch. They looked like Fourth of July bottle rockets, and they proved to be just as effective. It was clear that if technology was not going to overcome the problems with downing observation balloons, they would have to be overcome with sheer determination, courage, and skill.[5]

Enemy fighters often patrolled within sight of balloons, adding another deadly layer of defense. If a pilot were going after a balloon, he may have had one of his machine guns loaded with incendiary rounds while the other was normally armed. This cut his firepower in half against enemy aircraft. A pilot attacking a balloon didn't just have to worry about fending off enemy fighters while making an attack run on the balloon, he had to worry about the trip back to his lines. Even if he destroyed an enemy balloon, he would often have to fight off or flee from several enemy fighters on the way back to safety.

If a pilot opted to try to fly low, under the balloon, the web of cables suspending the gondola and controlling the balloon could slice an airplane in two. If a pilot opted for the most common approach, a strafing run along the top of the balloon at nearly point blank range, he might be spared the shots from ground fire but, a balloon carried a lot of hydrogen. When one exploded it left a sick, blackened scar in the sky. A plane caught in that blast could catch on fire, and the aircraft's fuel could explode. Balloon busting was one of the few air combat situations where success could be almost as deadly as failure.

Few pilots specialized in taking on German observation balloons. Though the general public thought that dogfighting enemy airplanes was more glamorous, experienced pilots had a much healthier respect for the men that went after balloons. Technically, they were considered EAs, Enemy Aircraft, but it was seen as much easier to take on fixed-wing fighters rather than try to shoot down a balloon. The tactics for doing it were not widely shared among the Allies either, mostly because the infrastructure for sharing such intelligence was limited at the time. Balloons were highly desired targets by upper command, but for those that were tasked with taking them out, balloon busting was a dangerous invitation to death.

Observation balloons were valued at over $100,000, including not just the balloon, but all of the equipment to pump the hydrogen, the winch truck or wagon, the crew, and the ground defenses. In a stretched, total war economy, every penny (or mark) counted. But as far as the American, French and British were concerned, downing an observation balloon counted the same as downing a fighter plane: one kill. You could become an ace shooting down balloons, if you lived to tell the tale.

Attacking a sausage required a certain detachment from the romanticism of the air war. It was not a test of skill against a fellow pilot but a contest with fate. Fighting an enemy airplane required gunnery and piloting skills; fighting a ballon, nerve and luck. What killed someone going after a Drachen was the random flail of hot shrapnel and bullets that defied the law of averages and hit pilot or aircraft.

Some aces refused to go after them as targets—the risks were simply too great. Many of the pilots who undertook balloon-busting did so alone, preferring to operate lone wolf style. This must have had some appeal to Frank, who had already developed a reputation for taking off on his own.

The greatest of the balloon busters was a pilot from Belgium named Willy Coppens. Willy would have the distinction of surviving the war, a rarity for balloon strafers, but the cost was his left leg. By the end of the war, he had taken out a confirmed total of thirty-five Drachen, the most being three in one day.

* * * *

All that the pilots of the 27th Squadron had in their arsenal to take on the menace of observation balloons was the Spad XIII. At first glance, the Spad did not instill a feeling of confidence. The aircraft was troublesome to maintain. The first few weeks they had the Spads, the 27th was plagued with mechanical issues. Many pilots had to make forced landings when the engines failed. A problem like that occurring in battle could spell the difference between life and death.

Spad was not a name but an acronym for *Société pour l'Aviation et ses Dérivés*. The Spad VII had been introduced in 1916 as a single-seated chasseur, or chasse ("chase") pursuit aircraft designed to take out other enemy aircraft.

As the war evolved, the Spad VII became slower compared to the airplanes it went up against. By December of 1916, redesign efforts were underway to replace the Spad VIIs with a new model, one that was equipped with a more powerful engine. By April of 1917, the first test models were ready for flight.

The aircraft factories during the Great War resembled furniture factories, because producing a standardized airplane was not unlike creating furniture: it was artisan's work. The mix of materials was similar as well: wood, canvas, and duraluminum tubing made up the fuselage and wings of the Spad. It weighed 1,807 lbs. when fully fuelled and armed.

The increased horsepower of the Hispano-Suiza motor came at a price. The Spad could fly over 130 miles per hour but such speeds were never recommended. While it could climb to 13,000 feet in 11 minutes, the engines were totally unreliable in those first few months of deployment. Even as late as November of 1917, a typical Spad XIII was grounded two out of three days. The problems were addressed, but this was done at the front line. With the war in full swing there was simply no time for proper design and testing. The new models simply *had* to be made to work, despite the risks associated with them. Ground crews in aerodromes around France each found fixes and workarounds to keep the Spads in the air and combat-ready.

Armed with two Vickers .303 inch machine guns designed to carry 380 rounds each, the Spad XIII doubled the firepower of its predecessors, and put it on par with its German counterparts. Spent bullet casings were funneled down and ejected from the bottom of the aircraft. It had considerable bite.

The Spad XIII had lines almost smooth and sleek compared to other aircraft of the day. The slightly compressed camshaft fairings on either side had an almost Art Deco look to it. It was fast and maneuverable enough to go toe-to-toe with German fighters.

Each squadron was allowed to choose its own paint scheme for their aircraft. The planes of the Fighting Eagles of the 27th Squadron were splotched with sweeps of greens and browns. The metallic cowl over the Hispano-Suiza engine was usually brightly painted, either blue or red. The tail bore the French and American colors of red, white, and blue, and an "S" for Spad. The number of the aircraft was painted on the side in blue just behind the cockpit. Just past that was the swooping eagle logo of the 27th Squadron. The rubber-tubed landing gear wheels were sometimes painted with a blue and white yin-yang pattern.[6]

The emblem of the Fighting Eagles, the swooping war eagle with open talons, was claimed by a few would-be-artists as their own. The truth was that Major Hartney had sketched the first design for the 27th Squadron's emblem. It was a shield emblazoned with stars and stripes, "USA," and the number "27." The shield was resting on an arrow. The air service was still attempting to come to grips with an identity and had adopted a metal wing for aviators that had a shield on it with stars and stripes—the forerunner of pilot's wings. When Hartney discovered that the USAS aviators were all to have the new design, he opened up the competition to all of the men of the squadron to develop a logo to represent the 27th.

Sergeant Harold Haggart came up with the artwork of the eagle, which closely mirrored the eagle on a Budweiser beer crate—far too similar to be a coincidence. Hartney accepted the design and the Fighting Eagles had their emblem.[7]

The evening of September 11, the ground crew for the 27th Squadron made their way from the Knights of Columbus Canteen and returned to the hangars. The aircraft waited there under the yellow lights, waiting for their pilots and the chance to do what they had been built for.[8] Each was lovingly checked one last time before the enlisted men made their ways back to their tents. There would be no sleep. The anticipation would have made that impossible.

For Frank and the other pilots of the squadron, the night of September 11 had to have been a long one. They knew that at dawn the offensive would be unleashed. Any time starting early the next morning they would be up in the air. From their prior experience, they had to have known that the Germans were not simply going to collapse or run without a fight. The rising of the sun the next day would change everything in Frank's life.

Chapter Eight

"He speaks of twelve things at a time, changes from past to future and to the present in one sentence, suddenly he sees a sausage, leaves us wondering and goes out alone for the enemy."

—LIEUTENANT EDWARD W. RUCKER AND LIEUTENANT L.H. DAWSON

Fire in the Sky
September 12, 1918

The roar of artillery fire erupted at midnight as the American Expeditionary Force unleashed its fury on the German lines of the St. Mihiel salient. It was a rainy morning, but anyone looking off toward the front lines would see the flash of explosions and hear the thundering rumble of the barrage. Colonel Billy Mitchell would later claim that the vibration from the attack was so strong that it shook the fuel hoses loose from the tanks on some of the Spads sitting in their hangars.[1]

The orders for the day came over the telephone to the First Pursuit Group, no doubt a security precaution. Aggressive patrolling and targeting of enemy observation balloons were the orders of the day. Regardless of the weather conditions, the First Pursuit Group was to get up in the air and be a dominating presence.

The pilots assembled for briefing and planning early that morning as the artillery barrage roared on in the background. There were two patrols planned for the morning, one for the afternoon. Both patrols would go up at 7:30 A.M. to engage enemy aircraft over the lines. If there were German observation balloons aloft, they were to be targeted and destroyed. The afternoon patrol was for alert—aimed at defending against a German aerial counterattack.

When the pilots gathered, one person was late—Frank. With the excitement and anticipation of the offensive, capped off by the artillery barrage, it is possible that Frank simply dozed off from exhaustion and came in late. His peers believed that he was simply being arrogant as always.

Frank's bragging, his flying off on his own, his "lone wolf," approach, had made him a pariah in the 27th Squadron. When he showed up late, it was perfectly in character. But there was a difference this time: the pilots of the 27th squadron had decided that they would put Luke in his place. Their intention was to give him the tough assignment, one that was going to force Frank, in front of everyone, to pull his stunt of breaking off to claim engine problems. In their minds, Frank was not as much a lone wolf as he was a sheep. Once and for all they would force the issue.

Frank was told that he had been picked to take out the Drachen.

During their briefing they had planned to have another pilot, Jack Hoover, take out the balloons while the rest of them provided cover. With Frank showing up late, they simply told him that he had drawn the duty.[2]

In a drizzle of rain, with the steady rumble of artillery in the background, the Spads of the 27th Squadron rose into the air and headed for the German side of the lines. Strong winds buffeted the tiny fighters. The orders were to fly regardless of the weather, and the American pilots were anxious to take the fight to the Germans.

* * * *

Frank had no idea that his fellow pilots had conspired to give him the duty of going after the balloons. He climbed aboard Spad Number 21, serial number S15836, which had had one machine gun replaced and fitted with a gun firing Buckingham incendiary bullets.[3]

Frank joined the other eight pilots who flew that day and swept out for the German lines, cruising to several thousand feet. Lieutenant Vasconcells led the flight. Lieutenants Clapp, Hewitt, Donaldson, Hudson, Hoover, Dawson, and his bunkmate Joe Wehner were with him. For Frank, this was a crucial day. Vasconcells's admiration for anyone willing to go after a balloon, spoken the night before, had to ring in his ears. Taking out a balloon would end the murmurs about his being a coward and vindicate his true prowess in battle.

Even the American balloons were not flying in great number due to the wind conditions that battered the tiny Spads. If a balloon was spotted, it was going to be hard to ignite. The rubberized silk bag was going to be wet from the rain. With the wind, the balloons would not be up very high, making the anti-aircraft fire an even greater threat.

Donald Hudson flew around over the lines and only saw three balloons, all of them American, and the only aircraft he saw were Allied. Donald W. Donaldson flew between Verdun and St. Mihiel, seeing only Allied aircraft fighting the drizzle and winds of the storm. At first glance it appeared that the weather was too foul for a balloon busting mission but the Germans were determined to keep an eye on the American build-up they had been watching for several days.[4] Eventually, balloons began to emerge from the shrouds of gray.

Joe Wehner spotted a German observation balloon near Montsec. He flew his Spad deep behind the German lines and came up on the sausage from their own side. Wehner sent 100 rounds blazing into the balloon. The ground crew spotted him and powered up the winch. He didn't burn the balloon but forced it to its nest on the ground. Undaunted, Joe banked off to an area northeast of St. Mihiel. He spotted seven horse drawn wagons attempting to retreat from the American onslaught. Diving, he blasted away at the tiny caravan scattering the horses.

All that left was Frank.

Frank spotted three enemy aircraft near Lavigneulle. He once again broke from the rest of the squadron, which was already scattering to individual patrols. Frank wanted those airplanes and gave chase.

The Germans spotted him and banked off towards Metz. Under the dismal, low-hanging clouds of the storm, the planes managed to elude Frank.

The cockpit was always cold at a few thousand feet up, and each drop of rain would have stung when it hit exposed skin. The open cockpit offered no comfort, no protection from the elements. Through rain-streaked goggles, Luke spotted a balloon hovering near Marienville. Like any balloon that was aloft that day, it would have been low so that the ground crew could control it.

Frank spotted the balloon and angled his Spad towards it. He was already high above the Drachen. He made sure his machine guns were ready. This was it. Hoover spotted him and gave the signal to dive. He headed straight in.

It stunned the other pilots up that day. The braggart they had counted on to run or feign problems to avoid the fight went right at the enemy balloon. Anti-aircraft fire erupted around it, black, sick puffs of smoke in the storm, dissipating quickly in the wind, sowing shrapnel in his path. Luke was undeterred by the storm of fire thrown at him. He blazed away with his guns at the balloon, and the shots stitched across its top. He was close, within yards of the sausage, as he fired at it.

Peeling off, he saw that the ground crew was wheeling to bring the balloon down. It had not exploded with his first salvo. It could have been the wet skin of the balloon or simply fate; Frank didn't care what the reason was. He sharply banked the Spad around and came for another pass. He left nothing to fate, he flew directly toward the balloon, only missing it by a few yards. The quickly descending balloon had still not ignited.

Frustrated, he maneuvered through the hailstorm of anti-aircraft fire for another pass. By now, the snap-thwacking of bullets and shrapnel punching through the canvas of his wings and fuselage was something that he simply ignored. All that mattered was taking out that balloon. He blazed away on a third sweep with his guns, but, again, no effect. But one effect of his last pass must have tied a knot in Frank's stomach. Both of his machine guns had jammed.

Frank knew that he was totally defenseless. He hammered at the guns and was able to clear the jam on the left one. Turning around, he saw with dismay that the balloon was almost on the ground at this point. He was going to make one final pass at it while it was in its nest. Diving to deadly range, where even the rifle fire from the infantry could riddle him, Frank dove again on the Drachen.

Suddenly, a flicker appeared followed by an orange ball of fire, rising into the air as if a volcano had erupted. It had most likely been a remnant of one of his previous passes, a hot piece of incendiary bullet that finally found the right mix of air and hydrogen and silk to fully ignite. The balloon blew upward and its blacked burning remains rained down onto the nest where it launched, destroying the winch and catching some of the crew there.

The anti-aircraft fire did not subside as he turned back towards the American lines and began to put on altitude—to buy some distance between him and the source of the shots aimed at his Spad. Tiny Number 21 rose up and headed back over the front lines, back to safety.[5]

In the burned funeral pyre of the German balloon, the observer's body was found. His name was Willy Klemm, and he had received his commission as a Leutenant just a few days before. One of Frank's bullets had hit him and he had been caught when the balloon's hydrogen had exploded. Klemm clung to life for a few days before he finally died.[6]

Frank knew that he had one remaining task, a lesson he learned from his August 16 efforts: secure confirmation of the kill. Without confirmation, his victory was simply going to be attributed to his bragging. This victim was a balloon; it had blown up and should have been seen from the American lines. His battered airplane fought the winds and made its way back. Frank was still looking for observation balloons, but this time he was looking for American ones.

* * * *

Frank spotted American 5th Balloon Company, which was in line of sight of his victory. It took a few passes, but he finally found a field and landed his airplane. It was tricky on a wet field, and there was a risk that his landing gear would lock up and he would flip face-first into the mud. This field had shell craters from an artillery barrage, making it more dangerous. There were telephone lines at one end that Frank had to navigate past, as well. And given the storm of fire he had been through, Frank really didn't know how badly off Number 21 was. But he made it.

He found two officers, Lieutenant Joseph Fox and Lieutenant Maurice Smith, who had seen the death-bloom of the sausage he had just blown up. Frank pulled out his forms that he had typed for confirmations and got both officers to confirm his kill. There would be no questions this time as to his victory. He had proven them all wrong.

Returning to his plane, he got it started and took off to head back to Rembercort. His motor began cutting out. He returned to the same field and landed again. He attempted to get the engine working but couldn't. Darkness crept in on the first night of the St. Mihiel offensive, and with it, Frank realized that his plane could not make the trip back. In the darkness it be too risky. Frank asked for a blanket from the balloon company and laid down under the wing of his airplane as shelter from the mist-like rain, eventually drifting off to sleep. The low rumble of artillery and the flashing of explosions like heat-lightning in the distance were all he had to soothe him to sleep. His great victory was celebrated alone, under the wing of his torn and battered airplane.

In the morning he rose and the balloon company arranged for a motor-cycle with sidecar to drive him back to his squadron. He took off, leaving his crippled airplane on the muddy field. The balloon company had called ahead to let them know that Frank was alive, and what they had seen him do. The tag of braggart evaporated when he arrived back at the squadron. The pilots who had witnessed his sheer bravery considered him as dangerous to himself as he was to the Germans.[7]

* * * *

On September 13, Frank's airplane was flown back to Rembercort. The maintenance team circled the airplane, awed at the damage that had been done. Nasty tears in the fuselage were everywhere and pieces of his wings were ripped to thin strips. One mechanic summed it up, "I never saw a bird come in with a ship like that but what soon he got bumped!"

It was a warning that Frank disregarded. He inserted his finger in some of the holes. One hole had come only six inches from his seat in Number 21. "Just look at that," he boasted to his ground crew. "They can't get me. Why didn't that one hit me?"[8]

Chapter Nine

*"In one swift, hectic fight, we accounted for five Boche, and we were
outnumbered three to one. But Luke never takes account of odds."*

—JOE WEHNER

The Dynamic Duo
September 13–14, 1918

As the American Expeditionary Force pushed forward, the 27th
Squadron's task was to cover the advances being made on the
ground. The rain finally broke but low, gray cloud cover made for
risky flying. Clouds provided perfect places for enemy aircraft to hide and
pounce from.

Two patrols flew on the 13th of September. Since Frank had not
returned until the morning, he was not included in either of them. When
he did finally arrive, gone was the ribbing he usually took when he described
his exploits. This time he had a confirmed kill, a highly visible victory. The
missions he was missing on were ground strafing runs in support of American
infantry, but the highly excitable young man had to be chafing at missing out
on the action.[1]

September 14 brought clearer weather and his return to flight duty. The
first patrol took off at 9:30 A.M. Their intent was simply to "patrol," but the
standing battle orders for the First Pursuit Group were to suppress enemy
air and observation activity. They were to look for targets of opportunity and

take them out. Specifically, Frank was looking for another observation balloon. His aircraft was equipped with one machine gun with incendiary bullets. Lieutenants Dawson and Thomas P. Lennon were assigned to work with him.

The Spads rose to an altitude between 3,000 and 5,000 meters, bitter cold even in the early autumn. Every exposed surface of skin would be windburned, cracked, or even frostbitten. There were thirteen aircraft in the patrol, the majority of the 27th Squadron.

Lieutenants Dawson and Luke spotted the observation balloon near Boinville first. It was attached to Ballonzug (Balloon Company) 121.[2] They were near the village of Moranville and saw the German sausage hovering in the morning light. Lieutenant Lennon followed Dawson and Frank as they headed toward the balloon.

The observer jumped, taking his chance with the silk parachute. Almost the moment he left the gondola the anti-aircraft fire erupted, targeting the three Spads as they maneuvered for the kill. Dawson went in three times as the ground crew began to lower the balloon. Three times he pushed through the ring of fire around the balloon. Three times he poured his shots into the top of the hydrogen bag. White phosphorous shots, the flaming onions of German ground fire, stretched out around his airplane. He emptied both of his machine guns into the Drachen but it did not explode.

Frank changed tactics from two days earlier. Rather than come in diving down on the Drachen, he decided to experiment with coming in low. While Dawson soared upward to make his run, Frank dropped down for his pass. Punching through the umbrella of anti-aircraft fire, Luke unleashed his shots at the balloon. His left machine gun, the one loaded with incendiary rounds jammed. He knocked it back into working order and made another pass, then another. The gun, the best weapon in the air for igniting the observation balloon jammed again—twice. Frank did not let up. While Dawson made three passes and broke off the attack, Frank kept it up. With each dangerous pass the ground crew furiously worked to bring the everdeflating balloon down. While it had not exploded, it was losing hydrogen and buoyancy quickly.

In the middle of this, Lieutenant Lennon jumped into the foray, diving on the balloon from high altitude. He fired 50 rounds from each of his machine guns and pulled out. The Spads were swarming around the balloon as if they were hornets after a farmer that had disturbed their hive.

The balloon didn't explode, but it was so badly punctured that it was transformed into a limp bag of silk, dropping onto its nest. Frank had made six passes through the hail of ground fire at the balloon and still had not caused an explosion. He had approximately 75 rounds remaining in his right machine gun and was still hot for a fight. Diving again, he strafed the anti-aircraft battery. The crew scurried for cover as he finally peeled away and headed back toward the American lines.

About twenty minutes later, Dawson turned to see if the balloon had been repaired or put in the air again. It hadn't. The Fighting Eagles of the 27th had done their job well. They landed back at Rembercourt, their planes pock-marked with holes in the canvas from the anti-aircraft fire. They had taken out the balloon the hard way.[3]

* * * *

In the afternoon, Frank was given another chance to go against the observation balloons that the Germans were using to direct their artillery fire. This time was different. When Grant gave him the mission, Frank asked that his bunkmate, Joe Wehner, fly with him.

Frank was steadfastly loyal to his friends in France, just as he was to Bill Elder back in Arizona. Joseph had his own baggage that he was carrying. It was no small secret that Wehner had been suspected of being a spy for the Germans. His time in Berlin up until the American declaration of war had made the quiet, thoughtful man suspicious. It was natural that he and Frank would gravitate to each other.

In many ways the two men were total opposites. Raised in different parts of the country, they had little in common other than their love of flying. Neither were popular in the 27th Squadron. Frank tended to be an energetic talker. Joe was soft-spoken, quiet. Frank was labeled as a braggart. Wehner was a man of few words. Still, there was a chemistry there that could not be fully defined. More importantly, they trusted each other.

Eddie Rickenbacker summarized his perspectives of both of them after the war: "Luke was an excitable, high-strung boy, and his impetuous courage was always getting him into trouble. He was extremely daring and perfectly blind and indifferent to the enormous risks he ran. His superior officers and his friends would plead with him to be more cautious, but he was deaf to their entreaties. He attacked like a whirlwind with absolute coolness but never a thought of his own safety.

" ... Wehner's nature, on the other hand, was quite different. He had just one passion, and that was his love for Luke. He followed him about the aerodrome constantly. When Luke went up, Wehner usually managed to go along with him. On these trips, Wehner acted as an escort or guard, despite Luke's objections. On several occasions he had saved Luke's life. Luke would always come back to the aerodrome and excitedly tell everyone about it, but no word would Wehner say on the subject. In fact, Wehner never spoke except in monosyllables on any subject. After successful combat he would put in the briefest possible report and sign his name. None of us ever heard him describe how he brought the enemy down."[4] What they lacked in similarity of character they made up for in teamwork.

In the previous weeks, Frank and Joe had been involved with several of the squadron's craps games. Frank, true to form, donated his winnings to the church. During one of the games, one of the new "shavetail" pilots had bet his pilot's wings, and lost them to Luke. Frank felt that the wings were too important to donate to the church—after all, he had given his beloved Marie a set of his own wings. Frank gave the wings to Joe Wehner instead. Joe had worn the wings on several of their missions.[5] Joe had also been given a "lucky ring" by a young woman that he had met in New York.[6] When he flew, he wore the ring and the wings. For him, they were symbols of luck.

Other people noticed the symbiotic relationship between Frank and Joe, and what it said about their characters. Reporter Frederick Smith was at the 27th Squadron covering Frank's exploits and got a chance to talk to both men. "Wehner talked to me about Luke, and Luke later confided Wehner was 'great stuff, but too damned modest.' Yet I could get little or nothing from Luke about himself."[7] It was obvious that Frank and Joe respected each other, and most importantly, they understood each other very well.

There were nine Spads in the second patrol of September 14 when they took off at 2:30 P.M. They were crossing the lines when at once they spotted an observation balloon. The plan that the two of them worked out was that Frank would deal with the balloon while Joe stayed high over the area to keep enemy airplanes away. The rest of the patrol was supposed to provide cover should the Germans show up in force.

Hovering between 2,500 and 5,000 meters, the planes crossed the front lines and moved towards the village of Buzy. At this stage of the war, Buzy had suffered badly from artillery, bombing, and strafing attacks, and was more of a pile of rubble than a functional village. It was also home to a German Ballonzug, the 14th Balloon Company. As the planes of the 27th neared Buzy, Frank and Joe dove off after the balloon.

Frank made a long pass on the balloon, his left machine gun rattling away at the silk top. The anti-aircraft fire broke as soon as his intentions were suspected, but he remained unwavering in his pursuit of the target. The two observers in the gondola reacted quickly by bailing out, discretion being the better part of valor.

In the warm, dry sun, the balloon material was much more vulnerable than his target's silk this morning. The balloon erupted in a ball of orange fire and sickening black smoke. The kill had to be satisfying but at the same time frustrating. Frank's machine guns had jammed again.

The problem of gun jamming was a common one. The more experienced pilots learned to load their own ammunition to make sure that the belts were straight and that the rounds were in good shape. When they fired they did not fire the long Hollywood-style burst of fire, spraying shots everywhere. Most pilots carefully squeezed off a few shots at a time to, hopefully, prevent jamming. Frank headed off for another nearby balloon and worked furiously to try to get his guns cleared and operational.

That was when he saw them. Eight Fokkers—most likely the deadly D.VII models. They dove down at Frank like avenging angels. He wasted no time, putting his stout Spad into a dive, he swung toward the safety of the American lines. Eight-to-one odds was not only dangerous, it was downright foolhardy, and Luke knew it. The Fokkers prepared to line him up for the kill when suddenly fate and Joe Wehner intervened. Joe's recounting of the events to a childhood friend in a letter described the fight in detail as he saw it:

I saw a patrol of Boche Fokkers further back across the lines so I began to climb for the ceiling as Frank started down toward the balloons. I aimed to get between him and the Fokkers and keep them off his tail when he started firing at the balloons.

Frank got the first Drachen before I could get between him and the Boche. He spit-aired through the enfilade of machine gun and anti-aircraft fire, and made a bee line for the second Drachen less than a kilometer distant. He scooted along at terrific speed not more than a hundred feet off the ground. But the Fokkers having height streaked even faster for him. There was a full Staffel of them. I piqued to head them off. The Staffel separated then into three flights. One went to my right, the other to my left and the center flight came at me hell for leather.[8]

From Luke's perspective he only saw Joe dive into the formation of Fokkers. Frank wanted to turn, his combat report said so, but without guns he was nothing more than a flying target for the trained killers behind him. Wehner went after them and Frank turned his attention to getting back over the lines. He saw a plane flying behind him in pursuit and it wasn't until he was safe that he realized it was Wehner's Spad. Somehow, Joe Wehner had scattered the eight Fokkers and had blasted the two that had been pursuing his wingman.

Frank landed as he had done before and got confirmation of the balloon kill. From Joe's account it seems Frank was entitled to a kill against one of the Fokkers but it is possible that Wehner imagined Luke's involvement with taking down the enemy aircraft. Having been deprived of his first victory for lack of confirmation, he was not going to make the same mistake again. He arrived back at Rembercourt a few hours after Wehner had.[9]

Once again Frank's plane was badly damaged, both by anti-aircraft fire and shots fired by the pursuing Fokkers. The story had grown while Frank had been gone. Wehner had shyly said that he had downed one, possibly two of the Fokkers.[10] There were no confirmations for these victims.

As the pilots gathered around his airplane, admiring the holes inflicted by the Germans, Lieutenant Leo Dawson exclaimed enthusiastically, "If anybody still thinks Luke is yellow, he's crazy. He's not yellow, he's stark raving mad. He winged on by me on that attack like a wild man. I thought he was diving right into the balloon. Then, after it was blazing, I saw him take another swoop down on it!"[11]

For his part, Frank wasn't done. His excitable personality had gotten ahead of logic. He chided his ground crew to prepare the Spad for another patrol, albeit unauthorized.

Major Hartney was in his office when Frank landed. The operations officer of the 27th called him on the phone. "Major, you'd better come down here quick and ground this bird Luke. He's ordered his plane filled up with gas. He's just run over to Wehner's ship and says they're going out to attack that balloon at Warcq. His machine is full of holes, two longerons and completely riddled and the whole machine is so badly shot up it's a wonder that he flew back here at all. He's crazy as a bedbug, that man."

Major Hartney took off at a full run across the field the quarter of a mile to the 27th's hangars. Lieutenant Grant arrived along with the flight leader, Lieutenant Clapp. Grant was not pleased with Luke attempting to take matters into his own hand. The crowd gathered along with his commanding officer did not calm his temper. Grant fumed: "You're his flight commander, Clapp. I hold you responsible. He's making a burlesque of the 27th and I'm just not going to stand it. Balloons or no balloons, we must have some discipline."

As if to emphasize the folly of putting Frank's Spad back into the air, the mechanics easily peeled off a torn piece of fabric that was nearly two yards long from the fuselage of Spad. The damage under the canvas was obvious.

Frank remained undaunted. He pleaded with Hartney to put him back in the air. "Won't you let me have Hoover's ship over there? It's all gassed up and Hoover told me I could use it in a pinch. Come on, Major, please."

This was too much for Grant. Frank was not just ignoring his authority but was going directly over his head—right in front of him. Grant issued an ultimatum. "Who's running this outfit, Major? You or I? I need Hoover's ship for the next patrol. We've got two balloons already today and this next one Wehner is after isn't so important."

It was a point that Hartney couldn't ignore. He was no longer in command of the 27th Squadron personally, that was Grant's responsibility. He had to concede the point to Grant. The major pulled Frank aside. "Listen, Frank, old boy. I appreciate all you're doing. I'm so proud of you I hardly know what to do. It's only a few hours since the Army called for the destruction of those balloons and you did it. No outfit can beat that. The famous French Cigogne group, with their great aces, Fonck and Garros, is over the hill there and they can't even get their new '220' Spads into service, let alone shoot down balloons. Have patience. In flying, patience is the best virtue you can have if you want to live to be an old man." As if to validate the younger pilot's skills, confirmation for his last balloon came in via the phone from the French 61st Balloon Company in Dugny who had witnessed it.

Frank reluctantly agreed. What he couldn't know is that the seeds had been planted in Hartney's mind for the next attack against the German balloon line. It was the evolution of a tactic that would propel Frank to even greater fame.[12]

* * * *

The German reports for the 14th of September were solemn. Eight balloons had been shot down, and two been had torn off their moorings. In the air, the Americans had pressed the observation balloons hard. Airmen in the gondolas reported seventeen "jump-offs." Six of the observers had been wounded. Their anti-aircraft batteries reported three men dead and six wounded, no doubt some of those coming from Frank's strafing attack at Boinville.[13]

For the U.S. Army Air Service, something more meaningful had occurred, though few at the time knew it. Frank Luke had found a wingman that he could work with, Joseph Wehner. Wehner had found someone that did not judge him by his name and background, but by his skill in the sky. Together they would carve out a place of myth and mystique in the history of the Air Force.

Chapter Ten

" ... 27th Squadron, twelve planes, proceeding two echelons (a) 2500 meters, (b) 3500 meters, via St. Mihiel, Vaviney, Chaillon, Creue, to patrol Woel, Etain, with specific mission of destroying all enemy balloons visible attacking between 17 hr 00 and 17 hr 15."

—FIRST PURSUIT GROUP OPERATIONS ORDER NUMBER 129,
SEPTEMBER 15, 1918

Roar in the Skies
September 15, 1918

The patrol assignments were posted the night of the 14th for the next day. Frank's mechanics had given up on getting Spad Number 21 back in the air for his use, instead he was assigned another airplane. Despite the fact that Luke had bypassed the chain of command the day before, Grant was meeting Frank's enthusiasm by giving him plenty of opportunities to get at the German balloon line.

Frank was quickly becoming the resident expert on taking down Drachen. The mission for the patrol was to proceed to Etain and take out the balloon operating near there. It was a sunny day but he was not on the first patrol, giving him some time to prepare. At 10:45 A.M. he took off with seven other members of the squadron on a patrol led by Lieutenant Clapp.

The flight was plagued with problems before it even got off the ground. As a last minute addition to the patrol, Joe Wehner was supposed to fly cover for Frank, but he was having problems getting his plane in the air, and he got into the sky fifteen minutes late. For Frank, this had to be like going into battle with one boot off—he trusted Joe and Joe knew how he fought and flew.

Almost immediately the other planes began to run into problems. The mechanical demons that terrorized the Spad XIIIs had once again reared their ugly heads. By the time the balloon had been spotted, only Lieutenants Clapp and Hoover were still in the air with Frank. The other five had returned to the safety of Rembercourt.

Frank signaled that he was planning to make his attack approach on the balloon at around the same time Clapp's Spad developed engine problems. Not wanting to risk going down behind German lines, Clapp nursed his Spad back. All that remained of the flight were Lieutenants Hoover and Luke.

The German anti-aircraft batteries were used to the balloon attacks by the American pilots. They opened up on the two aircraft, filling the air with explosions, smoke, and hot shrapnel. The crew of the sausage fired up the winch and began to retract their balloon, pulling it into the nest before it could be flamed by the Americans. Frank remained undaunted. He and Hoover fired at the grounded balloon, peppering the gas bag and spraying the ground crew.[1] Glancing back after their pass at the Drachen, Hoover and Luke saw that they were not alone. Six Fokkers pursued them about 500 meters higher. Realizing that the odds were against them, Luke and Hoover broke off their attack.

Postwar histories and biographies talk a great deal about Frank's recklessness in combat, but the balloon attack on the morning of September 15 showed Frank had another side. Perhaps it was Major Hartney's heartfelt talk with him the day before, or perhaps it was simply the reality of the situation. With six enemy aircraft and a vicious barrage of fire from the ground, Frank opted to not press his luck.

While Hoover and Luke put some distance between themselves and the Fokkers, Joe Wehner was about the face the gravest challenge he had yet dealt with in France. He saw a balloon near Etain go up in flames and assumed it was the one that he and Frank were designated to strafe. As he closed, in the same deadly accurate anti-aircraft fire battered and buffeted his Spad.

Wehner knew that if Frank was in the air he would not be satisfied with just one balloon so he began to scan the skies for a sign of his bunkmate. He thought he spotted Frank's Spad above the village of Rouvres. Coming in low at 1,500 meters, Joe swung in to join Frank when he then spotted seven or eight Fokker and Albatross airplanes swinging in behind the Spad that he was trailing.

Despite the odds, Joe slipped in behind the Germans and opened up with both of his Vickers machine guns. At the time, he thought he was providing cover to Frank, as he had done before. Joe's lucky ring and wings were suddenly working overtime. His targets were the planes at the rear of the German formation and his aim was true. As he crossed near the village of Waroq, Joe's shots found their mark on one of the Fokkers. It spiraled off of its intended target and spun into the mud and mire of no-man's land.

The Albatross fell into his sights and was peppered with his shots, finally falling off towards the ground in a steep dive. Joe assumed it was downed as well. The other German planes suddenly realized that their numbers had been reduced from a surprise behind them and broke off their pursuit of the Spad.

This time, when the planes arrived back at Rembercourt, it was not Frank who was in the limelight, it was the soft-spoken Joe Wehner.[2]

* * * *

During the afternoon patrol, Frank and Joe were once again assigned to go after a balloon. Joe got another late start and once again started looking for Frank so he could provide him cover. A few minutes into his flight, he spied a formation of airplanes heading toward him from the south and assumed that this was his squadron. In reality, the rest of the 27th was elsewhere.

Joe Wehner was alone that afternoon except for the Germans in the vicinity. He spied a balloon near Spincourt and headed off for it. The Drachen's defenders opened up with anti-aircraft as Joe strafed the balloon, letting loose with 100 rounds, spending his ammunition. He made more than one pass on the gas bag as the ground crew attempted in vain to reel it in. The balloon erupted in a hot orange and red blast.[3] Joe did not have time to gloat, as the explosive destruction of the balloon had attracted the attention of five German aircraft. They bore in on the tiny Spad seeking revenge and his blood.

Unarmed, his Spad was little more than a target for the Fokkers and Albatrosses. He piqed for the American lines, swerving towards the village of Chambley. The Germans were ready to pounce when they spied a formation of French Spads in the vicinity. Opting for better hunting grounds, they broke off their pursuit of Wehner and headed for the French aircraft.

* * * *

Frank was no doubt looking for his trusted wingman and bunkmate. With Wehner delayed from taking off with the squadron, he felt compelled to take off on his own. Frank broke off from formation and headed for the German balloon lines. Near Boinville, he found his first prey of the patrol. He dove into the balloon, unleashing his machine guns at it. The bag staggered as 125 rounds pock-marked the silk. There was a muffled explosion and a whoosh of hot flames and a searing black ball of smoke erupted. Even amidst the explosions of anti-aircraft cannons and the popping of machine gun bullets through his canvas wings, the explosion of the observation balloon dominated everything.

Banking away, Frank was already concentrated on his next victim. Another balloon was still up on its lines at Bois d'Hingry. He angled toward it and gunned his Spad. The Germans protecting the balloon at Bois d'Hingry had no doubt seen the results of his handiwork and were prepared. Shells began to explode, filling the air with shrapnel. The observer no doubt bailed as soon as he saw the Spad approaching. This was, after all, a plane that had just destroyed another balloon.

Frank opened up on the Drachen. This time fate was much kinder. It did not require multiple passes, and after only 50 bullets the German sausage was cooked up, a thick black mushroom cloud rising from where it had been. The empty gondola and tether lines dropped slack, pulling the burning pieces of cloth down to the ground.

The day so far had been a busy one, and it was far from over. But to carry on the fight, Frank was in need of petrol and ammunition, so he banked his Spad back toward Rembercourt. When he landed, his plane was grounded by his crew it had been riddled so badly. After all of the fighting he had been in, his Spad was simply deemed not airworthy.[4]

Frank was always causing headaches for Lieutenant Fred Ordway, the 27th's salvage officer. "Luke would land, taxi across the rough field at Rembercourt, and pull to a stop in a machine that looked like it would collapse any minute. 'Tell Fred Ordway to get me another; this bus is done in.'" Despite making more work for Ordway, Frank got along with Fred as much as he did any member of the squadron, and Fred thought a great deal of Frank. "He was a nice fellow once you got to know him," said Fred. "Yes, he was boastful and probably rubbed a lot of people the wrong way. He ran on nervous energy and was a very high-strung man. He always gave me the feeling whenever I talked to him that he knew he'd never see the end of the war."[5]

Hartney himself witnessed the frustration of the maintenance crew as they struggled with Luke's planes. When inspecting the 27th Squadron he was stopped by a crew member on Luke's maintenance team as he was looking over the repairs on Frank's machine. The mechanic was obviously frustrated. "Every day Lieutenant Luke comes back with his plane all shot up. I have told him he must fly higher or he will be killed, but he don't pay no attention!"[6]

* * * *

During the afternoon of September 15, discussion regarding the orders to take out the German observation balloons took place. Luke and Wehner heard that they were going to go on the early evening patrol from Grant. They would not be alone. In the presence of Grant and Hartney, they suggested an alteration of their tactics. The plan proposed was to hit the balloons at dusk, when they were being retracted.[7]

There were a number of reasons that this made sense. Striking at the balloons in the near-darkness of twilight, the archie fire from the ground batteries would be poorly aimed and perspective and distance could be distorted. The balloons would be low, near their nests. The Germans would not expect an attack at that time because night aircraft attacks, by non-bombers, were rare, and with good reason.

There were risks associated with such an attack. Pilots flying at night did so at great risk. There were no lights in the cockpits nor were landing fields lit. Flying in the dark with a Spad XIII was something that was done with blind luck and pure instinct. Navigation was going to be difficult if not impossible as the sun set. Lighting the landing field for a long period of time would invite enemy artillery attacks or even night bombers; so the field could only afford to be lit for a few short minutes, long enough for a plane to land. The solution that Grant proposed was to set up a dummy airfield nearby. Lit up, it would provide any German bombers the target that they desired. Luke and Wehner could then approach the "real" airfield. Using their Very pistols they would fire off a flare when they approached the field. It could be lit quickly, then the lights could be doused after they landed.[8] It was an approach done in total darkness, lacking instrumentation, requiring more insanity than bravery.

The evening of September 15 would be the first opportunity to test the technique. Frank bounded with impatience. His own plane's engine had been damaged in his earlier fighting and so his aircraft was grounded. Frank scrounged up another airplane, "disregarding the fact that he was unfamiliar with this machine and uncertain as to the reliability of its motor, he determined to risk it for night flying, a feat and incidentally an added hazard which would be required of him in returning after his attack on the balloon."[9]

* * * *

The final patrol of the day to test the new technique took off at 6:50 P.M. as the sun was setting. The combat plan had been approved by Lieutenant

Grant who was himself in command of the flight as the ranking pilot. The patrol was ordered to provide twilight reconnaissance near Châtillon-sous-les-Côtes where a German counterattack was suspected of forming. While the flight was focused on their intelligence gathering—attempting to locate target balloons—Frank was waiting for the chance to try the new American approach to balloon busting. There were three German balloons still up in the orange dusk sky. Levering the tactics that he had outlined before, Frank broke from the formation to go after the balloons. The Germans were not used to attacks in the evening. Many of the observation balloons had already been retracted to their nests for the night. The remaining screen of balloons was up to see if nighttime movements of the American and French infantry could be observed.

Frank peeled away from the patrol and headed to where one of the balloons was positioned near Chaumont. In the approaching darkness north of Verdun, Frank became lost in the darkness. He was flying at barely over 500 meters and with each heartbeat the black of night was sweeping in. He spotted a light in the distance in the air and at first assumed it was a German patrol plane. Carefully stalking the light, he closed with it and identified the massive gas bag of the balloon. Undoubtedly, the light was used by the observer in the gondola to see where he was.

The Drachen belonged to Ballonzug 35, commanded by Leutnant Bernard Mangels. Poised near the edge of the Dannevoux forest, the crew thought they were going to be spared an attack on that day. The balloon was at 300 meters altitude. Leutnant Mangels described the events: "Suddenly an aircraft appeared. Unnoticed it approached in low-level flight from across the forest and opened machine gun fire on the balloon. He missed on his first approach. After making a swing over the forest he came in for the second run. At this time we had the balloon already down to approximately 100 meters altitude. He missed again. When the balloon was about 10–15 meters above the motor winch, the daring flyer came in for a third dry and this time he set the balloon on fire. He then disappeared in low-level flight despite lively anti-aircraft fire."[10] Little did either Leutnant

Mangels or Lieutenant Luke realize that this was merely to be their first encounter.

Frank dropped low, probably in search of terrain that would help him find his way back to Rembercourt. North of Verdun he saw thousands of tiny lights, the lights of an army, flickering in the darkness. Frank continued until he crossed the lines. He continued to search for the landing field but could not find it in the darkness. Running low on fuel, he knew that further searching in the dark was not going to work. Frank came across a French wheat field and began to slowly drop. He had no idea if he was flying into telephone lines, or if his next few yards would crash his plane into a building or a shell hole in the darkness.

In the blackness of night, alone, he managed to bring his battle-damaged Spad to a landing. Frank slept there for the night, no doubt savoring his victory. His sleep came with the knowledge that he had taken off a pilot, but had landed an ace.[11]

Frank was missing, though no one was sure if it was a deliberate visit to the Cigognes or if he had been shot down. A French unit had seen his destructive work in the darkness, a brilliant ball of flame erupting from the exploding balloon, and they passed on word to confirm his kill.[12]

Frank was not the only pilot to not return that night. Joe Wehner had been forced to land somewhere other than the 27th as well. He took the time to call in to the squadron to let them know that he was all right.[13] Ironically, the two heroes of the day, the men that had prosecuted the war in the air so effectively, were not there to savor it.

Meanwhile, four kilometers away, the Prussian 5th Army (within the Imperial German Army) was assessing the extent of the damage that the American and French air services had inflicted on them. The losses were considerable. They had lost eight airplanes and had eighteen observation balloons shot down. One of their balloons had broken from its mooring and had drifted off. Thirty-three observers had been forced to bail out from their gondolas (known as jump-offs). The loss was more material than personnel, with only two casualties.[14]

One of Frank's survivors, Leutnant Wenzel of Ballonzug 18, had managed to safely parachute from his balloon before Frank had blown it up, making him one of the thirty-three jump-offs for that day. After the war, he commented that his balloon had been the target of numerous attempts by the French, Belgians, British, and Americans on several occasions. The only one to take it down had been Frank Luke.[15]

Chapter Eleven

"On every occasion this officer has demonstrated remarkable skill and endurance. He has no sense of fear, as evidenced by his record, and shows a remarkable devotion to duty."

—LIEUTENANT ALFRED GRANT, IN FRANK LUKE, JR.'S RECOMMENDATION
FOR THE DISTINGUISHED SERVICE CROSS, SEPTEMBER 15, 1919

Recognition
September 16, 1918

The weather was foggy at daybreak on the 16th of September, hindering long-distance observation, another sign that autumn was arriving on the battlefront. The normal routine at the 27th Squadron was shattered when Lieutenant Lennon ran Spad Number 10 into another one that was in the process of being worked on by the armorers. Two of the ground crew were seriously injured and splinters flew up from the crash, hitting Lennon in the face. It was not entirely Lennon's fault; the engine had gotten stuck with the throttle wide open. The technical kinks with the Spad XIII were still the problem of the squadron. It was also a sobering reminder of just how dangerous even daily life at a squadron base could be.[1]

Wehner made his way back to Rembercourt in the morning. Frank didn't return until 1:45 P.M. For Alfred Grant, this was simply another example of Frank's insubordination and disregard for authority. Frank simply had not been in a hurry to return to the squadron. To make matters worse for Grant,

Major Hartney had plans involving Frank for the evening ... plans that, if successful, were bound to feed Luke's ego even more.

The spectacular success of their twilight attack on observation balloons was the buzz of Rembercourt and among the leadership of the AEF. Hartney had spoken with General Mitchell regarding the success that had resulted from the tactic they had used, and Mitchell indicated that he would be coming out that evening to see the tactic employed himself. Grant played a role in pulling together the mission, though his contribution necessarily seemed small when compared to the star performances Luke and Wehner had given. Grant, it seemed, would always stand in the shadow of his subordinates.

There were some subtle modifications made to the plan from the previous night. Frank had faced extreme difficulties in finding his aerodrome after taking out the balloons. Lacking illuminated instrumentation or cockpits, it was only by sheer luck that he had found his own side of the trench lines and had not crash-landed in some unseen terrain feature or a low hanging electrical or telephone wire. This time the ground crews would fire off flares after (if) the balloons were taken out. This would give Luke and Wehner a visible reference for where the airfield was without risking drawing in German bombers.

There was no mistake—this was a show flight. Major Hartney had been bragging about the efforts of the two boys, and now he was going to prove it to General Mitchell. The details of their mission were carefully mapped out. Since Rembercourt was shared with other squadrons, there would be plenty of pilots and ground crew personnel on hand to watch. Before sunset, they picked their target balloons out on the sunlit horizon.

There was talk of coming up with a series of signals for the American ground troops so that they would not accidentally fire at him in the twilight. As Hartney said: "Equipping the machines in this manner meant delay, and Luke, boyishly remarking, 'they cannot hit me anyway,' went out as on other occasions, knowing full well that he would be shot at by his own as well as enemy troops."[2]

Billy Mitchell's interest in destroying observation balloons was hands-on. "I told Hartney to go back and fire out a new way of destroying the balloons,

I did not care how he did it. Hartney, who is an enthusiastic and able man, would keep cocking his head from one side to the other saying, 'precisely, precisely' as I gave him the instructions, but all of the time thinking how it would be possible to devise any new method which had not been tried in the last three years. The next morning, that is, September 16, Hartney told me that he had a solution."[3]

Rembercourt was abuzz that evening. Other pilots gathered, some because they had heard that General Mitchell was present, others because word had spread that Luke and Wehner were going to repeat the successes of the night before. Mitchell arrived with his staff in a captured Mercedes-Benz staff car.[4] The enlisted men distributed coffee for the brass that was present. The officers checked their watches, ticking off the minutes until the mission was underway.

Frank and Joe emerged from Major Hartney's headquarters. American ace Eddie Rickenbacker was there as Frank walked briskly to his machine. Frank pointed off at the balloons on the horizon. The sausages were about four miles apart. "Keep your eyes on these two balloons. You will see the first one out there go up in flames at exactly 7:15 and the other one will do likewise at 7:19."[5]

It was the piloting equivalent of Babe Ruth calling his home run hit against Chicago in 1932. Attacking balloons was hard enough, let alone being specific about the time. Joe would have to rely on more than his lucky wings and ring to pull off this attack. He was going to have to rely on Frank's cunning and dauntless ability to take out enemy balloons. Mitchell was there as were Colonels Milling and Sherman and Inspector General Donaldson. Mitchell commented, "Colonel Barnes is going to do a little extra shooting tonight with his artillery and his gunflashes will probably make the balloon line more active." As if on queue, the rumble of artillery started to launch thousands of pounds of shrapnel over no-man's land.

As the men kept checking their watches, Mitchell hesitated in his confidence. Shaking his head, he said, "Hartney, it's impossible. To get a balloon at all is a feat. To time its demise five hours ahead is beyond reason. And to do it at night is just not in the cards."

It was Lieutenant Grant who shattered the quiet at Rembercourt next. "Twenty seconds to go."

He had just completed his words when there was a brilliant burst of flame over the sky near Spincourt, the site of the first of the balloon targets. Sparks and burning pieces of silk rained downward as the ball of fire rose into the night sky.

"By God, there she goes!" General Mitchell exclaimed. The other officers began to cheer and howl. A few tense moments later, they were stunned to see another flash in the air—the second balloon. In the early evening sky, it was easy to see the explosions miles away.

* * * *

As Joe and Frank took off from Rembercourt, they headed northeast from the field, heading for Reville and away from the setting sun. The flight took them ten minutes. They spotted the balloon and both of them dove in on it, guns blazing. The anti-aircraft batteries sprang to life, filling the air with lead and steel as the balloon's observer jumped, preferring to take his chances with the parachute drop than against the fire from the Spads.

Incendiary rounds from their 11 mm Vickers slapped into the bag. Almost immediately the Drachen erupted in a ball of fire. The observer was caught in the raining gray and black flaming debris as he drifted to the ground.

The explosion separated the two pilots. Frank headed off to Remagne, while Joe edged along a landmark he could still make out, the Meuse River, trying to find another balloon. Frank's bearings were good. He found the second balloon. Their plan called for him to fire his Very pistol, a red flare, to help draw Joe in to engage the target. Frank aimed his Spad downward at the Drachen. Once more the anti-aircraft batteries and machine guns filled the sky as the balloon crew desperately tried to reel in the sausage. In the semi-darkness it was difficult for the gun crews to locate the Spads by any means other than sound.

Luke's Spad rocked as it took hits from the anti-aircraft fire. He caught the balloon near the ground and peppered the top of it with his gun. The balloon erupted just as it neared the ground, falling in flames onto the winch and crew. The ball of fire, orange and yellow was visible for kilometers.

Wehner spotted what he thought was a red flare in the night near Mangiennes. He assumed it was his wingman signaling him. As he headed towards that area, he spotted the silhouette of a third balloon in the night just above the tree tops. He dove in on it, firing at the dark black shape in the night. The anti-aircraft bursts around him rocked his Spad but his aim was true. The sausage was cooked, bursting brilliantly in the darkness.

Frank continued to fly, looking for more targets as nightfall swept the battlefield. He had lost Joe in the night and soon he would have a hard time finding the field. On his way back over the front he spotted several supply trains and strafed them with machine gun fire.[6]

* * * *

The gathered dignitaries watched as the balloons at Reveille, Remagne, and Mangiennes went up in great balls of fire. They had gone off at almost the exact moment that Frank had predicted. Grant knew that his men would be heading back and ordered flares fired off. In the darkness the unmistakable sound of a Spad motor could be heard. Frank circled the field and dropped, killing his engine and coming to a perfect landing in front of Major Hartney and General Mitchell. A few minutes later Joe Wehner's plane appeared and he, too, landed.

Mitchell came out and congratulated both of the aviators. Frank was laughing, quite pleased with the success of the demonstration. The crowd gathered to inspect the damage to the Spads. The anti-aircraft fire, even in the darkness, had done considerable damage. General Mitchell took his swagger stick and pulled loose large pieces of dope-covered canvas that covered the lower wing of Frank's plane. He did the same with Wehner's. Neither aircraft stood a chance of being ready for action the next day.[7]

General Mitchell was impressed. Could the same be done against the entire German balloon line? "Yes, sir," Hartney replied. "There won't be one left on the front in a few days."

That night the duo of Luke and Wehner were at their pinnacle. To perform such a public exhibition of their balloon busting tactic was incredible. For the newly minted Army Air Service, it was a vindication of the work that Mitchell, Hartney, and countless others had put in building an air force. While they and many of the command staff were filled with jubilation over the demonstration, Harold Hartney was worried. He understood Frank's personality; he knew he would want to go up again, to attempt to get more balloons. The damage done to their planes was testimony to how dangerous this fighting was, yet for now, the two pilots seemed oblivious to that risk. Silently, Hartney prayed that the next day would bring rain so that Luke wouldn't be able to fly.[8]

Across the barrens of no-man's land, the Germans were trying to determine what was happening. Their evening summary indicated "Active hostile fighter pilot activity in the east section and Ornes. Two of our balloons were shot down burning."[9] There were a total of six balloon losses for the day, of which half were accounted for by Luke and Wehner. At the same time, German pilots claimed credits for only two Allied balloons. The German observers were getting a great deal of practice for their jump-offs as a result of balloon busting operations. One hapless officer, Leutnant Hoefinghoff of Ballonzug 152, jumped three times on the 16th of September, landing safely each time.[10] The balloons that Frank and Joe had gone after were attached to Ballonzug 112 under Leutnants Finstre and Heicke. They filed reports regarding the night attack, doubtless with some apprehension.[11]

Chapter Twelve

"If I could only give you a picture of the magnificent fighter that your boy was. Within the last two weeks he downed four balloons and three Hun planes thus leaping into fame as one of the foremost American Aces. In the fight where he was last seen he was trying to protect his friend and working partner Lt. Luke from a great number of Hun planes."

—H. WHITCOMB NICHOLSON TO JOSEPH WEHNER'S MOTHER,
SEPTEMBER 21, 1918

The Darkest of Times
September 17–18, 1918

The day after the demonstration for General Mitchell was relatively quiet. The reason for that was the St. Mihiel offense was over. The salient south of Verdun had been crushed. The 27th put up two patrols in the morning and two in the afternoon. Their orders were to not cross enemy lines unless as part of an engagement with enemy aircraft. This was the mopping-up portion of the campaign and it was hoped that this day would buy the First Pursuit Group some much needed rest time.

The enlisted personnel enjoyed exploring the overrun German trenches and bunkers, pilfering and selectively looting. They confiscated food, writing materials, linen, tape, and even a small one-pound cannon. They were most disappointed that they did not find any German beer left behind.[1]

Even the officers were not immune to the temptations of looting. Lieutenants Hoover, Clapp, and Roberts, along with Sergeants Hessong and

133

Phopheter, confiscated a truck and headed to St. Mihiel. They found French magazines and books and even elaborate bunkers with furniture. Many of the villages were nothing more than smoldering ruins.[2]

The following day, September 18, the weather was partly cloudy, with a low fog early in the morning hours hugging over the trenches. The fog turned into drizzle, then outright rain, grounding the morning flights. "Luke literally chafed on his forced aerial inactivity. He spent most of his time that day actually working with his mechanics on his machine so that it would be serviceable at the first break in the weather. When he was not busy with his machine he was at the squadron or group headquarters discussing with senior officers possible new tactics for employment in the destruction of the Hun machines."[3]

The weather was going to break later in the day and that would once again put Frank and Joe in on the center stage. That evening they would take off again and employ the same tactic that they had used twice before—striking at the observation balloons in the early evening.

* * * *

In many respects, the mission was just like the ones they had already flown. But this time the two American pilots were facing an enemy of considerable skill and greater experience.

Across the lines another pilot was getting his orders at the same time as Frank and Joe. His name was Georg von Hantelmann, a young Leutnant in Jasta 15. He had been born in 1898 and was very young for a pilot of his quality. He also possessed the same sort of quiet demeanor that characterized Joseph Wehner, but was known to have a great deal of determination and concentration in his air battles. He had enlisted in the war two years earlier in the Braunschweiger Hussar Regiment Nr. 17. Their insignia was a "death's head." Hantelmann had adopted that as his personal insignia for his airplane's fuselage: a menacing skull and crossbones. His transfer into the air service in February of 1918 gave him months of experience over his American opponents.

His rise in the rankings was not nearly as meteoric as Frank Luke's, but was still very impressive. On September 12, he had shot down Lieutenant David Putnam—the leading American ace at the time. Putnam had 13 victories under his belt when he fell prey to von Hantelmann's guns. On September 16, he shot down Sub-Lieutenant Maurice Boyau of French escadrille Spa. 77, an ace with 35 victories—21 of them over balloons. By sunrise on September 18, Georg von Hantelmann had 15 confirmed victories—an ace three times over.[4]

His squadron, Jasta 15, had a reputation as a deadly group of aviators. Their distinction was that their aircraft, new Fokker D.VIIs, had a common paint scheme. Von Hantelmann's commanding officer, Hauptman Rudolph Berthold, had been a member of the Prussian infantry. Their old uniforms were a bright blue with red piping. The colors chosen for Jasta 15 paid homage to Berthold and the squadron's infantry roots.[5] The planes had been painted with blue fuselages, red noses up to the cockpits, and red wheels.

Thanks to an accident in supply, the blue paint had been somewhat translucent and if you got close to one of the airplanes you could make out where a black German cross near the tail had been on the planes when delivered—and painted over. The distinctive paint scheme was intended to let their enemies know who it was that was flying up against them. Jasta 15 wanted their reputation to stir fear in their enemies.

Von Hantelmann was on patrol over friendly lines in the late afternoon of September 18. His orders were to patrol on the German side of the lines, intercept enemy air incursions, and destroy them. He and the rest of Jasta 15 were on a collision course with Luke and Wehner.

* * * *

Frank and Joe took off earlier than they had in their previous attempts to hit the German balloon line, lifting into the air at 4:00 P.M. The plan was simple and direct. Frank would go after the enemy Drachen while Joe provided him cover. Wehner was flying Spad Number 21 on this day, patched up from his last mission.

They climbed to a comfortable but chilling altitude and headed over St. Mihiel, scanning the horizon for the dark gray-green shapes of the target balloons. Two were spotted near Labeuville. Their pair of Spads moved into a nearby cloud formation for cover, to conceal their approach on the balloons and to avoid an extra few moments of flying through the wall of anti-aircraft fire that was going to be thrown between them and their targets.

Diving out of the clouds they focused on the balloons. Frank and Joe both fired at the Drachen. One after another, the two balloons exploded with brilliant bursts of flames. Burning rubberized silk fragments rained down, billowing black smoke as they fell. The anti-aircraft fire was fierce but then suddenly stopped—an ominous sign to Frank and Joe that there were German aircraft in the vicinity. Bursting anti-aircraft shells had no friends nor did they discriminate between sides, so it was common practice for ground crews to hold their fire when an air battle was about to begin.

Jasta 15 arrived. Their brilliant blue and red airplanes dove straight at the pair of American Spads like birds of prey on the hunt. Joe Wehner was already somewhat higher and attracted the majority of the attention from the roaring Fokker D.VIIs. He turned away from Luke who was in the process of trying to rise up so as to provide Joe some much-needed assistance.

Two of the Fokkers careened into tight turns, coming onto Frank's tail. For the moment, Joe was going to have to wait. Frank careened his Spad around and charged straight at his would-be pursuers. He fired with both of his guns, both bullets and incendiary rounds, at the lead airplane. Head-on battles were always difficult, and the profile of the oncoming airplane was small and moving fast. The Fokker whizzed past Frank only a few meters away.

The lead Fokker reeled off to one side and angled nose-first for the ground. It was over in a few seconds as the mass of engine block, wood, aluminum tubing, and canvas slammed into the ground with full force and fury.

Frank swung around again after the other Fokker. He squeezed off a few rounds and the blue and red airplane dove to get out of his gun-sights. Instinctively he looked up, searching the skies for Wehner but could not see him—only the other aircraft of Jasta 15.

This was not the first time he and Joe had become separated in a battle, nor had it been the first time that Joe had tangled with a large number of Fokkers to protect his wingman. Frank decided to head back towards Rembercourt. As he was heading toward the American and French lines he spotted a Halberstadt near the village of St. Hilaire. The Halberstadt was an observation aircraft, a two-seater. The observer in the rear seat was equipped with a camera and a machine gun.[6]

The Halberstadt was being flown by Leutnant Ernst Höhne with Ernst Schultz as his observer. Höhne was focused on his mission and on avoiding contact with the enemy, playing cat and mouse with some French Spads from Spa. 68. Höhne was obviously on a photographic mission over the French portions of the lines. What Frank didn't know was that one of the pilots was Reginald Sinclaire of the Lafayette Flying Corps—an American still flying in the service of the French. Sinclaire was in the air with another pilot Adjutant Pierre Gaudermen. They had been attempting to engage the Halberstadt for some time but to no avail. Each time they closed with it, Höhne would swing away, keeping his distance.

They were playing a deadly game of cat and mouse when Frank's Spad arrived on the scene. All three Spads swung in, cutting off the German plane, driving him deep over the French ground positions. Frank came in low, rising behind his tail, firing away as Gaudermen and Sinclaire charged in on their prey. But Frank's rounds had already done the damage. The Halberstadt careened over and crashed near the village of Rattentaut.

The Halberstadt slammed into a field near a French infantry unit. Its pilot, Höhne, remained crushed in his cockpit. The observer, Ernst Schultz, was thrown clear of the wreckage. His body was a mangled mess, lying face down on the grasses in the field some distance from the pile of broken wood and canvas that had been the Halberstadt.

Frank brought his Spad down on the same field, landing a short distance away. Nearby infantry emerged and came to see the fallen airplane and the man who brought it down.[7]

Frank's mind had to be elsewhere, though. In a few short minutes, Frank Luke, Jr., had engaged two balloons and three enemy aircraft for five kills—one of which was in the field in front of him. When that Halberstadt had fallen, Frank had gone from being an ace to being America's Ace of Aces, edging out Eddie Rickenbacker. Five kills in just a few short minutes—it was incredible. Yet Frank had to have wondered about his wingman and good friend.

* * * *

The last few moments of Joseph Fritz Wehner's life were not recorded in any great detail but can be painfully pieced together. Today, information from the German records is fragmentary and terse at best, because many archives were destroyed in the Second World War. What is known is that, west of Conflans, Joe was maneuvered into the gun sights of Leutnant Georg von Hantelmann. The machine guns riddled the fuselage of the Spad, hitting the gas tank and the pilot. Several bullets separated by a matter of a second entered Joe's body. One hit him in the back of the head, blasting his jaws out. It was merciful and quick. His airplane crashed into the ground near Thionville. Almost every bone in his body was shattered in the impact and his head was nearly broken clean off at the neck.

Joe had died doing what he had done so many times before, providing cover for his friend—Frank Luke. Yet for some time his body lay broken and alone in the shattered remains of Spad Number 21, Serial Number S7555.

German infantry moved into the area. They buried the remains of Wehner wrapped in a burlap bag and noted the location. The German air service had felt the full fury of Frank and Joe's final flight together. For the day, they recorded the loss of four airplanes and four balloons—more than half of their losses being attributed to Luke and Wehner. Lieutnant von Hantelmann only accounted for one kill—Joe Wehner, number sixteen to his record.[8]

Joe always carried two lucky tokens with him: the ring given to him by a young woman in New York, and the "shavetail" wings Frank had won gambling. When the men of the 27th checked his personal belongings, the ring and wings had been left behind.[9]

* * * *

Frank was approached by the French infantry that had come to investigate the Halberstadt C that he had downed. A pair of American Signal Corps photographers who were in Rattentaut headed over to see if they could catch a photo image of the Air Service pilot and his victim. Sergeants C. E. Dunn and H. S. Druker arrived shortly thereafter. They snapped photographs of Frank and had him pose with the remains of the wrecked aircraft. They also snapped a photograph of Ernst Schultz, the observer who had died in the crash.

Pilots were known for taking mementos from their victims. Some cut off some of the dope fabric from the fuselage or tail, something to signify they had won in the battle. Frank did take a German cross off the wreck as tangible proof of his victory.[10] The nearby U.S. 4th Division came forward as well to see what the commotion was. One of their men, Captain Paul Coster, Jr., saw Frank cut the Iron Cross of the Halberstadt off. As Luke passed him, he casually asked if Coster wanted a souvenir. When he replied yes, Frank cut some of the cross off and provided it to him.[11]

For Frank, this was the first time he had come face-to-face with the men he was killing. It had to be a sobering moment. In the photographs that Dunn captured of Frank we are not exposed to the energetic and excitable youth. We see a young man who is tired, worn-down, and deadly serious.

Frank took off from that field but did not return to Rembercourt that night. Instead he went off to a rear-area field near one of the large 16-inch naval cannons that had been brought in to shatter the German trenches.

He contacted the headquarters to let them know he was alright and to check to see the status of Wehner. Officially, Joe was missing in action. While it had happened before, this time seemed different to Frank.

Major Hartney was well aware of what was happening. One of his pilots had performed an incredible feat—the destruction of five enemy aircraft in ten minutes. At the same time, word had come in that Wehner was not just missing but there had been sightings of a Spad going down. Also, Hartney was keenly aware that Frank's action that day had propelled him to the top ranking—the Ace of Aces.

Frank Luke, Jr., had been a pariah in his squadron a month earlier. Other pilots considered him a liar, possibly a coward, and definitely a braggart. On September 18, 1918, he became something else—the top American ace in France. For the highly competitive Frank, this title carried a burden. The men who had held it before him, Lufbery and Putnam, had lost that title by dying. Lieutenant Paul Baer had held the title but had been shot down, wounded, and captured by the Germans. Lieutenant Edgar Tobin had held the title for a few days but had been edged out by Lieutenant Rickenbacker. Frank's victories on the 18th had shot him past even Rickenbacker.

Chapter Thirteen

Frank Luke is flying high
Over the German zone
Good-by you Huns, the time has come
For the devil to claim his own.

The devil said to his friend, the Huns,
This much I will own.
I have sown the seed of murder
And hate.

And well has it flourished and grown.
You have done my work so well, you
Huns,
Henceforth you shall be my own.

Frank Luke is riding the clouds today –
A youth from our old town.
Love and pride we have for this lad
Who is bringing these devils down.

—CAROLYN P., MESA, ARIZONA

In the Limelight
September 19–24, 1918

The next morning, Hartney went to recover his boy. He took along Eddie Rickenbacker and Mrs. Welton, the YMCA representative at Rembercourt. They drove out to where Frank had landed and found a very remorseful and somber Luke. His question to Hartney summed up his worries: "Wehner isn't back yet, is he, Major?"

On the ride back the usually talkative and high-strung Luke sat quiet. What few words he did mutter were reflective of the worry he was facing. "Major, I'm glad it wasn't me. My mother doesn't know I'm on the front yet."[1]

His combat report reflects his understanding of Wehner's true fate. Despite the fact that Joe was declared as missing in action, Frank knew that Wehner would not be coming back. Instead of the usual "Confirmation requested" for the kills he got, Frank wrote a more telling line: "Lt. Wehner is entitled to share in the victories over both balloons." Only then did he request confirmation.[2]

The events that had unfolded the day before with the loss of Wehner had shaken Frank. He tried to take part in a patrol mission but even that went awry. His usual aircraft, Number 26, needed repairs from the fighting the day before. Frank was given temporary use of Spad Number 8. Rembercourt, always a muddy field even in good weather, was made worse with rains throughout the morning hours.

In the afternoon Luke climbed into Spad Number 8 and gunned the engine for takeoff. He roared down the field but the weight of the fully loaded and fueled Spad and the mud worked against him. Rembercourt held onto Frank's airplane, keeping the speed so low he couldn't take off. He crashed into the gun pit used for practice by the 147th Squadron. Number Eight was out of commission.

It was not a promising sign. It could be that it was simply the mire of Rembercourt that caused the problem—it could also be that Frank was still shaken by Wehner's death. Hartney was an experienced combat pilot, he had seen other pilots lose their edge before. He had a tiger by the tail in Luke. On one hand, the young man was the leading American ace; on the other hand, he was a rebel still contemplating the loss of his bunkmate. Each hour he spent alone in his room was a reminder to Frank that Joe was missing in action.

Major Hartney decided that a party would be thrown that night, September 19, to honor Frank. Major Hartney determined that his star pilot needed some time away from the front. With the St. Mihiel operation in a mopping-up phase, there was some time before the next offensive. The 27th could spare Frank Luke for a few days of much-deserved rest. And Paris was just the place for him to get it.

The party that Hartney pulled together involved all of the squadrons of the First Pursuit Group, with the 94th and 147th joining the Fighting Eagles. It was an affair for the officers to salute the new Ace of Aces. For Frank, it was praise overdue, validation in the eyes of men that had shunned him earlier. From Hartney's perspective, it was a party to show Luke that everyone appreciated the work he had done.

It rained the night of the 19th of September. The dinner hall where the party was held by the First Pursuit squadrons was a ramshackle building on the side of a hill. A truck went the village of Ligny to round up all of the food and drink that the locals could spare. The music came from a "liberated" German piano from Thiacourt.[3] For Frank, this dining hall probably bore resemblance to the dance halls of Ajo, Arizona.

Frank was not a dynamic public speaker. "When it came Luke's turn to respond he got up laughing, said he was having a bully time—and sat down!"[4] Frank was humbled—out of character for him.

Rickenbacker was being generous and had been part of planning the party. Luke had knocked him out of the top spot as Ace of Aces. Rickenbacker and Luke were both of European descent, but the similarities ended there. Rickenbacker was a very cool and calculating pilot, methodical in his style, whereas Frank tended to charge in boldly regardless of the risks.

Luke was given a present by Major Hartney: a seven day pass for Paris. The pilots had chipped in to provide Frank with some spending money, a wad of French francs.

Sending Frank to Paris to help him cope with the loss of Joe Wehner was well intended, but misguided. Paris was not a new city to Frank—he had been stationed at Orly, just outside the city, and had spent considerable time there when not ferrying airplanes. Getting Frank away from the front did give him some time to reflect and come to terms with the loss of Wehner, but it was wishful thinking to believe that Frank would be gone the entire time of his pass.

On September 20, Frank headed off to Paris as the leading American ace. A realization now must have come to Frank that his new title carried a price with it: fame. He was not unknown, even in the streets of Paris. And the reporters were submitting their stories about his exploits to the censors for publication in the States. Such stories sometimes took long days to go through approval by military authorities, and even longer to get to the U.S. and into the papers. But by the time he hit Paris, Frank was a hero—one of the very first heroes from the Great War for the Americans that had just arrived a few months earlier in France. His name was mentioned in the same breath as the members of the Lafayette Escadrille and a handful of other aviators that became publicly recognized.

What Frank suspected, and what had indeed already happened, was that the story of his meteoric rise had broken. The headlines of the *Arizona Republican* on September 19 came as as much of a shock to the Luke family as it did to anyone else in Phoenix: "Phoenix Boy Downs Nine German Balloons: Frank Luke, Jr., sets high record; balloon harder to down than airplane." The story had been telegraphed back by several different reporters and had begun to break in newspapers across the United States. Frank Luke was on the front pages from Washington, D.C., to Los Angeles.

"Phoenix is electrified. Downtown Phoenix was electrified last evening when *The Republican's* bulletin board gave the gist of the dispatch

Author's Collection. 1917 Phoenician. Frank is shown during the infamous freshman haircutting incident.

Author's Collection. 1917 Phoenician. Frank in 1915 in his baseball uniform.

Author's Collection. 1917 Phoenician. Young Bill Elder, Frank's childhood friend.

Author's Collection. Frank on the roof of Union High School in Phoenix preparing to jump using a wagon parasol.

Marie Jackson Collection. Frank, Sr., and Tillie Luke during their visit with Frank and Marie.

Marie Jackson Collection. This image was taken by Frank of Marie.

Marie Jackson Collection. Marie shows off her engagement ring with Frank at her side.

Marie Jackson Collection. Decked out in Frank's flight gear, Marie Rapson poses in San Diego during some of their last happy times together.

Courtesy of John Luke. One of the legacies of Frank Luke – the Luke Family poses in 1934. Front row
– left to right: Jerry Perry, Frank Perry, Peggy Flynn, Frank A. Luke, Teresa (Teedie) Flynn, Frank Flynn,
Frank Luke, Sr., Eta Flynn, Madgie Elaine Luke, John P. Luke, Frankie Mae Luke, Barbara Luke, Tillie
Luke, Marilyn Luke, Eddie Luke, Jim Luke, Sheila Luke, Mary Pat Flynn. Back row – left to right: John
A. Luke, Charles Luke, Eben Perry, Eunice Luke, Tom Flynn, Eva Luke Flynn, Bill Luke, Dorothy Luke,
Otillia Luke Perry, Regina Luke Perry, Beverly Wilson (baby), Carrie Liebenow, Maxwell Luke, Adolph
"Dolph" Liebenow, Ed Wilson, Irene Luke, Ed Luke, Sr.

Author's Collection. Joseph Fritz Wehner – Frank's close friend and wingman.

Author's Collection. Joe Wehner poses in his flight gear near a Nieuport.

NARA. This studio photo of Frank was taken stateside.

Marie Jackson Collection. Frank poses in a studio shot in his flight gear in San Diego.

Lafayette Foundation – Walter Williams Album. This image shows the birthplace of the Fighting Eagles, the tent city at Kelly Field, Texas. Amidst this old cotton field, the first American air force was forged.

NARA. Frank stands next to his Spad a short time before his death.

NARA. Frank poses with the wreckage of the Halberstadt he downed on September 18, 1918.

NARA. Captain Alfred Grant, Frank's commanding officer and a strict disciplinarian.

Marie Jackson Collection. Frank sits on a well in the French village of Cageaux.

NARA. Taken on September 18, 1918. Gone is the young man that came to the front only a few weeks earlier. With Joe Wehner missing in action, Frank appears aged several years.

Marie Jackson Collection. Frank poses with a captured German machine gun.

Author's Collection. The prey – a German Drachen.

Author's Collection. A German sausage.

Author's Collection. This is a typical German anti-aircraft machine gun emplacement. Numerous machine guns would ring a balloon nest, waiting for aircraft brave or crazy enough to make a pass.

Marie Jackson Collection. Frank takes time to play with a group of French children.

Author's Collection. This photograph was taken on the day before Frank died.

NARA. From left to right: Jerry Vasconcells, Alfred Grant, Fred Norton, and Harold Hartney.

Author's Collection. Just one of the many deadly defenders of the German balloon lines.

The Lafayette Foundation. Frank poses with a captured German machine gun along with his ground crew. From left to right: Lou Flanner, Unknown, Jackson, Rudy Shirek, Brady, and Toger.

NARA. This is all that remained of the Halberstadt that Frank downed on September 18, 1918.

Courtesy of the Smithsonian Archives. Discovered filed in the Smithsonian for decades, piece of airplane fabric (front) that Frank Luke shot down the day that Joe Wehner died. These pieces were on display until the 1950s when they were filed away until the author and Smithsonian officials rediscovered them.

History of Aviation Collection, Special Collections Department, McDermott Library, The University of Texas, Dallas. Leutnant Von Hantlemann poses in one of his earlier aircraft in the war. Von Hantlemann was responsible for the death of Frank's wingman and friend, Joe Wehner.

The Lafayette Foundation. A Canadian by birth, Major Harold Hartney was the father-figure for Frank, giving him much more leeway than Captain Alfred Grant.

Ivan Andrew Roberts

W. E. B. Du Bois Library, Special Collections and University Archives, "Massachusetts Agricultural College In the War," The M.A.C. Bulletin – Amherst, Mass., (Printed with Permission). Lieutenant Ivan Andrew Roberts, Frank's last wingman and one of a handful of American pilots from the Great War that remains missing in action.

The Lafayette Foundation. The maintenance crew of the 27th squadron poses for Joe Flanner.

Author's Collection. "Frank Luke – Balloon Ace." *St. Nicholas Magazine.* October 1920.
During Frank's advanced flight training in France, Frank sits in the cockpit of a Nieuport.

The Lafayette Foundation. Ernst Schultz, tossed clear of the cockpit of his
Halberstadt after Frank shot down the airplane on September 18.

History of Aviation Collection, Special Collections Department, McDermott Library, The University of Texas, Dallas. Franz Büchner – the pilot responsible for the downing of Ivan Roberts.

Liberty Magazine, March 24, 1928 Leutnant Bernard Mangels, Ballonzug 35. On more than one occasion, his balloon company found itself under attack by Luke. On September 29, 1918, a lucky shot from his ground batteries forced Frank down behind enemy lines.

Marie Jackson Collection. Frank leans back against his
Spad for a photo image sent to his fiancée Marie Rapson.

from the front recounting the truly marvelous performance of Frank Luke Jr. It was not long until word reach the theaters where slides announced the good news."5

Headlines around the country raved about his exploits in France with patriotic zeal. In many papers the story of Frank's feats were listed even above the 1918 World Series results. Many got the actual count of his victories wrong—some because of the cumbersome system of confirmations, others most likely because of outright distortions. Daily the story grew: "Frank Luke Jr. Gets Airplane to His Credit." "Frank Luke Jr. Is Now Ranked As Ace of Air." In Fort Wayne, Indiana, the spin was that Frank had done much of his flying with almost no gasoline left in the Spad. "Wins Air Victories on Thimbles of Gasoline: American Aviator Gets Three Enemy Balloons and an Airplane." Syracuse, New York, played off of Luke's energetic personality. "Luke Downed 25 German Aircraft in 10 Day Period: Hun Gasbags Are the Special Hobby of The Nut." The newspaper tallies of Frank's victories ranged from nine to twenty-six: evidence that the Army's censorship was willing to look the other way at the details of his exploits. America was looking for a hero from the Great War, and Frank fit the bill. What America got was a fiery youth that seemed to walk out of the pages of a Wild West dime novel. The details were irrelevant to the people reading the papers.

The Phoenix Chamber of Commerce sent an overseas cable to Frank. "On behalf of the citizens of Phoenix and Arizona we send you greetings and congratulations upon your splendid work. May it long continue and may God keep you in his care. Signed the Phoenix Chamber of Commerce, H. W. Asbury, President."6 Likewise, his mother sent a telegram to him: "We are proud God bless you. Mama." His brother Joseph sent him a short missive: "Congratulations, Joseph Luke."7

Frank had kept his family in the dark regarding his posting to the front. His writing of letters had dropped off to almost none since he had arrived at the 27th Squadron. At some point he took out some YMCA stationery and did something that was long overdue. He told his mother that he was at the front:

September 21, 1918
Dear Mother
Have not writing [sic] you in some days on account of being so busy. As you no doubt you have already learned. This is on a line to let you know that I am o.k. Now mother, remember that I have passed the dangerous stage of being a new player at the game. You don't have to worry for me. I now know how to take care of myself.

Love to all,

FRANK[8]

Letters and well-wishers poured onto the Luke property in Phoenix. For their part the family did not grant many words to the press other than to say that they were proud of Frank, and of Edwin, who was training in the artillery at the time. Their pride was also hurt by the fact that they had not received word that Frank was even on the front lines until the story broke with the *Arizona Republican*.

Frank's mother took a moment to pen a letter to her son, one that he would never get the chance to read:

September 21, 1918
My Darling Boy,
I am very proud of you. God bless you and keep you from harm. I am so excited. Everybody here in town is. Oh do be very careful Dear Frank, don't take any unnecessary chances my darling boy. You are a wonderful boy. I always knew you would be now [sic]. Do be careful because your country needs you my but I am so glad wish I was there to hug and kiss you for ever [sic] balloon and plane you brought down. The phone rings all day congratulating us and send my love to you and saying how proud everyone that knows us

also lots of strangers. The town is sure proud of you. We are going to send you the clippings as they don't take papers to send over there. I am so proud of my two hero boys, you know Ed is one saving fourteen people from getting drowned a few years ago, didn't care if he was drowned or not as long as he could save them. That is the kind of boys [sic] that needs to be over there I know Ed will do something great just like you if they only give him a chance, and he is so anxious to go. He will be at Fort Sill three weeks more than [sic] maybe he can come home for a few days hope so. We are so happy and proud of you. Mrs. Dumal sends her love and says you are her boy and she is so proud of you. My dear be very careful of your dear self. And keep the good work up and may god bless you and keep you in his care.

Love your loving mother.[9]

Frank's mother didn't mention the lilies that he had planted at their home in Phoenix, but by this date they must have surprised her by beginning to poke through the soil. It was unusual that they would bloom at all in their first year, and it was late in the season, but the lilies seemed to be emerging.

To newspaper readers in the states, Frank seemed to be more than just a young pilot. Many accounts referred to him as a cowboy, a ranch-owner, a genuine young man from the West. He seemed to embody what most Americans felt about Phoenix. And in Phoenix, he was seen as the first true hero that the state of Arizona had produced since it had joined the Union just a few short years earlier.

Another city where the word spread was San Diego. Young Marie Rapson was known to some of Frank's friends at Rockwell Field who most likely fed her name to the reporters for the city newspapers. Marie, like Frank's parents, was not aware that Frank was at the front. He had sheltered her from the worry. Suddenly she not only found out about where he was and what he was doing, but was tossed into the spotlight of the San Diego media. The local press was hot on the trail for any way to link this hero to their hometown and in Marie they had found the perfect angle for their stories. On September 24, Frank's sixteen year old fiancée found her photograph and life story spread out on the front page of the *San Diego Union*: "Frank Luke, U.S. Ace, May Be an Arizona Boy But San Diego Too Has a Real Claim on Him." Marie's mother, Cora, always the stern and protective matriarch, politely informed the paper that she was a senior in high school. In reality, she was two years younger.

Not that it mattered—young Marie was suddenly the luckiest girl in America in the eyes of many women. She was engaged to a dashing young pilot who was now the American Ace of Aces. Frank's photograph was everywhere and Marie appeared next to his image on papers in Detroit and New York. For the young and charming musician this had to be an overwhelming series of events. At the same time, it came with a concern that had to haunt her thoughts. Frank was at the front, as far as she knew, and many pilots at the front died.

Frank, Marie, and the Luke family were not the only ones to be drawn in on the sudden wave of publicity. Joe Wehner was listed as Frank's buddy, his stalwart friend. Because of the delay in the censors clearing the stories the word had not gotten out yet that Joe was missing in action and presumed dead. Some members of the press attempted to quote Major Hartney, only to have the censors block out his name and unit—an attempt to keep the Germans in the dark. Anyone in any paper who was a pilot in France was somehow associated with Frank Luke. Many gave quotes in interviews even if they were not in Frank's squadron or even on the front lines.

For Marie and the Luke family, it had to be a difficult way to learn how Frank was doing. Everyone was thrown into the turmoil of the moment. But back in Paris, only slightly aware of the stir that he was causing, Frank found himself in a big city with little to do.

* * * *

Frank returned to Rembercourt on the 24th of September, after only five days in Paris. Most men, when granted seven days leave in a war, would cherish being away from the front. When he was asked why he had come back early from his leave, his answer was simply, "There was nothing to do."[10] For a young man who gave his gambling winnings to the church, for the pilot who was committed to his fiancée back in the States, for the man who was focused on one thing and one thing only—busting balloons—his statement is painfully honest. Only Frank Luke could go to Paris in the middle of a war as a new celebrity and not find anything to amuse him.

While he had been gone, very little had been happening at the 27th Squadron. Lieutenant Grant rolled out the pilots and enlisted personnel at 5:00 A.M. for reveille, drill, and inspection. The enlisted men had schemed to steal a piano from the Knights of Columbus hall to add to their entertainment. Several Liberty Parties had taken place, trucks loaded with personnel out seeking covert fun. Lieutenant Rickenbacker organized an evening show with a local entertainment troop and the 27th's officers were invited to attend. To remind the squadron that they were, indeed, a part of the Army, Grant ordered general inspection of the day-to-day garbage around the field. When rain struck on the 23rd of September, the men finally had enough down time for the entire squadron to take baths, a happy and welcome diversion.[11]

There was a general sense of calm, but it was the calm before the storm. Infantry and artillery were massing again, the signs of a big push. With the St. Mihiel offensive already a fading memory, the Allies were turning north. The operation was called the Meuse-Argonne Offensive. The American thrust was to drive north along the Meuse River with the French on the flanks, driving into the Argonne Forest region. This would take the U.S. forces right into the heart of the Prussian 5th Army. It was hoped that the forests of the Argonne were less reinforced than the rear areas of St. Mihiel had proven to be.

Upon his return, Frank indicated that he was ready to get back into the air again even if Grant was hesitant to put him back in the cockpit. The day he returned, Grant and Hartney had devised a plan to get the B Flight under the command of Lieutenant Vasconcells closer to the action. There was an abandoned field and possible hangar north of Verdun. Russell Pruden and Jerry Vasconcells drove up to the field. They found that it had been the home to a French cavalry unit, and had a number of stone stables and a large barracks. Some heavy naval cannons used by the Americans had been brought into the area, and the best facilities had been taken over by the artillerymen. The two thirteen-inch guns shook the nearby buildings violently when fired.

The advance airfield could work for the 27th, but there were some risks. The massive artillery, every time it fired, could potentially draw counter-battery fire from the Germans. The artillerymen likewise were worried that having an airfield so close to their guns would draw unwanted attention from the Germans. This airfield was in range of the German artillery, much closer than Rembercourt was.

Vasconcells secured several farm houses at the end of the field to billet the maintenance crews that would work out of the advance field. On the morning of the 25th of September, trucks rolled out from Rembercourt for the B Flight's new field.[12]

Frank anxiously awaited his chance to get back in the air. It came on September 25, when he was assigned a new wingman—his replacement for Joe Wehner. Another young man from Massachusetts, named Ivan Roberts, was to fly with him.

Chapter Fourteen

"The enemy undertook numerous balloon attacks and our troops were troubled by low fliers. Several times [the enemy] squadron broke through but our own fighter pilots struck back."

—KOMMANDEUR DER FLIEGER 5, ARMEE NR.
15471, A.H. QU., DEN SEPTEMBER 25, 1918

Ivan the Missing
September 25–26, 1918

Ivan Andrew Roberts was a pilot who seemed destined to fall through the cracks of history. Most stories involving Frank's flight on the 26th of September simply refer to Roberts as Luke's "new wingman." Mentioning him by name seemed optional. After the war, he was ignored in such research tomes as *New England Aviators*, and even his hometown newspaper did not print him on the list of men serving overseas.

He was born January 24, 1896, in Shavertown, New York. His father, Thomas Lee Roberts, relocated the family to South Lee, Massachusetts, as he was growing up. His mother, Mary Ella Finkle, died and his father remarried. Thomas Lee became the headmaster for the Ascension Farm School, a facility for wayward boys.

Like Frank, Roberts had a fiancée, named Dorothy Thompson. Dorothy came from money; her grandfather was a well-off doctor in a nearby community. Dorothy herself was an architectural draftsperson, not a typical career for a woman in the nineteen-teens.

Roberts attended MIT for a year and spent time at the Massachusetts Agricultural College at Amherst. After war was declared, Roberts enlisted. On January 28, 1918, just a few days after his twenty-second birthday, he was commissioned a second lieutenant in the Army and, like Frank, attended pilot training in Texas. Ivan trained under Vernon Castle, another Massachusetts man known more for his dancing than his flying. Roberts was assigned originally to the 182nd Squadron, but was reassigned in March to the 27th Squadron. His brother, Thomas, was also in the Army and was destined to be in France at the same time Ivan was. Like Frank, Ivan's sister was in the Red Cross.

Ivan was well liked from the time he was transferred into the 27th. His nickname was "Robbie" with his peer pilots. There are no accounts of his vices or virtues. People generally liked Ivan, that was it. To judge by his combat reports and other fliers' comments on Roberts after the war, he was a good pilot. Prior to late September 1918, Ivan had three confirmed kills to his name, and one unconfirmed victory. On one occasion he was put in command of a B Flight for a mission. Yet he remained for the most part a mere face in the background.[1]

Plucked from his previous obscurity, Ivan Roberts was suddenly thrust into a new role on September 25, 1918, as Frank Luke's wingman. Ivan seems to have been a quiet man who kept to himself, and in that regard he was a perfect replacement for the quiet Joe Wehner. Wehner, on the other hand, was Frank's blood-brother, his bunkmate, his good friend. Ivan was simply a nice guy, a good pilot. Would the combination work? On September 25, they flew together for the first time.

Alfred "Ack" Grant was sensitive enough to know that sending Frank immediately up after a Drachen would be a mistake. Frank needed a mission that had less risk, that would get him back in the skies, get him ready for the big push that was coming. The mission that Roberts and Luke drew was one where they could fly together as a team, get to know each other a little bit, perhaps prepare themselves for a true combat mission. Luke hadn't been in the air in days and, with the loss of Wehner, there had to be some concern about his ability to engage. Grant most likely wanted to develop some understanding between Roberts and Luke. Whereas Wehner could anticipate Frank's moves and seemed to be able to read his mind, Roberts could not.[2]

Their mission was to fly over the American trench lines where the troops were massing. They were given candy and cigarettes and told to drop them down to the infantry below. It was a goodwill flight and Frank and Ivan returned without the typical Frank Luke mischief.

Later in the morning on the 25th, the American artillery roared back to life, pummeling the German lines. The Meuse-Argonne Offensive was about to commence and the artillery was a clear warning to the Germans that it was coming. With it was going to come some real combat assignments. There would be no more time to get Roberts and Luke to learn each other's strengths and weaknesses. The next day, the 26th, was going to be a return to the fighting.

That evening, Frank must have heard that Eddie Rickenbacker of the 94th Squadron, the number two American ace, had scored two more kills. He was just behind Frank in the race to be America's Ace of Aces and was closing. The 26th would change that, but at a terrible price.

* * * *

The orders for the evening of the 25th of September seemed written as if they had Frank in mind. The Fighting Eagles were responsible for the sector from Beaumont to Châtillon sous-les-Côtes. Specifically, the 27th was ordered to dispatch six planes to attack four enemy balloons:

33 Selfernet Ferme
34 Boinville
35 Bois d'Hingry
36 Straye

The plan called for a dawn attack on the balloons: 5:45 A.M. Mitchell's own Battle Order Number Eight called for aggressive action: "The First Pursuit Group (Hartney) will specialize in the attack of enemy low flying airplanes and balloons on the front Meuse River inclusive, west to the Argonne forest exclusive. Enemy low-flying airplanes will be destroyed and prevented from attacking our infantry liaison airplanes. Low patrols will be used and detachments of the group will be held on the alert close to the front lines, with warm motors ready to the air at once."[3]

Frank and Ivan were slated for the afternoon of the 26th for a combat patrol over the 33rd Infantry Division along the Meuse River. The Ballon-zugs there were going to be active, and their balloons would be up. For Frank, it was a chance to get back in the saddle again. Everyone hoped that Roberts would somehow fill the gap that Wehner had left.

* * * *

Franz Büchner was born on January 2, 1898 in the city of Leipzig. Like so many German pilots he enlisted originally in the infantry after his brother Max died in one of the early battles of the war. Büchner joined the 106th Saxon Infanterie Regiment at the age of sixteen, leaving school to avenge the loss of his brother. He fought at the first battle of Ypres in October of 1914, but came down with typhoid and was unable to resume his duties for several months. His superiors granted him leave to return to school, a decision suggesting that they did not think that the young man had much to offer the war effort. They could not have been more wrong.

In 1917, Franz got his commission as an officer and returned to his unit near Verdun. The fighting for Verdun was a meat-grinder for both sides in the Great War. This death-machine nearly consumed Büchner when he was wounded by a piece of shrapnel in the abdomen.

His injuries were so severe that he was deemed unfit for service in the infantry, but Büchner still wanted to serve Germany. He joined the air service, which had lower physical requirements than the infantry, and was assigned initially to Jasta 9, then Jasta 13. Like so many famous pilots, he was broken in by training with slower two-seat observation aircraft before moving up to more agile pursuit planes. He scored several kills from August to October 1917, but then seemed to enter a long dry period. Franz was flying with the squadron regularly during eight months of no kills. He became the commanding officer of Jasta 13, inspiring his pilots with his own bravery.

Something happened in June of 1918, either with Büchner's luck or his attitude toward combat. Büchner suddenly started racking up victories. By August 20, he had achieved his twentieth kill. While Frank Luke was reaching his pinnacle in September, so was Franz Büchner.[4] More importantly, Büchner was an ace killer. He shot down a Sopwith Dolphin piloted by Irish ace Joseph Callaghan, and a few short days later took out Canadian ace Merrill Taylor. Like Georg von Hantlemann, he flew under Berthold in Jagdgeschwader Nr. II.

The aircraft he flew was a Fokker D.VII, considered by many to be the best fighter the Germans put into the air. Büchner's had a distinctive blue fuselage and tail with a green nose. Just behind the cockpit it sported a green and white checkerboard pattern. These colors represented his region of birth, Saxony. Along the fuselage near the tail was an intricate werewolf's head emblem in gold.[5]

As the American offensive began to unfold on September 26, Büchner was ordered up on the German side of the lines to hold back the thrusts by the American pursuit planes. His patrol path was going to take him along the Meuse River where the Germans has placed several Drachen to observe the American infantry. He was set on a collision course with Frank and Ivan that evening.

* * * *

Frank had gone up earlier in the day on the 26th, most likely going alone looking for balloons or potential victims. There were no combat reports filed for these missions so the assumption is that he did not find what he was looking for. Rather than return to his squadron directly, he diverted to another field where the 91st Aero Squadron was based. George Kenney, a future general, spotted Frank landing and wrote in his journal:

"Lieutenant Frank Luke, the guy they are beginning to call 'Balloon Buster' because he has shot down ten or eleven of them since arriving on the front on the 12th of September, landed on our field this noon in a brand new Spad. He wanted some gas and ammunition for his machine guns. I took him down to the mess to get something to eat. I knew he had been sent to Paris to get a new plane and get a little relief from the fast pace of combat he had been setting, so I said, 'Frank, why don't you stay here tonight and get a little rest? The weather isn't too good anyhow.' He laughed and said, 'maybe you're right. I think I'd better go out to the flying line and see what they have done to my ship. Thanks for the lunch.' He left. About half an hour later we heard the roar of an engine and, looking out the door, saw a new Spad barrel-rolling as it disappeared into the haze headed east toward the front."[6]

At some point, apparently unable to find suitable targets, Frank returned to Rembercourt and joined his own squadron. The afternoon patrol was to be the first and last combat test of the combination of Luke and Roberts. They took off at 5:45 P.M. heading for the Meuse and the balloons that were known to operate between the villages of Sivry to the north of the front and Consenvoye, right near the front lines. Ivan was flying Spad Number 3,[7] tail number S7519, engine serial number 118935.[8] Frank was prowling for balloons and no doubt Roberts, filling Wehner's role, was to stay high and hopefully keep the enemy aircraft defending the Drachen at bay.

The attack did not go at all as planned. Most of the 27th Squadron's planes were assigned to duty with the 94th Squadron to provide air support for an observation mission. Over the Meuse, Luke and Roberts were after a balloon tethered in the valley when they spotted a patrol of German aircraft in the vicinity. They rushed at the five Fokkers and were joined by another unidentified pilot. Firing controlled bursts from his machine guns, Frank saw one of the Fokkers career over for what he presumed was a crash. It was his first victory since that fateful day that had cost him Wehner. Two of the Fokkers swung wide and managed to come in behind Frank.

Luke dropped low, to only 100 meters over the surface, weaving wildly to avoid the airplanes that pursued him. The winding river meandered through the rolling hills, every spot hiding anti-aircraft guns and Prussian infantry. As much as Frank wanted a confirmed kill, two enemy aircraft dove in behind him and kept his attention focused. He once again faced the curse of a jammed machine gun. He managed to get the one gun working but was forced to fire very short bursts otherwise it jammed repeatedly.[9] It was frustrating work, flying, firing, fixing the jams, watching the enemy, hand-pumping fuel, all at the same time.

Somewhere in the near distance he saw Spad Number 3, Roberts's machine, hotly engaged with several other Fokkers. At least one of them was painted a distinctive blue with a green nose and a golden werewolf's head on the fuselage.

Franz Büchner swept in on Ivan Roberts and fired. Roberts's plane went down, carrying the wingman into an obscure footnote in the history of the U.S. Army Air Service. Büchner, for his part, was far from done that day. Ivan was merely the first of four confirmed victories, bringing the German's tally to 33. Büchner tore a nasty wound into the First Pursuit Group on September 26 by taking out Alan Nutt, a pilot from the 94th Squadron, Rickenbacker's friend, killing him. Another pilot from the 94th, Lieutenant Alden B. Sherry (nicknamed "Madame Sherry"), was forced down, as well. Four planes were shot down by the Germans over the Prussian 5th Army lines on the 26th of September, and Franz had accounted for two of those kills.[10] Büchner was a precise killing machine on the 26th. Ivan Roberts was merely one of the men who fell victim to his meticulous skill.

* * * *

What happened after Büchner's shots tore into Roberts's airplane will probably never be known. There are several conflicting accounts of the event. The known facts are that Ivan was shot down between the battered and burned villages of Consenvoye and Sivry in the Meuse River valley. Several accounts indicate that his plane was on fire as it went down, but this was never confirmed and must be taken as hearsay.

Another account (in this case, given in the 1960s), from a German Ballonzug commander, places Robert's last mission some eight kilometers away. Bernard Mangels, whose full role in the story of Frank's Luke life was to be played out a few short days later, conveyed a somewhat different account of Robert's last flight: "We were at Lion on the Côte St. Germain—when after retrieving our balloon we scanned the sky and horizon. Suddenly we discovered two aircraft at great altitude (approximately 5000 m) which were descending in circles. Coming lower they separated and one of them flew over our balloon and set it on fire. The aircraft, however was hit by anti-aircraft fire, caught fire and crashed. The other aircraft, piloted by Frank Luke, set course for the neighboring site where he shot down a balloon before managing to get away unharmed."[11] It was not uncommon in the fury of battle for someone to mistake what downed an aircraft, but this account, which is close to the date and circumstances around Roberts's death, still is based on memories decades after the war. While Mangels's telling seems to contradict some known information, and the kill confirmation for Franz Büchner that day, it may offer yet another tantalizing clue in the search for the truth about the fate of Ivan Roberts.

The most probable set of events centers on Roberts surviving his crash landing. Chances are Ivan crashed and was alive after his plane tore into the mud and sod in the Meuse River valley. If so, he was almost certainly captured by German infantry. Grant's letter to the Roberts family a few days later detailed the search to confirm his status:

"Robbie went missing Sept. 26 in the evening. We were working hard, and he, in company with Lt. Luke (now missing) started out for a German balloon which had been giving trouble. Robbie was furnishing Luke protection and attacking also when possible. Our other planes were scattered throughout the sky and saw the balloon burn, but could not see Ivan. Luke, who was flying below, did not see him either, after the attack started.

"Now this is the news that we saw, but I have a report from our balloon companies who at that time and place observed a plane of the type we use, land in Germany. It was so far away that they could not see much of the machine except that it landed with out turning on its back. The pilot was seen to jump out and run for a shell hole. We now know this must have been Ivan. Their report coincides exactly with ours, so in our minds there is no question that he is a prisoner."[12]

Ivan was behind enemy lines. The American army with the French on its flank was advancing to where he was held. There was still a chance that he could be saved. Or would he be lost in the fog of war?

Roberts had found the crack in history and had slid into it.

* * * *

Frank often became separated from his wingman, so losing sight of Roberts, even in the wake of Wehner's death, did not strike him as unusual. Hartney saw Frank for the first time since his early return from leave, recounting to other pilots his earlier battle. Hartney noticed that "[i]n this and the previous fight against enemy planes, Luke's ship, strange to say, came home without any bullet holes." Kenneth Porter of the 147th, one of the very best commanders in the group, undertook to kid Luke in his usual 'put-you-on-the-spot' manner.

"What's the matter, Luke? No bullet holes must mean no balloons. Are you slipping?"

Luke came back in characteristic fashion.

"Oh, you'll see. I'm letting everyone take a crack at that bag over Bethenville and if, by the day after tomorrow, you all fail I'm going on over and bring it in."[13] These were hardly the words of someone worried about losing his wingman.

For all of his bravado, when word finally reached Frank that Ivan had not returned, he must have been disturbed. He had flown twice with Roberts assigned to him since returning from Paris, and had lost him. The specter of Wehner was casting a shadow over Frank. There are those, that after the war, referred to him as "Unlucky Luke" after this incident, though none would have had the courage to do that to his face.

Chapter Fifteen

"There is only one sad thing about it, he can't keep it up. He will not stick to formations. I have warned him. I told him he will be picked off sure as fate, perhaps today, perhaps tomorrow, but he does not seem to be able to understand such things. We simply have to trust chance."

—MAJOR HAROLD HARTNEY IN AN INTERVIEW WITH GEORGE H. SELDES

Crescendo
September 27–29, 1918

September 27 was a dreary day, with poor visibility in the morning hours. The artillery barrages, on and off again, rumbled like low thunder in the distance as the French and American forces drove forward along the Meuse line. Given that Frank and Ivan had gone up on the last patrol of the day, Luke was spared assignment that day. He absented himself from the squadron, without permission. Frank took his airplane over to a French airdrome to work on his motor with Captain Nungesser.[1] For Frank, it was a chance to spend some time with a great ace who might understand what he was going through. For Lieutenant Grant, it was most likely viewed as another example of Luke's flagrant violations of orders and military discipline. Technically, he was absent without leave.

The French ace Charles Nungesser was a legend at the front. He had 43 confirmed victories but since August had been assigned mostly training duties. The French ace had transferred into the air service in 1914 and had been something of a legend. He had suffered numerous wounds including a broken jaw, a fractured skull, a burned hand, and two broken legs yet still, somehow, he survived. Nungesser had destroyed more than half a dozen balloons himself, and Frank's time with him had to be one of both respect and mutual admiration. While the details of their meeting have been lost to time, it is safe to say that Charles Nungesser was one of the few people who could understand the pressures Frank was facing.

In the evening, Frank went out looking for balloons, but the Germans apparently were not offering him any targets. Rather than return to Rembercourt, he diverted to the advance field near Verdun. That night, Frank remained with Vasconcells and the B flight at the forward field.[2] The ground crew there refueled his Spad and rearmed him, indicating that he had fired at least a few rounds while out scouting the balloon line.

September 28 was a gray day, with thick fog and rain that made flights before noon almost impossible.[3] Frank was undaunted by the weather. Lieutenant Grant arrived at the forward airfield that morning to go over flight operations when the weather finally cleared with Major Hartney. The discussion turned to the prospect of allowing Frank to go up alone against the observation balloon at Bantheville later in the day. This is the same balloon that Frank had been teased about several days earlier by Kenneth Porter of the 147th squadron. While Hartney and Grant were discussing sending Frank after the balloon later on, Luke opted to take matters into his own hands. Without permission or filing a flight plan, Frank went to his Spad, Number 26, and roared off alone.

The sausage at Bantheville had been the target of several pilots of the Fighting Eagles, but so far no one had possessed the luck and skill to take it out. Frank went after it just before 6:00 a.m. The German air squadrons were grounded, with the strong winds and cloud cover being so thick that reconnaissance was deemed impossible.[4] The rubberized silk of the massive gray bag would have been wet from the fog and rain, almost impossible to ignite, but that prospect did not hinder Frank. He was modifying the tactic that had served him so well by attacking at dawn rather than at dusk. The other major difference was that from now on he did not work with a wingman. No Joe. No Ivan. Frank's dangerous approaches were not going to place other men at risk.

Frank angled Spad Number 26 north towards Verdun, cruising 500 meters over the battle-torn landscape. He spied the balloon near Bantheville, near St. George. It was already reeled down to its nest when he dove in on it, blazing away with both of his machine guns. The anti-aircraft batteries roared to life, filling the air with deadly, hot pieces of shrapnel. Frank stitched his bullets along the balloon's gray bag and pulled back on the stick to break his dive. As he swung away, the sausage cooked off, blasting a ball of hot flames into the air.[5]

The Germans were aware that their balloon line was being victimized and were preparing a trap for would-be balloon busters. Several German balloons were set up as aerial ambushes without observers and ringed with extra anti-aircraft batteries. These balloons were tethered at a low altitude, so gunnery aim would be accurate. Anyone going for one of the decoys would be facing much more firepower with no gain if he did, somehow, manage to reach the balloons.[6] The Germans had good reason to prepare for an assault on their balloon line, courtesy of an American propaganda effort. American fliers dropped leaflets near balloon companies with a warning: "Watch out! The balloons of the Huns will start burning soon." Capitalizing on Frank's efforts, the Americans were putting the Germans on warning. But rather than intimidating the Germans, it prompted them to be more prepared than ever.

Luke looked around but could not see any other potential prey. He maneuvered off towards the Allied lines. Rather than return to his own field at Rembercourt, Frank decided to pay a visit to the French Cigognes squadrons. Landing at their field, Luke spent the evening with the French pilots.

The next morning Frank rose and fired up his Spad and headed off for Rembercourt. Once he arrived, he reported to Lieutenant Grant's office. His purpose was to file his combat report and pick up his assignment for the day. What he found was "Ack" Grant in an ill mood. The commander of the

27th had endured about all that he could of Frank's streak of disregard for his authority. When Grant pressed him as to where he was the night before, Frank replied, "The Cigognes." Frank filed his combat report with Grant but that only added fuel to his fire. Frank had gone after the balloon without permission. Luke was fragrantly flaunting his position as the Ace of Aces, and doing so with a commanding officer who was a strict disciplinarian. It was a combination that was destined to lead to trouble.

Grant pressed the matter. Why had Frank landed with the French squadron? Luke used his time-tested line of having engine problems. This time, however, Grant was not inclined to accept that answer.[7]

Frank had been violating orders more than he had been following them. Grant was furious with the young man. His word to Frank was simple—he was grounded until the late afternoon. To be specific he was not to take off after the balloon line until 5:56 P.M. The operations orders for the day were cut with Luke in mind and Grant was hoping to hold him back for that mission. "The 27th and 95th will detail volunteer dusk of the evening balloon straffers to report by telephone to these headquarters before 18 h 00, leaving the ground not earlier than 18 h 15."

Luke was the perfect candidate for the assignment. All he had to do was sit and wait.

Chapter Sixteen

"It isn't courage exactly. He has no imagination. He can't imagine anything happening to him. He thinks he's invincible. If he ever finds himself he may be almost as good as he thinks he is."

—JERRY VASCONCELLS

"Watch for burning balloons ahead ..."
September 29, 1918

Peorle are defined in many ways in their lives. There is a tendency to look at September 29, 1918, as the defining moment in the life of Frank Luke, Jr. It was not. His life, as a whole, must be considered. For it was his character, his courage, and his sense of invulnerability that led to the events on September 29.

Frank knew that Grant was watching him closely, and it was preventing him from doing what came so naturally. He knew that there were balloons up on the German line. The weather had cleared somewhat from the day before. Did it really matter at what time the balloons were destroyed? Why wait? Frank knew that he was not going to get away with anything with Grant watching him. The solution was to get out of Grant's sight.

He made his way to Spad Number 26 and gunned the engine. The mechanics assigned to his plane protested. It generally took an hour to ready a Spad for battle, checking the engines, topping off the fuel, rearming the aircraft. Frank disregarded their protests. They had had only half an hour from the time he had arrived at Rembercourt to look at his plane. They had not even topped off his fuel. It is entirely possible that Frank had had his plane refueled and rearmed while with the French the night before. His maintenance crew would swear for decades though that he took off without enough fuel.[1]

Luke's destination was not the German battle lines. Instead he was heading for the B Flight's advance airfield. He arrived at the field and found himself the butt of a practical joke that Jerry Vasconcells had become fond of playing with visitors. The forward airfield at Verdun was sharing the grounds with massive naval cannons. Vasconcells had developed a working knowledge of the firing times of the cannons, since loading and firing them was done on a fairly regular schedule. While Frank was conferring with him and Major Hartney, Jerry poured Frank a full cup of hot coffee. The major, who had already been the butt of the joke, knew to set his cup down—but Frank was unaware of what was coming.

The massive cannon roared right on schedule. The concussion of the gun was so great that it would blow the out the candles in the billets where the crews slept, even through the curtains made from exploded balloon scraps.[2] Frank was shocked by the roar of the blast and spilled the coffee, much to the amusement of Hartney and Vasconcells. The men roared with laughter.[3]

Frank was "wild with impatience to get going." He was "pacing around the field like a caged lion."[4] In the meantime, Lieutenant Grant had finally realized that Frank had taken off in defiance of his orders. Alfred Grant was not a fool, and he figured out that Frank had most likely taken off for the advance airfield. A furious Grant called Vasconcells. Luke had been ordered to stay on the ground until 5:56 P.M. and had blatantly violated those orders. As such, he told Vasconcells that Luke was supposed to be placed under arrest.[5] Grant would send a pilot down to the advance field to fly Spad Number 26 back. Frank could come home in a car. For the time being, his flying was over.

"Arrest" was an inaccurate word. The authority to place a pilot under true arrest resided with Major Hartney, not Grant. What Grant could do was ground Luke, as he had done before. The thought that the American Ace of Aces would be arrested for attempting to go up in the air and engage the enemy in battle is laughable.

Chauncy Daniels, Grant's clerk, asked him what he would do next. His high-pitched Texas twang was clear. "I'm going to recommend him for the Distinguished Service Cross. Then, by God, I'm going to court martial him!"[6]

Hartney was out in the hangar area tending to his Sopwith Camel, unaware that Frank was supposed to be under arrest. He was having difficulty getting the engine started and the ground crew was assisting him. It was still almost thirty minutes before Frank was supposed to take off. At one point he looked over at Frank and saw him casually leaning back, grinning.[7] The major was aware of the time of the attack, but most likely was not aware that Grant had specifically grounded Luke.

Frank slid into his Spad and fired it up. Hartney checked his watch and saw that it was a good sixteen minutes early. "Do you see that?" Hartney howled to his ground crew. "Go over and pull him out of that ship and tell him if he doesn't obey orders, I'll stop his flying and send him to the rear."[8]

Vasconcells emerged from the operations shack, no doubt having heard the commotion and realizing that Luke was once again openly defying Grant's authority. Surveying the scene, the Lieutenant headed over to Frank's Spad. Hartney was shaking his fist at Frank, and Vasconcells had him shut down his engine.

Frank then decided to play the trump card that had served him so well in the past. Major Hartney and Frank had a special relationship. As long as he brought down balloons, the major seemed happy. He assumed that Hartney would overlook the indiscretion if he took off early. The major had looked the other way when Frank's rebellious nature had taken over before. Vasconcells had not told Major Hartney that Frank was not supposed to be going up, though there is evidence that he was present when Frank pressed Major Hartney for permission to take off and target the balloons. Hartney hesitated, then acquiesced.

Why didn't Vasconcells say something and possibly ground Frank? The answer is most likely a simple one. "… Vasconcells, thinking that Luke's offense may be [sic] minor, decided to let Luke go on the mission rather than expose him before Major Hartney."[9] It was a decision that Jerry Vasconcells would have to wrestle with for the rest of his life.

The B Flight crew made sure Frank's Spad was fueled and armed. Number 26 rumbled down the field and took to the air. It was only then that Hartney heard from Vasconcells that Frank was supposed to be grounded. Hartney's tendency to work directly with Frank, going around the obstinate, authoritative Grant, had sent Frank up on his last flight.[10]

* * * *

At the same time, at Rembercourt, one of Frank's few good remaining friends, Granville Woodard, fired up his Spad XIII. He was going to head out for the balloon line, as well. Woody had not had a chance to speak much with Frank in the last few weeks, but still considered himself a good friend. He angled his own Spad off toward the German lines, oblivious to the fact that Frank was in the air near Verdun heading off for the same targets.

* * * *

Frank flew over the American 7th Balloon Company before crossing no man's land. The 7th was based in a wrecked French building in what had once been the village of Avecourt. The company's machine gunners scrambled as the plane approached at 1,000 feet against the gray skies. In the early evening light they were unsure if the plane that was approaching their balloon was friendly or hostile. Ammunition was loaded and they waited for the order to fire. At the last minute, Lieutenant Karl Axtater ordered them to stand-down. It was a Spad flying over them. This one dropped a metallic cylinder with a white streamer attached to it. The cylinder was recovered by the balloon crew and delivered to Axtater.[11]

He opened it and read the message: "Watch for burning balloons ahead. Luke."[12]

The men of the 7th Balloon Company turned to face the Meuse River line where the German balloons were hovering on their tethers.

Frank roared in on the first balloon, most likely the one from Ballonzug 95 near the village of Liny. The details of the battle itself are not important. The men of the 7th Balloon Company saw the orange ball of flames and the sickening streak of black smoke and burning rubber and silk rising in the air.

A few minutes later, a balloon near the village of Milly, near Briere Farm, became the target of Frank's furious assault. It was Ballonzug 64, one of those closest to the American lines. Vice-Sergeant Meyer jumped off from the gondola and successfully landed by parachute, the third time he had cheated death. This balloon too went up a ball of flame as the anti-aircraft fire seemed to tighten its noose around Frank's Spad. Good old number 26 held together though. As the ground crew of Ballonzug 64 scrambled for safety from the falling scraps of their sausage, Frank angled off for the final balloon—near Lyon and the village of Murvaux.[13]

Frank had, in the period of just a few minutes, destroyed two observation balloons. One more remained in his sights—that of Ballonzug 35.

* * * *

Granville Woodard and his wingman, Denny Holden, angled off for the balloon line unaware of Frank's actions nearby. Like Frank, his plane was equipped for balloon busting—one machine gun armed with standard bullets, a larger gun mounted for incendiary rounds. He got separated from his wingman but came along the Meuse River and spotted a balloon in a large open field. From the German records, it seems likely that this belonged to Ballonzug 115.

The anti-aircraft fire erupted around him, filling the sky with flaming onions and hot lead. Woody dove on the balloon from 6,000 feet up as it was being reeled into its nest. He opened up with both machine guns, riddling the balloon. As he pulled out of the dive, one round clipped his right thigh, tearing his flesh. Wincing, he turned just in time to see the balloon erupt in a ball of fire.

Woody was bleeding and knew he had to make for his own lines. As he executed the turn, four enemy Fokkers appeared. They came in step formation and dove in on him. He swerved and managed to avoid the first two, sending bursts of fire in their general direction. He tried a virage maneuver, but a Fokker came at him from underneath, peppering his tail section. His elevator controls would not respond, and his virage suddenly evolved into an uncontrolled side-slip, then a sickening nose dive.

His Spad was dying all around him from the bursts of fire it had taken. It took all of his strength to level the airplane out, but time had proven to be an elusive ally. Painfully, the aircraft crashed into the ground on the German side of the lines. Woody was knocked unconscious, and when he came to he found himself pinned in the wreckage of his plane. A German infantry platoon came over and pulled the shattered remains of the Spad off of him, and eventually got him to a field hospital.[14]

Woody had gone down only two miles from where Frank was as he turned to go after Ballonzug 35.

* * * *

On September 29, 1918, twelve-year-old Georges Reguier saw a furious combat unfolding in the skies near the tiny village of Murvaux, and he marveled at the daring airplane that was defying the Germans. At a distance of five or six kilometers, he could make out the sequence of Frank's attack.

> "I was just at the southern tip of my village when the sounds of a machine gun drew my attention in the distance of Dun and Milly; there was a big balloon (which we congenially called 'sausages') going down in flames. I'd seen four, moments before, scattered

between Dun and Lion, which lies just North of St. Germain County. It was the one closest to Dun that had been hit. That's when I noticed a plane flying rather low, straight towards the second balloon, it burst into flames at the first stream of bullets. The plane lost no time in chasing the third airship which had now been made to drift down. I could see the look-out man already on his parachute glide towards earth. Before striking this "sausage," the plane swished around in circles and spirals and finally set it on fire as it touched ground. The plane then set its course on the fourth airship that had been brought to the ground in the meantime. I could no longer see the action and the plane's activity but I heard separate shots and got a final glimpse of the plane as it barely made it over the hills of St. Germain. Then, I lost it. Moments later, more shots, then a dead silence."[15]

Chapter Seventeen

"You have suggested I make a statement comparing the flying technique, courage, and skill of Frank Luke Jr. with that of Richthofen. That's a pretty broad request, but I would be willing to wager odds in favor of Luke on a single combat in the air between these two men, provided they were each flying the same type of machine and motor. In my opinion there is not the slightest doubt that under these conditions, a staged bout, it as it were, Luke would down Richthofen."

—LETTER TO JOHN KNOX FROM COLONEL HAROLD HARTNEY

Into the Setting Sun
September 29–30, 1918

September 29 was a day of battle and confusion. Memories over the years were destined to cast doubts as to the events that unfolded. Frank's account of the events was never to be heard. September 29 was his last mission, the last day of his short life. Versions of his death became distorted over the years, both deliberately and unintentionally.

It was one year to the day that Frank had reported for duty to begin his military career. He had arrived at the front a mere fifty-three days before. It was forty-four days on from his first, unconfirmed victory. In that time he had gone from being "the Arizona Boaster" to "America's Ace of Aces." He had stepped out of the Wild West of Arizona onto a worldwide stage as a celebrity.

There are some facts that are undisputed. Frank had blown up a sausage from Ballonzug 64 and turned to go after the nearby Drachen commanded by Ballonzug 35. He was shot down and died. Everything else depends on your willingness to believe a particular version of the events that took place.

* * * *

The village of Murvaux, France, was little more than a cluster of small buildings and a church, which formed the center of its community. War had stripped the veneer of quaintness from this village. The trees had been cut down for either firewood or the material of war by the Germans. The fields had been torn and plowed by the fury of exploding artillery shells. While the structures of Murvaux remained, its dignity did not.

On September 29, Ballonzug 35 was based between Murvaux and Lion, having relocated there a few days earlier. It was under the command of Leutnant der Reserve Bernard Mangels, and was part of Feldluftschiffer Abt. 12, attached to the Prussian 5th Army. The Drachen that Ballonzug 35 put aloft on September 29 was tethered at 1,200 meters.

Ringing the hills around Murvaux were numerous machine guns and two 4.5 cm anti-aircraft cannons that were placed about 100 meters from the Drachen's nest. Leutnant Mangels was thirty-one years old and had seen a lot of the war so far. He knew his Drachen was a possible target and knew that Frank Luke was operating in the area. His company and the nearby Ballonzug 64 had tangled with Luke more than once so far since the Americans had entered the war. On September 15, Luke had attacked and blown up their balloon. This Drachen was a replacement. Mangels later recollected:

"Our entire defense was on alert when we retrieved at dusk. We learned our lesson from previous experiences. On 29 September, at approximately seven o'clock in the evening we were retrieving a balloon and were ready to moor it when *he* came in low-level flight. This time our defenses reacted swiftly. Before Frank Luke had a chance to open fire, we let loose with a machine gun barrage. The pilot lost control of his aircraft which crashed with great impact near the balloon. Fortunately it did not catch fire. When our people rushed up to the wreckage to rescue the unfortunate from the desperate situation, he showed only weak signs of life. He passed away shortly thereafter. A machine gun bullet which hit the radiator ricocheted and struck his chest. Our people removed the body of the brave enemy and put it in an empty room in our camp."[1]

While Leutnant Mangels indicated that his balloon was not taken out by Frank Luke, the official German report for the day differs with this account, given decades later.[2] "The balloons 64, 35, 95 were burning shot by hostile fliers. Vice-sergeant Meyer jumped off for the third time in the parachute. All observers landed smoothly. The defense of the balloon course 35 shot the attacking hostile flier after successful attack. Unsuccessful attack against B.Z. [Ballonzug] 115 by good-lying defense fire repulsed."

French civilians still sheltered in what was left of Murvaux claim that Frank fired a machine gun burst into German troops on the ground—killing anywhere from six to eleven infantry in the assault. According to the French, Frank did not crash but landed his aircraft.

The French civilians claim that a mortally injured Frank crawled out of Spad Number 26 and staggered to Milly Creek near the outskirts of the village. There, he produced his pistol and opened fire on the Germans as they approached. A gun battle ensued with the Germans shooting and shortly after it began, Frank succumbed to his injuries.

The original French version of events has the angry Germans kick his body and loot it of any useful identification. They forced the French civilians to load his corpse into a wagon and take it to the church in the center of town. It was too dark to bury Frank's remains. While the French narrative of what occurred is suspect, it was this version of events that the American media decided to write about.

* * * *

For the men of the 27th Squadron, something was different about this mission. Frank had a reputation for landing at other fields and not returning, but on the rainy evening of the 29th of September it seemed obvious that something was wrong. Frederick Smith, a reporter from the *Arizona Republican*, was at the field and witnessed the vigil for Frank kept by his peers. "In a large tent on a bleak, rain swept Lorraine hill, I passed the night in was a score of American aviators. They sat about on the edges of crude bunks, talking in low tones, but always keeping eyes on the flap at the end of the tent, facing the darkened aviation field. At intervals a man would put on a fur jacket and go out on the field, picking up a route with the aid of a pocket flashlight.

"Occasionally a rocket lofted into the dripping clouds, or a flare was sent up, momentarily illuminating a dreary picture and casting dark shadows about the looming hangar.

"The squadron was waiting for Lieutenant Frank Luke, school boy from Phoenix, Arizona, who had gone over and had not come back. In the long months of training both at home and in France, these airmen form friendships which are cemented into rare comradeship when they reach the front, and share the perils of the fighting line side by side. But Frank Luke not only had more than his share of these warm friendships, he had won the affection and admiration of the entire aviation section of the army by his incomparable courage."[3] The efforts were in vain. With each passing minute the likelihood of Frank having enough fuel to return dwindled. On this mission there was no call from another squadron reporting that Frank was there and staying for the night. Eddie Rickenbacker noted the evening in his flight diary with the ominous words: "Frank Luke, the marvelous balloon strafer of the 27th, did not return last night!"[4] The story of Frank's last day, his defiance of Alfred Grant, his bravado in telling the 7th Balloon that he was going after enemy Drachen, all of this had come to the other squadrons of the First Pursuit Group as the stuff of legends. For Rickenbacker, the news was not welcome. Once again Eddie had become the American Ace of Aces, but there was no glee for him in how he was assuming that title, and possibly the fate of the men who had held it before him.

Grant himself offered little of the details of the day, especially of the grounding of Frank. "One sector patrol 17h 15 to 18hr 30, one plane, Lt. Luke—altitude 500 meters. Lt. Luke landed at Riacourt and has not returned."[5] He gave no hint that, once it was learned that Frank was not at Riacourt, he was considered lost—either a prisoner of war or dead. Then again, from Alfred Grant's perspective, the days of Frank flouting his authority were over.

* * * *

The next morning, Jerry Vasconcells took to the air on a personal mission. He was searching for Frank. His flight was early in the morning and was not on the normal roster of scheduled missions. Doubtless Major Hartney approved the solo mission. The motivation for Vasconcells to seek out Luke was never stated. Was it guilt over allowing him to take off the day before? Or was it a kinship that only brothers in arms can understand? Vasconcells never spoke of his search.

He flew along the front using a bulky set of binoculars to look for any sign or trace of Frank's Spad. There were several planes that had gone down the previous day, including Granville Woodard's Spad. On the flight of the 30th of September Vasconcells found no trace of the missing men. Lieutenants Pruden and Vasconcells went up on October 2 searching for Frank and located an American Spad XIII near Cumières. The cockpit was splattered with dried maroon-brown blood, but the aircraft belonged to Alan Nutt, who had been shot down earlier.

On October 5, Vasconcells set off again, this time with Lieutenant Lennon, still attempting to spot some sign of Luke's aircraft. Jerry surveyed the terrain with binoculars and, according to his flight log, he spotted a downed Spad XIII just over the German lines in the vicinity of a village that could have been Murvaux or Lion. He was fairly sure that the Spad was Frank's.[6]

For the men of the 27th, this was potentially good news. If the plane was on the ground and relatively intact, there was a good chance that Frank may have survived the encounter. Planes rarely landed intact on their own, meaning that the pilot might have been alive when it came down, and that he didn't die from the crash. Frank was well known to the Germans as the American Ace of Aces. Pilots who were captured were generally treated well. Perhaps, just perhaps, word would come soon that Frank was a prisoner of war.

* * * *

In the morning, the men under the command of Leutnant Mangels took Frank's body to the graveyard. The grave site did not have to be dug. The hole was there where a German officer had been buried and recently disinterred. Frank's body was wrapped in burlap, a common practice given the lack of wood near the front lines. "The next morning we buried Frank in the garden of the Lion castle. [Note: This is an error on Mangels's part, an easy mistake to make decades after the fact. Frank was actually laid out at the church in the center of Murvaux.] After paying homage to the brave enemy and saying the Lord's Prayer, we put his body to rest. Requiescat in pace!"[7]

Leutnant Mangels did not deny that Frank was buried in a shallow grave. In his view, Frank was given the same courtesy in death as his own men. "I have lost several of my men near Lion by enemy artillery fire, and also other soldiers who were killed by shells were buried in the same way as we did it with Frank Luke. Because of the situation there was mostly not much time for it, but it sufficed for a pious Pater Noster." The French claimed that Frank's body had been mistreated; the Germans claimed they treated him with all the respect that they would their own men. The truth will never be known but is probably somewhere in between.

However, the Germans did take souvenirs from the downed ace. "In the pocket book of the dead flyer we found a letter of commendation written by his commanding general. The lettered mentioned that Frank Luke is an outstanding flyer, that he flies daily sorties at dusk, which are carefully planned, for the purpose of destroying 'Huns" balloons and that he had already destroyed 20 balloons."[8] "A soldier brought to me the small black badge with the four letters U.S.A.R. or U.S.A.F., I don't know it no more, which American flyers wore on the breast fastened with a needle. I did keep it as a souvenir of the brave opponent."[9]

On September 29, a judgment call had to be made by Lieutenant Grant and Major Hartney. Frank was declared "missing in action." Telegrams were prepared by the War Department and sent to two cities: to Phoenix, Arizona—to Frank's parents—and to San Diego, California—to his young fiancée, Marie Rapson.

* * * *

In the pulp magazines of the 1920s, where the stories of Frank Luke and other Great War aviators were told, pilots rarely crashed. They were rarely trapped in burning cockpits, seared alive as the airplane burned around them. These men were heroes and their deaths were expected to be romanticized.

As such, most books referred to a pilot's death as "flying into the setting sun," or "flying into the western skies." Magazines would say that if a pilot died, he had "gone west." Rather than face inglorious and often agonizing death, the heroes were seen as simply flying off into the distance. The language conjures up romantic images, of daring men in open cockpits, wagging their wings as they headed off into the twilight.

While the actual events in Murvaux have been difficult to interpret over the years, tainted by the French hatred of the German occupiers and the popularity of Frank Luke, one thing is for certain: On September 29, 1918, while the rest of the world wondered what had become of Frank Luke, the truth was that he simply turned his plane into the setting sun of the western skies and left this Earth.

Half a world away, Tillie Luke knew something was wrong with Frank. This went beyond mere mother's intuition. On his last leave, Frank delayed going to play football with his friends at his mother's behest. She had asked him to plant some lilies, in the front of the house. He did it just before leaving to join his friends one last time. They shouldn't have bloomed at all the first year and it was very late in the season for them to be poking out of the ground.

On September 29, 1918, the lilies unexpectedly bloomed.

When Tillie saw the flowers she knew something had happened to Frank. Some witnesses claimed that they formed a cross, but Mrs. Luke, a devout Catholic, insisted that they were not a religious symbol. She said they were in the shape of an airplane. Obviously Frank had arranged the bulbs that way. Regardless of the form of the flowers, they were taken as a sign of Frank's passing.[10]

Chapter Eighteen

*"And so these two, Wehner and Luke, flew from this earthly scene, just
a little way yonder over the Western Horizon. Pals in life and danger;
undivided in their last hours on this earth."*

—THE LAFAYETTE FOUNDATION, DEDICATION FOR THE JOSEPH WEHNER
VFW, EVERETT, MASSACHUSETTS

When Time Stood Still
October–November 1918

There was an abrupt stop when Frank was declared missing in action. The momentum, the whirlwind of action and excitement that he brought to the 27th Squadron, was replaced by an eerie calm. Vasconcells's sighting of the airplane aside, there was little that the Fighting Eagles could do for Frank. He was either alive and a prisoner of war, or dead.

While the Army had been quick to publicize Frank's incredible rise in the rankings as an ace, they did not announce that he was missing in action until October. There was no rush to report bad news to the rest of the AEF. It wasn't until ten days before the end of the war, November 1, that an article appeared in *Stars and Stripes* saying that Frank was missing.

Oddly enough, the laurels and accolades he was due in life came only after he was downed. His promotion to first lieutenant had been in the works from the start of the Meuse-Argonne Offensive. Grant had also had recommended him for the DSC, the Distinguished Service Cross—a new award just below the Congressional Medal of Honor. On October 1, Frank's promotion to first lieutenant came through. The squadron was told the news, but it did not ease their sense of loss at Frank's disappearance.[1]

Alfred Grant, the officer who had tried so hard to impose strict military rule on Frank, had to write the Luke family and tell them what he knew. The usually short and direct Grant wrote a surprisingly long letter to the family.

October 8, 1918
Mr. and Mrs. Frank Luke
220 W. Monroe
Phoenix, Arizona
My Dear Friends:

I know you are anxiously awaiting news regarding your son Frank, who will be reported "missing in action" by the War Department by the time ere this reaches you.

It is now ten days since we last saw him, hence he is carried as missing. None of us are overdepressed, for we feel, and trust you will feel with us, that he is a prisoner, yet alive and well.

I can do no better than to write as fully as censorship will permit in order that you get the picture of conditions. On Sept. 12 Frank went out with a patrol, but, due to the clouds, he became separated from the others. Finding himself over an enemy balloon, he at once attacked it and brought it down in flames. He then landed near our balloon lines and brought home a confirmation of his work. This was his beginning and his first official victory. He was very happy, as were we all, for only those who have gone after balloons realize how hard it is to combat them.

After this victory I gave him a new plane with especial equipment. He and Lieut. Joseph Wehner were great friends and worked together for their results.

From this time till the 29th, when he went missing, his record is one whirlwind of achievement. We thought he was going too fast, so we sent him on a four days' leave. He came back rested and with added enthusiasm for work.

On one occasion he, with Wehner, went out at dusk to attack some balloons previously identified. Lieut. Wehner on this occasion protected from above while Frank attacked. Just as the show started a formation of Huns attacked them but Wehner fought the group and Luke continued his attack until three balloons were burned: he then turned and shot down one of the attackers. He was starting home alone and saw our anti-aircraft guns shooting at a plane on our side of the lines. He flew to it, attacked and sent it to the ground. Five confirmed victories in the space of 30 to 40 minutes. This has seldom or never been equaled. The "cross" which you will find in his trunk is taken from this last plane.

On the 27th of September he went out in the evening and spotted several balloon locations. He did not return that night. He stayed at our advance outpost up near the front. The crews there went over his plane and filled up gas and oil.

He stayed with our boys there the next night, 28th. On the 29th he got a plane. Then in the evening same day he went up about 5 o'clock. He did not want any protection or help; a few minutes later he passed over our balloons and dropped a note asking them to observe for burning balloons. Ten minutes later two were observed to go up in flames. At this time it was too dark to see, hence our observers could not tell what happened. We have had no word since then or have we located any plane parts. He was in the general vicinity north of Verdun.

Do not worry over his treatment, for Luke is undoubtedly the best known American aviator. The Germans know his record, as well as ourselves. His career was meteoric, for he was easily the most wonderful pilot we have ever seen. The ease and grace with which he flew were remarkable. Imbued with the enthusiasm of his age, he made an ideal pilot.

It is truly a great loss in the air service that he is lost, to say nothing of the personal loss which all of us feel. Every officer and man sympathizes deeply with you, even though we think him to be now in a prison camp.

Your cable to him arrived too late, (on October 3). All of his mail is being returned as we will not know for several months his location.

The International Red Cross in Geneva, Switzerland, will notify you direct of any news they obtain. It sometimes requires several months to get this information. Just recently we have heard from boys missing since July, as I trust that you will try and wait patiently. I do not write you optimistically to build false hopes in your hearts, but to assure and comfort if possible during the time we do not hear from him.

I have just received notification from the chief that his promotion to be a First Lieutenant has been approved and forwarded. Also you will receive his Distinguished Service Cross which has been recommended and is sure to come through.

I cannot tell you more except to say that your son is the premier air man of the American air service. He has made this record through study, enthusiasm, and a remarkable keenness and ability to think rapidly. We all honor him and you are justly proud in feeling happy to his record. He has not only brought distinction upon himself and yourselves, but upon his squadron, his uniform, and the entire Allied cause.

I shall cable you all permissible information we may be able to obtain, and believe me in saying that we are using every available means to secure it.

Accept the sympathy, honor and respect of his brother officers, the enlisted men of this squadron, and the entire air service.

Most sincerely,

ALFRED A. GRANT[2]

Grant glossed over the conflicts he had had with Frank. He omitted the fact that, in a fury, he had ordered the Lukes' son grounded. He made Frank's overnight stays with the French pilots seem either accepted or outright endorsed. It was courteous of Grant not to tell the family Frank's story from his perspective. Rather than tell Frank's concerned parents that their son had cut short his leave, Grant simply changed history: Frank had a four-day leave.

Some of Frank's brother airmen made sure his personal gear was packed up—and in some cases liberated some of it for their own. Chauncey S. Daniel, the clerk for C Flight, took a compass out of Frank's personal gear as his own souvenir.[3] Lieutenant William J. Hoover, who flew with Frank on several missions, at some point came across a letter that Frank had not mailed. It bore the name "Marie" on the envelope. Rather than entrust this to the Army to deliver, Lieutenant Hoover kept the sealed letter. It was one letter that he would deliver himself. Hoover was one of the dwindling handful of "original" members of the 27th Squadron, having joined the unit when they had been stationed outside of Toronto. In taking that letter he was assuming a sacred trust to deliver it.

Marie, unaware of the letter that Lieutenant Hoover had found, was also getting letters of encouragement regarding Frank, sowing the seeds of optimism in her. It was a time of confusion, when optimism and hope were blurred by letters that were hopelessly delayed by the distance involved with delivery. Mutual friends from Frank's time at Rockwell Field clung to hope in their letters and praise of Frank's exploits.[4]

Marie, like the Luke family, had reason to worry, but at the same time was courted with optimism. Other men found out in different ways. Granville Woodard, shot down at almost the same time that Frank had been, eventually ended up in a prisoner of war camp with his friend and fellow-pilot Norman Archibald. As they swapped stories, Woody updated Archibald on what had been happening since he had been captured.

"Remember Luke?"

"Luke? Why of course, Woody. We four, Luke, Beauchamp, you and I were on the train together the day we joined the group. Do I remember, why I can see the little crossroad where we parted. Luke and Beauchamp bound for the 27th and you and I for the 95th."

"Well, Luke is the sensation of the Front."

"What do you mean?"

"Just that! Luke is the most talked-of man in Europe! He's the Ace of Aces; known everywhere as 'The Great Luke.' He got fifteen official victories in less than two weeks. He'll get killed at the rate he's going, though. We gave a banquet for him and he was told to take it easy, that he was worth more alive than dead. But Luke just laughed. Said he was a different person the minute he got into the air. Wehner used to fly with him, remember, but after eight victories was shot down in flames. Luke goes it alone now. He's a wild man in the air! He's gone crazy! Why, he told his commander that with protection, he'd clean up the entire German balloon line!"

"Luke? ... well I'll be ..."

"On September 18th he shot down three Fokkers and two balloons in less than seven minutes!"

"What? ... Five in seven minutes! I am dumbfounded. Luke, that little Arizona towhead, had told the truth and fooled us all."

"Yes, and all confirmed. It's the greatest record ever made at the Front! No aviator of the entire Allied Armies ever equaled his victories. His name blazes the headlines of every Paris paper. He's the idol of France."[5]

* * * *

The war ended at the eleventh hour of the eleventh day of the eleventh month. When it did end, the quest for Frank Luke and the details of his last mission could begin in earnest. The International Red Cross was the first to speak of Frank's true fate. This came via a letter to the Luke family on November 26, 1918. The message was short and left no doubt as to the fate of their son. ·

My Dear Mr. Luke:

I am very sad to have to tell you that the International Red Cross reports, out of Germany, that Lieutenant Frank Luke Jr., your son, was killed in action on September 29.

We have found almost invariably that these reports coming out of Germany are to be trusted, but our office in Paris, nevertheless, cables that they are vigorously continuing their investigation for verification of this report. This word was sent to my office in Paris at the request of Mr. Brophy.

If this report should prove true, as I fear there is every reason to think it must, we send you the very sincere sympathy of the Red Cross. We know that you will always be proud of the fact that your son gave his life so finely and in such a splendid cause.

Sincerely,

W.R. CASTLE, DIRECTOR[6]

What had taken so long was that Frank's name had not been listed as one of the dead on the American rolls. Instead he had been listed as a British pilot. An administrative mistake had kept his true fate from his loved ones. Now though, there was no question as to what had become of him.

* * * *

When the war ended, the U.S. Army Air Service began the process of documenting its efforts during the conflict and stepping back to a peacetime level. One man, however, felt that his work was just beginning. Captain Frederick Zinn proposed a concept that had never been considered in the aftermath of a war before. He proposed that he stay in Berlin and track down the nearly 200 missing airmen. It was a gutsy suggestion. America did not have a good record in wars of bringing her boys home. What Zinn proposed was that the effort be made—at least with the airmen.

Every war leaves men who are missing in action, and the grueling conditions and excessive use of artillery made recovery of every person impossible. Zinn insisted that the airmen of the USAS were different. They were a subset of the overall contingent missing in action, and the documentation that the Germans had on the men was bound to be better than for the typical missing infantryman. Captain Zinn was proposing, for the first time, that the air service remain after the war and collect their honored dead. He was the first man to suggest this, and the tradition continues on today in our military service.

That isn't to say that Zinn didn't have his own reasons for wanting to fulfill this mission, reasons above honor. Zinn had been the commanding officer of the personnel section of the Air Service. It had been his responsibility to send all replacement pilots from their rear area duties to the front line. Frederick Zinn had sent these men off, many to their deaths, and now he was proposing that he personally head up the effort to bring them home.

The Quartermaster Corps, Graves Registration Services, had the ultimate responsibility for recovery of the remains of soldiers and returning them home. Zinn and a small group of officers were a resource for the Quartermaster Corps. They would find new ways of accessing the German records to look for the honored dead. They would provide the details for the families so that they would obtain final closure and learn what happened to their loved ones.

Zinn worked out of a dark, dank little office. He had a crude little wooden set of cubby holes, each one representing every missing pilot, observer, and bombardier. He and his small staff pored through the German military archives to try to piece together where every aviator who was missing might be found. They pursued every scrap of information, every interview, every hope. Some, like Quentin Roosevelt, were easy to find—the Germans had taken pictures of his grave. Zinn and his team provided validation that indeed, the pilot in that grave was the former president's son.[7]

Frank Luke, Joseph Wehner, and Ivan Roberts were all names on Zinn's meticulously maintained list.

* * * *

A former prisoner of war and brother aviator, Captain Merian (also spelled as Marion in official records) D. Cooper, had connected with a Mrs. Clarkson Potter, who was searching for information on her son, who had been downed in the same region as Frank. On their trek to various villages trying to find information, they came across a hopeful tale. The people of Murvaux told Cooper a story about a daring aviator that the Germans had shot down.[8]

They claimed that the young man laid to rest in their churchyard had destroyed three German Drachen, then downed two enemy aircraft. He then "descended low over the ground and killed eleven Germans with either hand bombs or machine gun bullets. While flying low his plane was hit from the ground and he himself was apparently wounded. He made a successful landing, got out of his plane and while the Germans called on him to surrender replied by drawing his automatic and opening fire. Thus standing he continued to defend himself until killed."[9]

Cooper contacted Captain Zinn in Berlin and Zinn, in turn, contacted Captain McCormick of the 301st Graves Registration Unit. McCormick had been a field resource for Zinn and had spent his days following up on leads that Zinn gathered, scouring French villages attempting to piece together any local stories regarding aviators. He journeyed to Murvaux and gathered the same basic story that Captain Cooper had. Under his authority, he ordered the body of the aviator exhumed.

The body in the shallow grave lacked any identification but did possess an Elgin watch, #20225566. Frank owned such a watch. From the description of the engagement, no matter how fanciful, there was little doubt as to the identity of the pilot. It was Frank Luke.

The body was moved to a U.S. Cemetery, and placed in a plain pine box. Frank was still wearing his uniform but was already so badly decomposed that he could not be identified. There were no visible wounds on the body.

Captain McCormick obtained an affidavit from some of the citizens of the village who had witnessed the event. The obtaining of the affidavit was not standard procedure in the identification process for unknown aviators.

AFFIDAVIT

The undersigned, living in the town of Murvaux, Department of the Meuse, certify to have seen on the twenty-ninth day of September, 1918, toward evening, an American aviator, followed by an escadrille of Germans, in the direction of Liny, near Dun, descend suddenly and vertically toward the earth, then straighten out close to the ground and fly in the direction of the Briere Farm, near Doulcon, where he found a captive balloon, which he burned. Then he flew toward Milly, where he found another balloon, which he also burned, in spite of an incessant fire directed toward his machine. There he apparently was wounded by a shot fired from rapid-fire cannon. From there he came back over Murvaux, and still with his guns he killed six German soldiers and wounded many more.

Following this he landed and got out of his machine, undoubtedly to quench his thirst at the stream. He had gone fifty yards, when seeing the Germans come toward him still had strength to draw his revolver to defend himself. A moment after he fell dead following a serious wound he received in the chest.

Signatures of the following:

Perton	Valentine Garre
Rene Colon	Gustave Carre
Aguste Cuny	Leon Herny

Henry Gustave	Cortine Delbart
Eugine Coline	Gabriel Didier
Odile Patouche	Camille Phillips
Richard Victor	Voliner Nicholas

The undersigned themselves placed the body of the aviator on the wagon and conducted it to the cemetery:

Cortine Delbart
Voliner Nicholas

Seen for legalization of signatures placed above, Murvaux, January 15, 1919.

The Mayor
August Garre[10]

The alleged "myth" of Frank's demise was the spreading of the account to the media before all of the facts were in. Much of this blame has to lay with Captains McCormick and Cooper. Frank was already a known hero, a celebrity, now the legend was able to take root. The account gave people something more than the grim reality of trench warfare that had dominated Europe for years. This was the story of a true, red-blooded American hero shooting it out, against the odds, against the evil Germans. Frank Luke's last mission became a modern story of the Alamo, though this story was based on unconfirmed information.

On the 20th of November, Alfred Grant, most likely at the suggestion and prodding of Major Hartney, initiated the process to place Frank's name in the queue for the Medal of Honor. None of the instances surrounding his death or final mission were mentioned in the application. While many people place great weight on the details of Frank Luke's demise, the truth is that his Medal of Honor was awarded for actions *prior* to his final flight.

While Grant and Hartney pressed to get Luke the Medal of Honor, Captain Zinn paid a visit to Murvaux to further the investigation himself. After interviewing the citizens, Zinn found that the versions of the stories gathered by Captains McCormick and Cooper were full of errors. Most seriously, the story of Luke's gun battle with the German troops with his automatic weapon was brought into question, prompting Zinn to personally step into the investigation. Zinn believed that the source of the mistakes was easy to understand. "... I think the variation was due to the fact that Captain McCormick, who had received it from civilians, did not speak French and misunderstood some of the statements. All of the civilians who witnessed it are very sure that no shots were fired after the aviator landed, either by him or the Germans."[11] There was no government conspiracy to make Frank's story larger than it was—it was simple miscommunication and the zeal of the press.

The problem was that by the time that Zinn had uncovered most of the truth behind the final minutes of Frank's life, the version drafted by Captains McCormick and Cooper had become instilled in the public's imagination. Frank's original recommendation for the Medal of Honor was "amended" to include information on how he died, and then was changed one more time so that the events in Murvaux became the key reason for him to receive the medal. There was a reluctance for years to attempt to clarify the official record. Zinn's version of Frank's death was only partially incorporated into the official records, only where it was felt that it didn't diminish from the first version created by McCormick and Cooper. The two versions were different enough that Zinn personally contacted the Luke family to attempt to provide them with the absolute truth as he knew it.

The "myth" of Frank Luke's final moments had fertile ground to grow in. His infamous gun battle against overwhelming odds rang true of a western epic. Arizona was a new state, ready to embrace its first true American hero. The truth would remain suppressed or simply forgotten by official sources for decades. Any research Zinn did, other than the account provided to the newspaper in the interview regarding Frank, was lost either accidentally or intentionally. The world, America, and Arizona wanted the "final stand" myth wrapped around Frank Luke, Jr.

Chapter Nineteen

"Little did we think the fair haired boy who once played in our streets and mingled with our children possessed of such unfaltering courage and patriotism. As a boy the love of adventure was strong in him. This in turn developed into bravery of an unusual quality and spurred him to efforts which made him one of the greatest heroes of the World War."

—NOVEMBER 11, 1930, ARIZONA GOVERNOR JOHN C. PHILLIPS AT THE FRANK LUKE STATUE DEDICATION CEREMONY

One Man, Many Lives
December 1918 to Present Day

Surviving parents and wives were given a solemn choice when their loved ones were found after the war ended. They could have them returned to their homes for re-interment, or they could be reburied in one of the Quartermaster Corps designated military cemeteries. Frank Luke's family never explained their choice to leave Frank back in France to be buried with the other honored American dead. Perhaps stripped of their privacy already, the family worried that Frank's grave would never know peace in Phoenix. His body was removed from Murvaux and placed carefully into a plain pine coffin identical to thousands of other coffins used to inter the honored remains. He was moved to the Meuse-Argonne cemetery in Romagne-sous-Montfaucon. Frank was placed in Space 1232, Section 56. His simple white-cross grave marker reads: "2nd Lieut. Frank Luke Pilot

27th Aero Sqdn. September 29, 1918." It is almost indistinguishable in the sea of white crosses against the lush green grasses.[1]

Posthumous medals and awards came in for Frank from every conceivable source. His Distinguished Service Cross came through just after his body was located and identified. He was awarded a medal as the first graduated pilot from Rockwell Field to down an enemy aircraft in battle. A film company cast their own special medal for Frank and gave it to the family. The French honored Frank, as did the Italians, as was customary with soldiers of such distinction. It wasn't until his passing that Frank received the formal recognition that he had so deservedly earned over the muddied fields of France. But then again, Frank wasn't fighting for the medals or for the recognition. But that fact would not prevent him from winning the highest medal for heroism offered by his country.

* * * *

Phoenix had become obsessed with the idea of commemorating Frank Luke, Jr. There were discussions of statues, of building homes for veterans, libraries, and schools in his name. Some of those would follow in the years to come. In the end, the U.S. government found the best way to exalt the fallen aviator, America's Ace of Aces. Frank was awarded the highest honor the nation's military could bestow on him, the Congressional Medal of Honor.

From the time that Hartney and Grant submitted Frank for the Medal of Honor, the various versions of Frank's final mission became intertwined with his application. This appears, from the paper trail, to have happened after Major Hartney forwarded the application on, with the most significant editing and addition taking part at the hands of Lieutenant Colonel O.C. Aleshire.[2] The Army Air Service chose to adopt parts and pieces of the affidavit and the work done by Captain Zinn. The result was that, on paper, a significant reason that Frank was receiving his Medal of Honor was because of the information gathered from the French citizens of Murvaux.

Frank was the first U.S. Army Air Service aviator to receive the Medal of Honor. There would be other medals awarded through the 1920s and '30s either as political favors or because of lobby pressures. That does not diminish those awards or the brave men who won them, but it is important to note that Frank was the first winner, and that the only lobbying that took place on his behalf came from a single letter Frank, Sr., wrote to the War Department.

Four companies of student military cadets were on hand in April 1919 when the award was to be presented. Acting Governor McGillen and Supreme Court Justice Baker presided over the ceremonies. The speeches were long, colorful oratories designed to stir the patriotic spirits of those in attendance. Frank had, in his death, taken the long step from military aviator to legend, and the speakers did what they could to carpet that path for him.

Dean Scarlett said, "The spirit of 'Don't give up the ship' was in him. He died in the field of glory—far over his lines, in enemy territory. His body may rest in France, but his spirit is triumphant just the same and will forever inspire the sentiments of his countrymen. America will never forget Frank Luke, and his friends will cherish his name and emulate his example. Phoenix is very proud of this brave son."

Brigadier General Hickok, as one of his last acts before retirement, was on hand to present the medal itself. And it was not the medal alone that would honor Frank at the ceremony. It was also that announced the air station on Ford Island in Hawaii had been renamed Luke Field.[3] In the time since Grant and Hartney had put in their application for Frank to receive the medal, Frank's story had ceased being only about his brave career in the air. It was now also the story of the events that allegedly unfolded on September 29. The award of April 19, 1919, included the following description:

Frank Luke, Jr., Second Lieutenant, 27th Aero Squadron, First Pursuit Group, Air Service. For conspicuous gallantry and intrepidity above and beyond the call of duty in action with the enemy near Murvaux, France, September 29, 1918. After having previously destroyed a number of enemy aircraft within seventeen days, he voluntarily started on patrol after German observation balloons. Though pursued by eight German planes which were protecting the enemy balloon line, he unhesitantly attacked and shot down in flames three German balloons, being himself under heavy fire from ground batteries and the hostile planes. Severely wounded, he descended to within fifty meters of the ground, and, flying at this low altitude near the town of Murvaux, opened fire upon enemy troops, killing six and wounding as many more. Forced to make a landing, and surrounded on all sides by the enemy, who called upon him to surrender, he drew his automatic pistol and defended himself gallantly until he fell dead from a wound to the chest.[4]

The bands played patriotic tunes—John Philip Sousa and the like. The cadets performed drill ceremonies for the crowd in the already warm sunlight. Frank Luke, Sr., accepted the medal for his son. But as the night closed in and the medals Frank earned were placed on public display downtown Phoenix,[5] the people of Phoenix sought to find another way to preserve the memory of what they had lost with Frank's passing. While the nation had honored Frank, his hometown and state still were struggling to find the right way to commemorate the boy and man that they had known.

One of the first ideas that generated both public interest and seemed the most appropriate way to honor Frank was an air show. This was just before the age of barnstorming, and air shows were packed events. The airplane was just over a decade old and it still captivated the public. While several citizens' committees were formed to try to come up with ideas for commemorating Frank, it was the one led by his friend Pidge Pinney that came up with the idea for the Luke Memorial Air Tournament. There would be racing, exhibition aircraft displays, and captured German Fokkers. The guest of honor was to be Eddie Rickenbacker, the greatest living American ace. At the last minute Rickenbacker had to cancel, but on June 28, 1919, the air over Phoenix roared to life with airplanes, including a flight that came in from San Diego, from Rockwell Field, honoring the young man who had learned to fly there.

When the very first American Legion post was formed, Post 1, it was named after Frank Luke, Jr. His sister Anna was present to accept the gracious acknowledgement on behalf of the family.

In the 1920s, it was decided that a statue was the best way for Phoenix to remember its favored son. The sculptor, Roger Noble Burnham, turned to the Luke family for the person who most resembled Frank to base the statue's face on. It was decided by the family that Anna, his sister, was the closest. Several different models of the statue were cast before the final design was settled on. And the people of Arizona and Phoenix felt that there was only one place fitting for a statue of the first Arizona winner of the Medal of Honor—in front of their new State Capitol building.

On November 11, 1930, Armistice Day, at 10:59 a.m., Governor John C. Phillips rose to the podium with much pomp and circumstance, for the unveiling of the statue. The statue of Frank towered over the crowd. Frank had his back to the capitol and was looking upward into the sky, his flying cap and goggles in hand. The names of the 318 other Arizona men who died in the Great War were carved into the base of the statue. The Luke family was there in force that day, as were many Phoenicians who had known Frank. The passage of eleven years had not diminished Frank's popularity.

There was one seat, however, that remained empty at the ceremony. An invitation had gone out to Marie Rapson, now Marie Jackson. She did not attend the ceremony but had been sent a special invitation to the event which she lovingly kept her entire life.

* * * *

The Luke Family maintained some contact with Marie Rapson after the death of Frank, especially his sisters and sisters-in-law. Charlie Luke and his wife Eunice struggled with having children, losing several when Eunice was at various stages of pregnancy. The Lukes preserved the name Frank each generation. In this case, Francis (Frankie). At one point her middle name is listed as "Marie" but changed at some point to "Mae." Frankie Marie was the only child raised by Charlie and Eunice that did not have a birth certificate. Her birthday was remarkably close to the time when Marie Rapson began to go back to school again after her eight-and-a-half months of being away.

Not long after the war ended women began to surface, women claiming to be the fiancées of Frank Luke. Some wore cheap rings that they claimed Frank had given them, others showed up at the family homestead. More than one claimed Frank had proposed to her. It was part of the price of Frank's fame that such frauds emerged. People wanted to be associated with the hero they had read about. Such rumors and women appeared in San Diego where Marie lived and grieved, as well. None of these pretenders was ever proven to be more than a liar. The only woman Frank ever wrote about between 1917 and 1918 was his beloved Marie. Still, the false claims stung Marie deeply.[6]

In May 1919, word came of Frank's final letter to Marie. Captain Hoover had recovered the letter addressed simply to "Marie" after Frank had been killed. After the war, Hoover was traveling the country in a barnstorming expedition that the government had put together to promote the selling of Victory Bonds. The Victory Liberty Loan Flying Circus was put on by war veterans piloting surplus and captured aircraft. The circus traveled from city to city putting on flying acrobatics demonstrations to help the government pay for the war effort.

Captain Hoover arrived in Phoenix with the letter and took it to the Luke family. They provided him with the address for Marie and sent the letter on with him, unopened. Hoover personally carried the letter with him to San Diego and presented it to Marie. For her, it would be the last time that Frank communicated with her. At a time when she was still likely grieving, the letter must have come as a sudden reminder of the life that she and Frank almost shared.

There is a saying that we never forget the first true loves of our lives. This has never been truer than it was with Marie Rapson.

In 1919, Marie met a young naval officer Gordon MacAlister Jackson. "Red" Jackson was a graduate of the Naval Academy and was stationed on destroyer duty in San Diego. He was a headstrong young officer. His Academy yearbook quoted one cadet's account of dealing with him: "Jackson, if you don't lay off of me I'll blow your brains out one by one." Red was apparently quite smart and highly disciplined. In many respects, he was the opposite of Frank. Marie and Red married within the year. While Gordon filled a gap in her life, she never forgot Frank. In fact, she clipped every newspaper article, every story in a magazine about Frank and kept it in a scrapbook, carefully preserved.

Gordon left the Navy and they moved to Oklahoma. Marie had two young boys by him, Donald and Douglas. Gordon opened an engineering business associated with the oil industry. Marie embraced her music as she always had, teaching piano lessons to earn extra money. The marriage didn't work out. Marie held Red to some high standards—the life she would have had with Frank. As she once told her daughter-in-law, Charme, "He just never measured up to the first love I had in my life."

Donald Jackson followed in his father's footsteps and attended the Naval Academy, becoming a naval aviator. With the outbreak of war, Douglas, too, became an aviator, learning to pilot B-29s. With her mother Cora passing away in 1942, Marie had her daughter-in-law, Charme, Donald's wife, move in with her while the boys were off at war. "There were times she would get sad and go upstairs to look at her box of photos and articles about Frank." She warned her daughter-in-law of the risks of falling in love so deeply. Surrounded by the rich sounds of her pianos, she could find solace. Marie embraced her music.

When Donald earned his wings, Marie went out and purchased *The Big Blue Book of Aviation* for him as a present. She gave it to him, carefully folding down the corner of the page about a great American aviator—Frank Luke, Jr. Donald had a bright future as a naval pilot. He had been highly decorated for action in the Pacific during World War II. He flew with such men as a young John Glenn in an exciting age when jets were in their infancy.

Marie had lost the first true love of her life to the gods of the skies, and now those same gods reached out once more into her heart and soul. In 1955, her son Donald was piloting a jet aircraft on maneuvers near Patuxent Naval Air Station. His plane collided with another jet piloted by the son of an admiral, a pilot known to have issues with controlling his aircraft. His jet plummeted into the earth near a small subdivision while the other pilot managed to eject in time. The ruling was that the collision was due to pilot error (the other pilot), but that did little to ease the loss. Marie had lost her first son to flying. She arrived in time from the California for Donald to be buried in Arlington. Most women hope they never have to make the supreme sacrifice to the nation's defense. Marie had done it twice.[7]

* * * *

Joe Wehner's family struggled to locate and bring him home. Graves Registration, fed on information from Fred Zinn and his small team, tried several locations in France, exhuming the bodies of men only to discover they were not Joseph Wehner. They met an American soldier named Fred Smith in the Rhineland after the war, and he discussed an unidentified pilot that he had buried near the end of the war. The soldier had a photograph which was then published in a Newark, New Jersey, paper. One of Joe's former roommates saw the photo and realized that the dead pilot was Wehner. Armed with this information, Graves Registration had a location they could focus in on—near Thionville.[8]

Almost every bone in Joe's body had been broken during his crash and with his jaw missing, his identification had to be done using archival records from Berlin and parts of the uniform that had not yet decayed. In April of 1919, his body was moved to a temporary grave location while the family decided where he should be interred permanently. Their decision was that Joe should return to Everett, Massachusetts.

His father went alone to the docks in New York when the body arrived. It had been placed in the sort of same military-specified plain pine coffin that Frank had been interred in. The ship had arrived in the late evening and Joe's father had to sign off for his son's remains in the dingy darkness of the New York docks. It was a long journey into the night to bring Joe home.

On June 20, 1921, a lone biplane flew over Everett and dropped roses on front of caisson that carried Lieutenant Joseph Fritz Wehner solemnly to the Woodlawn Cemetery. With full military honors he returned home, the only wingman who flew with Frank to do so.

Later that year, the VFW Post 834 in Everett opened as the Joseph Wehner Post. The ceremony for one of the first Massachusetts aces was long. The program that had been written by William Wood and Henry Lawson wrote of Joe's exploits and personality. They wrote of Joe's silent sacrifice and of the special bond he and Frank had. "And so these two, Luke and Wehner, flew from this earthly scene, just a little way over yonder Western Horizon. Pals in life and danger; undivided in their last hours on this earth."[9] Even in commemoration in his home town, Joe's accomplishments were always tied to those of Frank Luke.

* * * *

Frank Luke, Jr.'s official victory tally at the end of the war was 18, with 14 of those being enemy observation balloons. Hartney always believed that Luke had deserved many more credits, not the least of which was his first engagement on August 16, 1918. In retrospect, that victory is one that the Air Force should have awarded Frank after the war but didn't. Some amateur lists credit him with 20 kills, others 21, some with fewer than 18.

There are a number of reasons for this confusion, not the least of which is that authors have either made mistakes or inflated Luke's kill-count for their own purposes. On top of that, the Air Force opened the door for dispute when it recalculated the kills for World War I pilots in the 1960s. As one former Air Force historian stated during the research for this book, "the

Air Force has been busy re-writing its history since the day it was formed. Some of that is to justify having an Air Force, some of it is to make it seem more important to itself." Frank's records were adjusted in an effort to level the playing field for pilots who had fought under the newer shared-kill system. Frank's victory count was reduced as a result of this new system since his kills were equally divided among those he shared victories with.

Ultimately, it doesn't matter which count method you wish to use. Frank ended the war as the U.S. Army Air Service's number two ace. To the young man who played sports hard to the winning play, who fought with such fury to win every battle, the final score would not be what was important—all that mattered would be the victory itself.

* * * *

When Captain Zinn's work was finished in Berlin he had managed to identify or locate the remains of all but five or six airmen who had flown in the war. The last ones were elusive and remain such even to this day. One of those pilots was Ivan Andrew Roberts.

The final resting place of Ivan "Robbie" Roberts is unknown even today. There was a report in October 1919 to his family from the International Red Cross that Ivan had died of "wounds from his fall," and had passed away on October 1, 1918—some six days after he had been shot down. Like Frank Luke, Ivan's name had been logged accidentally with the British aviators' fatality list. The difference in the days implied that he had, indeed, been captured by the Prussian Army troops when he had been shot down on September 26, 1918.

But the prisoner of war reports do not list Ivan Roberts. This implies strongly that Roberts was not taken to one of the Germans' POW camps, which had a very detailed process for logging prisoners and informing their families as to their fates. It is most likely, based on the evidence, that Roberts was indeed injured and died on October 1 but that he had not been made a POW. He simply may have been too badly injured from his final flight to be taken to a POW camp. Instead, he most likely perished in a field hospital. With the Prussian 5th Army in retreat, his burial would have been quick and the records may have been lost amidst the collapse of the German forces. The true location of Ivan Roberts is likely a slit trench where his body, and those of dead Germans, were buried together as the Prussians retreated.

Robbie's father, Thomas, left the Ascension School where he was super-intendent for a personal leave in 1919. While the scars of the fighting still had not healed on the landscape of France, Thomas Roberts went looking for his son. Alone he wandered the Meuse River valley, asking a war-weary population if they had seen or heard anything about his beloved son. Sadly, he had no luck and returned a month later without even a clue as to the whereabouts of Robbie.

Elizabeth Roberts, Ivan's sister, took up her father's quest to find Ivan next. She was in the Red Cross and transferred to Paris in an effort to begin to search for Ivan or his remains. Elizabeth was indeed a force to be reckoned with. She had the Army meet her as soon as she arrived in France at the train station in Paris. They took her to the sites of four different burials. Elizabeth stood by while the long-buried men were exhumed. One site was a burial trench with several bodies in it. She crawled into the wet mud, fighting the stench of the dead, and sought in vain for her brother. Some of the remains were nothing more than a few burned bones. At other locations she had the Army exhume other dead officers searching vainly to end her family's pain. One was simply the upper portion of the body, the rest having been burned away to the bone. Others wore uniforms that were half-rotted. It was a grim scene of death for this young woman. From her observations, none of them were Ivan.[10]

Elizabeth was not alone in her quest to find out Ivan's final fate. His fiancée, Dorothy Thompson, moved to New York to be near her family and, thus settled, wrote several letters asking for more information on Ivan's fate. Dorothy became one of the first Navy Yeomen and worked in a variety of jobs, including as a draftsperson. She eventually gave up hope that Robbie would be found.

Ivan's brother, Thomas Roberts, Jr., also pursued the quest for his brother, writing the Army pleading for new information and hope. But Ivan remained elusive. All efforts by the U.S. Army to locate his remains were futile.

In the list of the Berkshire, Massachusetts, Honor Roll of those men and women who served in the military from the town, his name is forgotten on the list while his brother's appears. Likewise, even authoritative books such as the two-volume *New England Aviators*, which lists all pilots from New England, oddly omits Ivan Roberts even though pilots with fewer kills than him appear. Whatever crevasse in history Robbie had located, he huddled there and remained unknown—remembered often as "Frank Luke's other wingman who died."

The Roberts family did not give up on Ivan. Their correspondence is a portrait of war grief in miniature. In some letters, they will admit that they are sure Ivan is dead, while in others they raise the specter that he may yet be alive. In others they just don't know. Frank Luke's last wingman, quite literally, flew off to the final sunset and was never seen or heard from again.

Chapter Twenty

*"He was a boy possessed of the most superb self-confidence that I have
ever encountered. There was no feat so difficult nor so dangerous that he
did not consider himself as capable of performing it and there was con-
sequently nothing that he was not ready and willing to undertake."*

—FEBRUARY 14, 1919, EDDIE RICKENBACKER

The Stuff of Legends

The Gold Star Mothers' Pilgrimages were a series of trips, set up by
the U.S. government and administered by the Quartermaster Corps,
to take the mothers of soldiers killed in action to France to pay their
final respects to their departed sons. Almost from the start, the pilgrimages were controversial. It took twenty years for Congress to get the funding
and the appropriate rules put in place. Many people complained that at the
same time that the economy of the United States was showing the strains
of depression, tax dollars were being spent to send people on trips overseas.
But it was a unique gesture in the history of the United States—sending
grief-stricken mothers to the grave sites of their children to obtain some sort
of closure.

The people chosen to go were chosen by lottery, by state. Tillie Luke,
Frank's mother, was chosen to go on the 1930 pilgrimage. Like most invitees,
she didn't want to go without her husband, which was allowed but at his own
expense. At the last minute she became sick and was unable to attend. She

went on the next pilgrimage, however, touring Paris and finally making the long, painful trek to Frank's grave site.

Ivan Roberts's step-mother, Hattie Decker Roberts, had to get special dispensation to go on the trip. Ivan's status as Missing in Action in addition to her being his step-mother required the personal intervention of her congressman. She attended the 1930 pilgrimage but for her, there was no grave site to visit, simply a stone wall which bore her son's name among the honored missing. If Tillie Luke had been able to attend, it's not hard to imagine that they would have met each other—they shared a common bond.

The mothers were treated regally by the U.S. and French governments. They were taken to Paris and taken to scenes where the American army had fought and where their sons had died. Grass covered the still visible but fading trench lines of the war. Farmers returned to the fields and plowed where men had battled for each meter of ground and where the skies had been filled with the sputter and roar of aircraft.

The capstone of their journey was the trip to the grave sites. Taken in limousines solemnly to the cemeteries they were greeted with honor guards. Tents were erected to shade them. Nurses and doctors provided by the Quartermaster Corps were at the ready for the mothers that were destined to swoon as they found their boys.

Frank's mother, Tillie, would have found a pristine cross with Frank's name. Hattie Roberts would have been led slowly across the green grasses to the wall where the names of the men who were never found were carved. There would have been tears, sadness, and in Hattie's case, a sense of frustration.[1]

* * * *

Bill Elder, Frank's childhood friend, went on to have a happy life. He married in 1925 to a woman named Dorothy. He became a general building contractor and worked in construction most of his life. When he retired, he moved to Long Beach, California. Bill joined his old friend Frank on April 12, 1953, and was buried in Phoenix, Arizona.[2]

* * * *

There are times when fate has a less-than-subtle way to remind us of our past. On January 11, 1947, Frank Allan Luke, a nephew of Frank's and son of John A. Luke, was piloting an airplane in the Arizona desert near Papago when he lost control of the plane and crashed. At the age of twenty years old another Frank Luke had perished in an airplane. It was a chilling reminder of the loss the family had suffered decades before. The loss of another Frank, in a plane accident, was so shocking that the family kept it from Tillie Luke out of fear that it would disturb her physical condition.[3]

* * * *

Albert "Pidge" Pinney went on to leave Phoenix after ensuring that a proper memorial was erected to Frank. Pidge had gone to training in 1917 as a naval aviator but never made it to the war. He attended Stanford University for a few short months studying journalism but left school unexpectedly. By the 1930s, he took over the family sporting goods store and was instrumental in setting up a commercial basketball league in Phoenix. Pidge was one of the first of Frank's friends to join him, having died on June 25, 1931, of a peritonitis attack.[4]

* * * *

Some of Frank's former comrades returned to Europe to seek their own form of redemption or to recapture past glories. Lured by the myth of Frank's famous last stand, some went to Murvaux and spoke with the locals. The French were willing to perpetuate this myth. One veteran airman, Charles D'Olive, tried to retrace Frank's last few minutes. "I found the farm and talked to the old French lady there who had seen the whole thing from her upstairs window. The farm houses are built like a U. The pigs, chickens, and family all live in the round and the manure pile is in the middle. The house has a little sloped roof. She was upstairs and saw all of this.

"When he landed the tail of his ship was pointed slightly toward the farm. He got out on the other side, sitting on the trailing edge of the wing, leaning up against the fuselage. He had been shot through the lung. When these German soldiers ran down there they went off the tail of the ship and he killed seven of them with his two forty-fives. He was an excellent forty-five hand gun shooter."[5] The locals and alleged witnesses of the events that "took place" at Murvaux were content to wax ecstatic about Luke's Wild West gunfighting death for a generation.

The members of the 388th Fighter Bomber Wing of the United States Air Force erected a marker to identify the spot of Frank's epic last stand in 1957.

The Air Force historian Royal Frey was renowned for helping sort out World War II combat kill confirmations, and was a World War I aviation expert. Building on the work that Frederick Zinn had started decades before, in the 1960s Frey began to research the story of Frank's last mission, going back to Murvaux to talk to some of the survivors who might still remember the events of September 29, 1918.

His 1962 version of the Murvaux affidavit changes a number of minor points of the myth of Frank Luke's demise but takes nothing away from what Frank accomplished in the war or his final few minutes of life. What Frey determined was that Frank did discharge his pistol but the Germans did not fire on him. Frey also determined that Frank did not strafe the streets of Murvaux. But Frey knew, from his notes and follow-up communications with the witnesses, that his version of the story flew in the face of those that wanted to believe an epic last stand for Frank. Adding to the problem, he was interviewing people in 1962, forty-four years after the events. One of his witnesses was four years old at the time. Frey, a detail-oriented historian knew that his version was not necessarily 100 percent accurate. Ultimately it did not change history, but it provided some interesting details.[6]

By 1963, Frey had tracked down many of the surviving witnesses of the key events of Frank's military career, including Bernard Mangels, the German officer most responsible for Frank's demise. Without the benefit of the Internet, Frey tracked them down like a sleuth and contacted them via the mail, obtaining sworn statements and documents pertaining to the events. The efforts of Royal Frey were invaluable in the writing of this book.

* * * *

In 1941, the U.S. Government purchased an immense piece of property outside of Phoenix, Arizona, for use as an air base. Famous men, such as Captain Barry Goldwater, have served there. The Air Force's elite flying squadron, the Thunderbirds, was created there in 1953. More than 12,000 pilots logged over a million hours of flying time during World War II at the base. The dogfighting tactics that are taught there would have honored the man for whom it is named.

Luke Air Force Base.

Today Luke remains the largest fighter training base in the world. While many have heard the name, few know the story of the man it is named after.

And, as we have read, a field on Ford Island in Hawaii was named for Frank, but it was renamed just prior to the start of World War II, releasing its name for Luke AFB.

* * * *

Eddie Rickenbacker assumed command of the 94th Squadron, the famous "Hat in the Ring" squadron, so named for the Uncle Sam top hat flying into a ring (a literalization of the metaphor "to throw one's hat into the ring," as America upon entering the war). Rickenbacker became the

American Ace of Aces upon the death of Frank Luke. If Frank had lived, there was a good chance that he would have been assigned to fly under Rickenbacker—but that never was to be.[7] He eventually achieved a total of 26 confirmed kills before the war ended in November 1918. He survived the war and his name was recognized nationwide, while Frank's name became a fading memory. Parades were held in his honor in New York and Los Angeles upon his return.

Rickenbacker started a car company and eventually became president of Eastern Air Lines. In 1930, he received the Congressional Medal of Honor, at which time he commented, "If Frank Luke had lived I wouldn't be here." Throughout his life Rickenbacker expressed only words of high praise for Frank. On several occasions he stopped by the Luke household to pay his respects.

During World War II, Rickenbacker was flying with a bomber crew in the Pacific delivering a message from the Secretary of War to General Douglas MacArthur when his plane was shot down. He survived on the open seas in a life raft for twenty-four days before being rescued.

Rickenbacker remained an aviation icon throughout his life. He was invited to Cape Kennedy to watch the Apollo 11 moon landing. In 1973, "Captain Eddie" flew the same last mission that all pilots eventually do—he flew off into the western sunset.

* * * *

Walter Williams, an enlisted man in the 27th, was the unofficial historian for the 27th Squadron. He and a handful of the faithful men who served in the Fighting Eagles kept in contact over the years, meeting from time to time to share war stories and hopefully rekindle the flickering light of fading memories. In 1970, fifty-two years after the war, they came to Phoenix to hold one of their last reunions and to pay tribute to the most famous member of their squadron. The list of attendees was less than a page in length, and some, like Rudy Shirek of Los Angeles, clutched at his copy of a black-and-white photo of Frank Luke.

Williams kept a diary which he updated, amended, and sometimes outright changed during his time in Europe. Upon his death, he donated it to Maxwell Air Force Base and the Air Force's Historical Archives. While it is a jumble of mixed memories and post-war edits added long after the fact, it provides a valuable reference still used by historians today.[8]

* * * *

Franz Büchner, the man who downed Ivan Roberts, Frank's last wingman, survived the war as one of Germany's top aces. His Jasta's aircraft were turned over to the American 138th Squadron after the Armistice. He had been awarded the Saxon Knight's Cross of the Military Order of St. Henry, the Mérite and Albert Orders, and the Knight's Cross Second Class with Swords. Just before the war ended he was awarded the Pour le Mérite—the Blue Max.

On October 10, 1918, a month before the war ended, Büchner was flying a mission with his brother Felix and another pilot, Gefr. Arnold Michaelis. They spotted a lone observation aircraft and dove in at it at an altitude of 4,000 meters. The still raw and inexperienced Michaelis turned sharply and unexpectedly and rammed Büchner's Fokker. The jolt was so hard that all four of his safety straps broke and he was thrown out of his seat over the upper wing of the aircraft.

The German pilots had one benefit that American pilots did not: parachutes. In the rush of air Büchner's chute opened but the jolt was so violent that it almost tore free from him. He physically had to hang on to the straps of the parachute during the descent to the ground. He was assigned another D.VII to replace the one destroyed in the mid-air collision.

A sergeant in the American 138th Aero Squadron, Walter Wood, carefully cut out the proud werewolf's head emblem from Büchner's Fokker. For the 138th, a squadron that never tangled with Büchner in battle, the werewolf head was simply a trophy—a souvenir of war. The emblem was sent to the Army Aeronautical Museum at Wright Field as a trophy of American victory, though Büchner himself had not been shot down by the Americans. The head was either lost, destroyed, or stolen in 1940.[9]

After the Great War, Germany was thrown into turmoil and chaos. Civil war broke out as various political factions tried to fill the vacuum of power left after the Kaiser stepped down. Franz Büchner joined the Freikorps, plying his military skill in an effort to maintain order and control in Germany during this chaotic period of political revolt.

On March 18, 1920, Büchner was flying a single-seat fighter on escort for another reconnaissance airplane near his hometown of Leipzig. Local communist forces were known to operate in the area and Büchner's unit was charged with locating them so they could be suppressed. Bad weather forced the plane he was charged with protecting down but Franz continued on alone. He located the communist ground forces but was hit by ground fire.[10]

His airplane spun into the ground near Mockau, killing him on impact. He had survived four years of fighting and had destroyed over 40 confirmed Allied aircraft, only to be killed by fellow countrymen a few miles from his home after the war. Like all pilots of all countries of all wars, his destiny lay in the setting sun with his comrades and foes alike.

* * * *

There was talk in Congress at one point of awarding Joseph Wehner the Congressional Medal of Honor. His mother requested that the issue not be pursued. Joe was not a person who sought out publicity or recognition for his efforts and most likely would not have considered ever asking for the medal himself, had he lived. Joe Wehner, forever tied to Frank's exploits in France, slowly faded into obscurity even in his home town. He remains buried in Everett, Massachusetts, with a humble marker.[11] An outstanding aviator on his own, Joe is almost always described in one way: the wingman of the incredible Frank Luke.

* * * *

Brigadier General William "Billy" Mitchell commanded all of the combat aviation assets of the AEF during the Great War. After the war, he pushed for the Army Air Service to become its own separate entity in the military rather than being under the Army. His proposal ruffled feathers.

Colonel Mitchell (his rank reduced to pre-war levels) said that aircraft could obsolete battleships. Again, the military experts scoffed at him, until he sunk a surrendered German battleship with some biplanes. Rather than embrace his ideals, the military turned on Billy Mitchell.

Mitchell was a maverick and criticized the War Department publicly. He was brought up on charges and a court martial. Mitchell did not waver. His show-trial became a sensation and a platform for his belief that air warfare was going to play a dominant role in the next war. He was found guilty and was suspended from rank, pay, and command for five years. Years before World War II began, he wrote articles that warned that Japan would one day put aircraft into service that would obsolete or even destroy the American Pacific battle fleet.

Mitchell didn't live to see the war he predicted. In 1936, his heart finally gave out. Eddie Rickenbacker was one of his pallbearers, an honor that would have pleased Billy. Mitchell, no doubt, climbed once more into the cockpit and joined the men he led in the Great War off in the setting sun.

* * * *

Bernard Mangels, the commanding officer of Ballonzug 35 on the fateful day that Frank Luke died, survived the Great War. After the war, he joined the "Tin Hats," a politically active veterans' organization. He completed his education and went on to be a secondary school teacher—instructing in Latin, Greek, and French—as well as a sports instructor in Münster, Germany. The rowing team that he instructed in Münster was known as "the Four Helmsmen," and went on to the Berlin Olympics in 1936.

During the Second World War, Mangels re-enlisted and rose to the rank of major. He served in Holland as a radio operator. His home in Germany was destroyed in a bombing attack, taking with it his few mementoes of his encounter with Frank Luke on September 29, 1918.

Mangels went on to be a high school teacher later in his life. He felt that the American press, especially the *Chicago Tribune*, had besmirched his name. Even late in life he claimed that the publicized accounts of Frank's alleged gun battle and "last stand" against German troops were a fraud. He was disturbed at the insinuation that he and his men had mistreated Frank's body. Even in later life, he referred to Frank Luke, Jr., as "der fliegende Cowboy." While he admired Frank, he felt that the American media and the French civilians of Murvaux had painted him as a war criminal.

Bernard Mangels died on December 3, 1969, at the age of eighty-two having never successfully cleared his reputation in the eyes of many Americans.[12]

* * * *

Alfred "Ack" Grant was promoted to Captain in October of 1918 and commanded the 27th for another month when the war ended. He left the military and for short time he ran the family grain business in Denton, Texas. Grant never achieved public popularity for his contribution to the war effort. He is thought of as the tough disciplinarian who locked horns with the upstart pilot and hero. His role in history was to be the whetstone to Frank's rebellious nature. As much as he and Frank were polar opposites, their names would always be recognized together.

In the Denton papers, he was lauded as a war hero, but at home he would have to come to terms with the death of his brother Silas and his decision to remain with the 27th Squadron in lieu of returning home for the funeral. There was a parade for him and the other four "war heroes" from the town, but none of this brought back Silas.

Grant wrote about Frank only once after the war, contributing the entry on Frank Luke to the *Big Blue Book of Aviation*. The words he wrote in that book were his only full account of the events of September 29, 1918.

In his own words, third person, Grant summed up his relationship with Frank: "Captain Alfred A. Grant, his commanding officer who had opposed Lieut. Luke's 'irresponsible' conduct, as a matter of discipline, was the first to urge America's highest award for bravery for the great flyer, whom he had previously ordered under arrest."[13]

Grant later in life moved to California and practiced law in Los Angeles. He did not maintain close relationships with the men who served under him, but did run into them from time to time. Grant died of a heart attack on January 10, 1950.

* * * *

Georg von Hantelmann, the pilot who killed Joseph Wehner, survived the war. He achieved his final victory on November 4, 1918—his twenty-sixth confirmed kill. The Armistice came into effect the following week, ending his career as an aviator. He was nominated for the Pour le Mérite but the elusive Blue Max was only conferred by the Kaiser, who abdicated his throne on November 9, 1918, and in doing so, denied von Hantelmann the honor.[14]

Von Hantelmann returned to the family estates in East Prussia after the war. He lived there in relative peace until September 7, 1924, when a group of Polish poachers attempted to drive him off of his property. The proud von Hantelman refused to give up and resisted the poachers. He was shot ingloriously attempting to defend his home. Like all airmen, his final trip to the unknown was into the setting sun.

* * * *

Frederick Zinn had brought home or determined the fate of all but a handful of aviators, nearly finishing the cleansing of his soul that he had sought. He was one of the last members of the Air Service to return after the war, having stayed behind to find his boys whom he had sent to the front. Zinn, having pioneered the techniques for identification and recovery of missing airmen returned to the family business and property holdings in Battle Creek Michigan.

When the Second World War broke out, he offered his services once more. With two sons already in the Army, the fifty-two-year-old Zinn was reactivated at the rank of major. The U.S. Army Air Services were having problems recovering bodies of air crews when ground forces overran enemy positions. Prodded by some of the officers he knew from the Great War, Fred offered his thoughts to the Army, which realized what an asset he was in this field.

Zinn was brought in as a consultant to the OSS, the precursor to the CIA, specifically to help train teams of individuals in the techniques he pioneered in the Great War. He served in the OSS in Africa, France, and Italy during the war. As he had done in the previous war, Fred Zinn made sure that many American families learned the final fate of their missing loved ones.

In 1960, he died after a successful political career in the Michigan State Legislature. In 1962, the last surviving members of the Lafayette Flying Corps, his old unit, assembled in Battle Creek at his simple grave site. A replica red Fokker triplane was flown over the gravesite and dropped roses over those gathered to commemorate their comrade. Baron von der Osten, a World War I pilot who had flown in Richtofen's Flying Circus, came to the United States to lay a wreath on Zinn's grave. Most of the former pilots were in wheelchairs, but all remembered their comrade fondly. Teary-eyed old men saluted Zinn and fading memories of the times they had spent together. With this tribute from his peers, blessed with the tears of aging heroes, Fred Zinn climbed once more into the cockpit of destiny and flew to the setting sun to join the men to whom he had given final peace.[15]

* * * *

Harold Hartney, the almost father-like figure, left the military, as well. He would always be remembered as the man who could get the most out of Frank Luke. After the war, he helped Colonel Mitchell prove that aircraft could sink a battleship—proof of the changing face of warfare. He wrote his memoirs, *Up and at 'Em*, in 1939. He also published an aircraft recognition guide in 1941.

Hartney's last memory of Frank was his takeoff on September 29, 1918, for his last flight. On that occasion, Hartney had shaken his fist at Luke. In *Up and at 'Em*, Hartney wondered about the boy he had lost that day. "Did I treat him right? I think so. Did I give him too much leeway? I think not. In any other branch of the service requiring routine discipline he would have been unhappy, unruly, totally lost. In the Air Service his dynamic, rebellious, reckless, fearless individuality found expression."[16]

The year following the release of his last book, the much beloved Major Hartney flew west into the sunset to join Frank, Joe, Ivan, and the other boys he had had the privilege to command.

* * * *

Jerry Cox Vasconcells was the first World War I ace from Colorado, but he did not revel in that title. Jerry did not talk about his time in the war, either out of modesty or because he had painful memories. Like so many veterans of war, he struggled to cope with things he had done, or not done, or witnessed. "His wife Marietta says he was tortured by terrible nightmares in which he relived the horrors and war and in which he saw, again and again, his best friend shot down in flames."[17] Today, his condition would be diagnosed as post-traumatic stress disorder. At the time, nightmares were simply called nightmares.

Despite being married to a reporter, Jerry avoided conversations about his war years or his contribution. He became a successful lawyer and community leader, running a highly profitable investment business. He was one of the people responsible for the construction of Stapleton Airport in Denver, Colorado.

Pushing aside his own painful war experiences, Jerry Vasconcells was responsible for forming the first Colorado Air National Guard unit.

On only one occasion, during a trip to California shortly after the war, did he speak of Frank Luke, Jr., when pressed by a reporter. He spoke of Frank's unwillingness to worry about the risks he faced. At the age of fifty-eight, Jerry Vasconcells suffered a fatal heart attack. As he flew into the western horizon of life, Jerry put his nightmares to rest.

* * * *

A number of people profited off of Frank's story. A screenplay writer for the movies and radio, Norman Shannon Hall (not to be confused with the World War I Ace), wrote a series of articles for *Liberty* magazine about Frank Luke in 1928. These articles were later reassembled and further edited for the book *The Balloon Buster*. Hall's account was based on his trip to Phoenix and correspondence with Major Hartney. While his rendition of the events of Frank's early life was fairly accurate, since it was based on interviews with the people involved (though corrections have been provided in this book), his accounts of Frank's combat duty were highly fictionalized at best. Hall even went so far as to falsify combat reports and present them as historical fact. Ultimately, the place the Norman Hall account must be shelved is "Historical Fiction."

Arch Whitehouse, a World War I pilot and prolific author, wrote his own highly stylized account of Frank's life in *Hun Killer*. In this version, Frank has his epic gun battle with the Germans in the graveyard of Murvaux.

Frank's image and representation continues to be used even today to market products. He has appeared in comic books, on model airplane kits, even on packaged candy cards. In 2001, the Matchbox company released a model Spad XIII patterned to look like Frank Luke's aircraft as part of a collector's series.

* * * *

Perhaps the saddest story that came out of the events of Frank's military career was the agony that Ivan Roberts's family endured. Fred Zinn found his search frustrating, as did the Robertses who simply wanted to know Robbie's final disposition. It was a burden on the family that stayed with them for years. Ivan's father and step-mother divorced in the years that followed. Thomas Roberts, Sr., wrote letters almost annually to the government attempting to get information about Ivan's remains or, just possibly, find Ivan alive. Ivan's fiancée Dorothy Thompson pressed for answers as to "Robbie's" fate, too, but to no avail Eventually, she moved on with her life in New York City. Ivan's father could not let Ivan go so easily. The hunt for his son was an obsession that dogged him throughout his life.

His last letter was an impassioned plea sent to the Secretary of the President on February 3, 1938—some twenty years after the war had ended and his son had disappeared. "I go to Arlington about every year and make my duty at the Tomb of the Unknown. Can this boy be mine? Has he given this child of my loins such anonymous glory? Am I making a fetish out of this hero worship of mine?" The raw emotions of a grieving father searching for answers about the fate of his lost son, are on every line of his last letter. "Where is Ivan Roberts?"

The Army sent him a letter back. "As it is now over 19 years since your son's death, and the investigations made immediately after the war proved fruitless, it is not believed that anything would be gained by attempting to reopen the case at this time." The letter went on to confirm for the father that the odds of his son being in the Tomb of the Unknown Soldier were infinitesimal.[18]

The search for Ivan Roberts was officially closed as far as the Army was concerned. His paperwork was processed and shoved into a thick folder in the U.S. National Archives. Ironically it was a "Burial File," though no one knows where Ivan's final resting place is.

His name was etched into the stone on the wall of the missing at the U.S. military cemetery at Romagne-sous-Montfaucon. While his body was never found it is sure that "Robbie" made his final flight to the western horizon in 1918 and awaited many of his comrades there.

* * * *

Granville Woodard survived the Great War as a German POW. He was expatriated and gave his deposition to Fred Zinn. Woody, who had gone down within minutes of his friend Frank, paid a visit to the Luke family after the war to pay his respects. They gave him a photograph of Frank that Frank's father signed, "To Woody." He kept that photo of he and Frank together his entire life. He went on to work in the Far East as a consultant in Shanghai. He was one of the individuals who helped build the first Chinese air force.

After a long and successful career and life, Woody joined his comrades and friends in the light of the setting sun on August 10, 1982.

* * * *

The Luke family thrived and grew despite the loss of Frank, Jr. Frank's parents enjoyed their golden anniversary in 1934, and several years of good life after that. They were a prosperous family and swelled in numbers. Frank Luke, Sr., was a man known to wear a suit coat even in the blistering heat of the Phoenix summers. When the subject of Frank, Jr., was brought up, his father would talk about him. His mother, Tillie, did not. If Marie was mentioned, oddly, both parents were silent. Perhaps it was the fact that she remarried so soon after the loss of Frank—or that the love their son was denied because of his death was too painful for them to discuss.

Frank's father died on a business trip a few short years later. Tillie followed him in 1947. She lived long enough to pin pilot's wings on her grandson James Luke's chest at Luke Field in 1944.

The Lukes still remain as icons of the pioneer spirit of early Arizona, though today people in Phoenix are more familiar with the Bill Luke Chrysler Jeep and Dodge dealership than they are with the family's most famous son. At the last Luke family reunion a few years back, 108 relatives assembled.[19]

The Luke home on Monroe Street fell into disrepair as the neighborhood became seedier over time. Part of if suffered in a fire, and it was abandoned for years before finally being torn down. A local TV station covered the plight of the home and its famous occupant, but it was not enough to rally the locals to save the home or restore it. All that remains today is a parking lot—not far from where the statue of Frank Luke still stands on eternal duty in front of the Capitol, his back to authority, staring into the skies.

* * * *

Marie Rapson was Frank Luke's one true love. He loved her until the end of his life, sadly before their dreams of a future together could come true. Marie loved Frank her whole life, as well. Her scrapbook, carefully saved, was added to even in the late years of her life.

Over the years, Marie's role in Frank's life seemed to diminish in the eyes of the Luke family. When John Knox wrote his ten-part series on Frank's life in 1928, Marie was not mentioned. The icy removal of her from Frank's life story seemed to be deliberate, as the family endorsed the Knox series as the most accurate telling of Frank's life. Still, she received clippings for her scrapbook over the years from the Luke family, articles from Phoenix, each carefully marked with her name and sent to her.

Frank never left Marie. In the 1970s, when a Scottsdale, Arizona, wax museum added a display of Frank Luke and Eddie Rickenbacker, Marie not only dutifully clipped the article for her scrapbook, but went to the museum. There Frank was as he had been: the young, dashing pilot in his cockpit, not touched by the passage of time. Marie snapped two photographs of the image, a reminder for her of a life that might-have-been.

Some of Marie's friends were traveling to France and extended to her a chance to go with them. While her friends set the itinerary for the journey, it would be hard to believe that she did not visit Frank one last time at Romagne-sous-Montfaucon.

Marie married again when she was in her eighties. Her son Douglas said, "She finally found some happiness." Marie never gave up her music. She played the piano for years and worked in a music store where one of her duties to was to pick up the concert pianists and musicians and bring them to their venue. For Marie, it was a taste of the life of a professional musician that she had never gotten to enjoy.

After the death of her second husband, Marie contracted breast cancer. She died in 1992, requesting that her ashes be scattered at sea beyond the Golden Gate Bridge. It is no small coincidence that she chose the western horizon as her final resting place. It is easiest to believe that her one true love was waiting for her there—in the setting sun where all aviators and their lovers go. She never let go of Frank, and he never wavered in his love for her.

Afterword

*"Man, how that kid could fly! No one, mind you, no one, had the sheer
contemptuous courage that boy possessed. I know he's been criticized for
being such a lone-handler, but, good Lord, he won us priceless victories by
those very tactics. He was an excellent pilot and probably the best flying
marksman on the Western Front. We had any number of expert pilots
and there was no shortage of good shots, but the perfect combination,
like the perfect specimen of anything in the world, was scarce. Frank
Luke was that perfect combination."*

—MAJOR HAROLD HARTNEY

When you stand in front of the statue of Frank Luke, Jr., in front
of the Arizona State Capitol, a few things stick in your mind.
Frank has his back to the Capitol and is facing the other Arizona
war memorials in the park across the street. In death, as in life, Frank has his
back to the symbol of authority. It is enough to raise a grin. His eyes stare
out at the other mementos of Arizona's sacrifice at the altar of freedom, the
anchor of the USS Arizona, the Vietnam Memorial. This lone statue does
not stand in the park with these other monuments ... part of the privilege of
being the state of Arizona's first great hero.

Frank is facing east, out of the west, and again the symbolism is not
lost on a visitor. Frank's is gazing slightly upward, into the sky. Luke always
said that he was a different man when he was flying. There is a yearning in

the statue, the expression of a man who wants to climb once more into the cockpit of a Spad and take to the air.

The medals that Frank earned during his life are presented as brass casts in the base of the memorial. Whereas a dark patina covers the statue, these emblems are polished—not by the State of Arizona but by the fingers of those that come to the statue. They touch those medals, often, as if they were able to provide a tangible link to the young man towering above.

Even in the middle of winter, the warmth of the Arizona sun shines through. As you look up, you will find yourself stepping into the shade of the statue itself to get a better look at the young man it represents. Frank's shadow is a long one, even in death.

As you look at the face of the statue, when the light is just right, a wry smile appears. The boyish, almost impish expression portrays Frank perfectly. He was a young man who never had a chance to grow up.

* * * *

In writing a book such as this, one accumulates an immense amount of information that is contradictory, or outright fabrication. Some of this came into being because that was the style of the time—authors were allowed to "enhance" their stories or books to make them appealing to a broader audience. Some of it is simply down to the whims of writers who thought stories are stories, and facts be damned.

Each change or error causes a ripple effect. What appears in print first as a simple mistake or an innocent addition to the facts gets duplicated a hundred times over as other writers repeat the error. In this way, myths are born.

Norman Shannon Hall's Account

Many people's only exposure to Frank Luke is via the account written by Norman S. Hall. Originally, this account was a ten-part story published in *Liberty* magazine in the spring of 1928. Later, these stories were repackaged as a successful book, *The Balloon Buster*. For many readers, this was an introduction to the life and legend of Frank Luke, Jr. No better or worse than we might expect it to be, Hall's account is to be read with caution.

Hall was a successful screenplay writer for movies, television, and radio. In 1927, he traveled to Arizona, according to the newspaper from his hometown, to write a series on Frank Luke. He interviewed many of Frank's childhood acquaintances and family. He contacted Major Hartney via the mail and obtained much of his information regarding Frank's time in France from a series of questions he sent to Hartney.

Norman Hall was a writer who chose to edit history his way. He took two combat reports that Frank filed on September 14, 1918, and combined them, adding in a provocative note about the target balloon's observer: "Jumped after he fired a shot at me." Hall then goes on to describe the observer, by name, and writes up a discussion that Frank "had" with another pilot as to why he didn't shoot him as he parachuted to earth.

It is fiction.

The source material at the National Archives shows that some of the "subtle" changes that Hall opted to include in his account were just "changes," and not subtle, either. Hall's accounts are always vivid, and always doubtful.

Thus, Hall's account of Frank's combat on September 26 has him shooting down a German ace, Lt. von Ziegesar, the commanding officer of Jasta 15. Von Ziegesar did exist, and he was in the air on September 26, but nowhere near where Frank Luke and Ivan Roberts were flying—nor was he shot down on the 26th. Archival evidence from the National Archives and the Lafayette Foundation helps correctly identify the type of aircraft shot down on any given day, and by whom. These data are further supported by the outstanding works of Norman Franks, Frank Bailey, and Rick Duiven in *The Jasta War Chronology*.

Perhaps the most cruel and inconsiderate lie that Hall put forth in his articles and book was the alleged letter that one Jack La Grange, M.D., sent to the Secretary of the American Legion, to be forwarded to Captain Grant. Allegedly drafted in 1920, it tells a heroic version of Ivan Roberts's death.[1]

Dear Sir:

Please forward the following information to the family of Lieut. Ivan A. Roberts.

Lieut. Roberts on the evening of September 25th, 1918, rolled, engine trouble, to the ground about 12 kilometers east of Sivry. On the morning of Sept. 26, 1918, he was picked up with lacerated scalp and slightly wrenched hip by H.M. Prussian Guard, 42nd Squad.

On Oct. 2nd, 1918, he arrived at the place where I was held prisoner, a temporary structure on the Murg River in Baden about 50 kilos from Sackingen. I will not detail our experiences.

On Oct. 7th Lieut. Roberts and myself managed to effect our successful escape leaving three of his Majesty's Prus. G's in the Murg. However, Roberts sustained a bad cut running from ear to collar bone.

We traveled westerly to the Rhine River and northward to Strassbourg. We were subsequently arrested by two men on horseback who had probably observed our departure from the house. After the little "difficulty" there was one horse standing. We both mounted and traveled for Nancy. After perhaps three hours traveling, the horse stepped in an old well and Roberts pulled me out, rather done for, don't you know?

We layed around the well, until the twelfth of Oct. and resumed our way toward Nancy. Roberts' temperature jumped to "top" and he became uncomfortably talkative in view of our close proximity to village homes. Of course we had no medicine of any description. Had I thought there was any degree of salvation for Roberts in surrendering him I should have done so. But as I knew we were wanted real bad and in view of my past experiences I decided to do for us, myself, what I could and which was pitiably little indeed.

We arrived at a small densely wooded cañon about noon on October 14th. We were about 5 kilos from a small and beautiful place called Wasselbonne. We climbed to the bottom of this cañon. Roberts insisted upon bathing his feet despite his physical condition. So it was there, near Wasselbonne, in the canon laying with his burning head in my dampened jacket, and his feet dangling in the pool, that Ivan offered up a few trinkets and a letter to my care to be taken home. I did the best I could with rocks, limbs, etc., a heartache and a big lump in my throat.

The Lieutenant's little personal things together with my own are present en route from Paris, where I left them with a friend. I will forward them upon receipt of address. Please treat this letter as it is given. In confidence as I have no desire for notoriety. I am sick of it all and trying to forget. Also pardon mistakes, grammatical, etc., as I am anything but well.

Sincerely,

JACK LA GRANGE, M.D.

This published account does not stand up to scrutiny on many levels. It has all of the hallmarks of a fictionalization by Norman Hall. It references real places and provides some specific details, but nothing that can be verified. There is no account of this letter ever arriving for the Secretary of the American Legion—per their archivist. In fact, this would have been one of the last places it would have been sent. The YMCA or the Red Cross would have been the well-known and logical recipients of such a letter. There is no reference of the letter being in possession of the Grant family.[2] There is no copy or reference to it in Ivan Roberts's burial file in the National Archive where all such correspondence regarding missing airmen is filed. Given his father's obsession with finding Ivan and his family's letter writing campaign, one would expect that there would be references to this letter numerous times in his files. There isn't a single reference to it.

The only place this letter appears is in the Norman Hall accounts. His attempt at filling space in his article and book, at the expense of the mourning Roberts family, lacks dignity and, at the same time, accomplishes nothing.

Norman Hall's errors are numerous. One researched by Royal Frey in the 1960s concerns the note Luke dropped as he started his final flight. Hall's account says, "Watch three balloons on the Meuse." Frey checked with the actual witnesses and people who read the note. Frey's work is the basis for the version of the story presented in this book. He notes that, even in Hartney's account, there were more than three balloons visible that day. This is substantiated by the letter of witness written July 22, 1981, by Georges Reguier. Which three would Frank have been referring to?

The errors that I have highlighted here are but a handful of those that were found. But Hall's articles seem to stand up to checks of archival documentation. He does alter facts, but most of these stories were based on interviews with people and family who were still alive, so he stuck much closer to the truth than in the parts of the story dealing with France. Like most writers of his era, Hall simply added color to the stories, which sometimes negated their truth.

An example of this is Frank's boxing in Ajo in his youth. There is archival evidence of a James Breen who was a miner in Arizona, and that account is provided in this book. Hall's version also describes a match against a "Battling Haney." Checks of census records, California and Arizona boxing records, and the newspaper archives in Ajo offer no one by this name nor any boxing match promoted involving him. As he did so often, Hall took a nugget of truth and expanded it.

Most of Hall's misrepresentations were detailed in nature, enough so that people would take them as truth, yet often difficult to verify.

The truth of the matter is that many writers have taken the works of Norman Shannon Hall as 100 percent valid and based articles or chapters in books totally on their content.

Arch Whitehouse's Account of Frank

Arch Whitehouse, himself a World War I pilot, wrote numerous books and articles after the war about pilots and air battles. His account in *Hun Killer*, a highly stylized account of Frank's life and death, is more fiction than reality.

William Haiber in his book *September Rampage* points out some of Whitehouse's failings. He altered a combat report by Frank on September 14, adding a line for color: "I saw Lt. Wehner dive through the enemy formation and he attacked two planes on my tail." In the style of writing of the time, such additions were commonplace, but this type of imaginative storytelling prevents one from using *Hun Killer* as anything more than a secondary or tertiary piece of reference material. Whitehouse adds dialogue that often is impossible, out of character, and most likely pure fiction.

Whitehouse's account in *Hun Killer* is little more than a novelization of Frank's life and death. His account of Frank's death, covered later in this chapter, is nothing short of pure fiction.

The Frank Luke Diary

Two authors from the 1920s refer to Frank Luke's diary in their works—Norman Hall and Laurence La Tourette Driggs. Hall's integrity as a researcher has already been impugned. Driggs refers to the diary in an article in *The Ladies' Home Journal.* He claims that he read the diary and from it determined that Luke confessed having lied about his kill on August 16.

However, Driggs's later book *Heroes of Aviation* refers to the same incident but gets the date wrong by one month. In this version, Luke does not confess to lying about the kill. One would assume that if Driggs had access to such a sensational bit of information that he would have included it in both places.

Driggs and Hall, who both reference this diary, do not have data between the two of them that would indicate that they were looking at the same document. If Hall had taken the effort to plagiarize Driggs, it would have added some validity to the fiction of the diary.

The Luke family has no record of a diary by Frank, nor do they reference it. The family donated all of Frank's letters and photographs to the Arizona State Library and Archives to preserve them and make them available for historians. There is no diary listed in the collection.

Frank's Collecting of Machine Guns

Several writers have suggested that Frank was collecting German machine guns to send back to Arizona after the war. The alleged justification for this is that the Mexicans had crossed the border in 1916, and Frank thought Arizonians might put the guns to good use. Both Hall and Driggs describe remarkably dissimilar variants of this story.

On September 17, Frank would have had the time and opportunity to do this. Given the retreat of the Germans from St. Mihiel, it is entirely possible that he could have liberated some machine guns for shipment back to the states.

There is a photograph of Frank posing with a captured German machine gun with his mechanics lined up behind him. This was obviously a posed shot and does not prove that Frank was shipping machine guns home. At most, it may serve as the starting point for such anecdotes.

There is simply no evidence. No archival sources, diaries, or letters substantiate this. Also, the machine guns would have been worthless without German ammunition. Frank understood guns very well and flew with two machine guns of different calibers. Sending the guns home, even if it was possible, seems a waste of effort.

Frank's Boxing for Money in Ajo

Several magazine articles state that Frank made money during high school riding off to Ajo on the weekends and boxing. This is pure fancy. Yes, he did box. That was validated by the letter that Frank wrote his future mother-in-law, Cora Rapson. Riding off to Ajo on the weekends to box for money seems romantic, but it simply was not realistic given the distances involved.

"I won't be taken alive"

One poignant element of the mythos surrounding Frank was that he swore that he would not allow himself to be captured. In the writing of this book,

I went to find the source of this statement. The quotation seems to originate with writers of the period, rather than with Frank.

The most referenced source is John Knox's 1928 series "Aces Up," which refers to the party just prior to Frank's departure to Paris. There he allegedly utters that comment, after he swears to make the Germans pay for what they had done to Joe Wehner. The source of this line is never quoted and it is to be assumed that it was John Knox himself. A number of other writers have lifted the line for their own works, some claiming that it was in letters he wrote home.

Rickenbacker, who was there, indicates that Frank said very little that night. Surely such a boast would have earned comment in his autobiography.

None of Frank's original correspondence suggests that he held this attitude. Frank, a devout Catholic, was making plans with his fiancée to travel to the Far East after the war. They were planning for a life together. Why would he say such a thing?

Two facts go against this. Frank was so concerned about his family's feelings and worries that he did not even tell them he was at the front. Chances are he never would have written home to tell them that he was willing to die rather than be captured—it would have served to only alert them that he was at the front and scare his poor mother.

Second, the pilots of the 27th Squadron knew that Joe had been shot down but did not know his fate. Even as late as September 21, members of the squadron were writing Mrs. Wehner that her son was most likely a prisoner, as evidenced by the letter on display at the Museum of Flight in Seattle. Frank could not swear revenge on Joe's death because no one knew at the time he made the statement that Joe was indeed dead.

Like most elements of the Frank Luke myth, this starts with a simple line or two by a period writer to add flavor—and we can assume that it is fiction that people have treated as fact.

Frank's Frame of Mind—His Alleged Depression

Many authors have claimed that Frank was depressed after the death of Joe Wehner. Some have indicated that depression drove Frank to totally reckless behavior which resulted in his final mission and his death. More than one has used the word "suicidal" in their accounts.

There is no doubt that Frank took the death of his friend Joe Wehner seriously. But was he depressed? His primary concern at the time was informing his mother that he was at the front. A party was held for Frank before he went to Paris, and by all accounts he was happy and enjoying himself—hardly the behavior of a man in the depths of depression. Major Hartney, who knew him as well as any man in his unit, said that he was impatient, but never describes Frank as depressed or despondent.

Frank was writing Marie at home to plan their life after the war. He was concerned over his mother worrying about him. These are simply not the indications that he was suffering with deep depression that drove him over the edge. Yes, the events of August and September 1918 impacted the young man. Even evaluating the changes to his photographs in the period shows the changes and aging that seem to have taken place. But how he felt on the ground was one thing—how he acted in the air was another.

The Origins of the Balloon Busting in the Evening

One self-published book on Frank Luke, Jr., *September Rampage*, highlights a common problem in such efforts. In that book, the author presents a copy of the Herbert letter, written by a balloon corps veteran named Craig Herbert to Royal Frey. In it, he claims that Luke landed at their balloon site for two days, and during that time he explained to Frank how he could take out an observation balloon by attacking it in the evening when it was near its nest.

The letter shows some of the problems that Royal Frey had to deal with decades after the events. Frank was never laid up for two nights at a balloon company. He did stay at Herbert's company on September 14. Did Herbert tell him how to blow up balloons? Highly unlikely.

The real impetus for the dusk balloon busting can be found in the orders that came down. Billy Mitchell wanted the German balloon line suppressed for the Meuse-Argonne Offensive. Those orders went to the First Pursuit Group. Major Hartney assigned the 27th Squadron to take out those balloons. Grant had his orders and had to find a way to do it. Frank had already demonstrated his abilities by the time he landed at Herbert's balloon company and would not have had a reason to inquire as to how to deal with Drachen.

In the end, like so many sensational pieces of evidence, the Herbert claim simply does not hold water.

Frank did not originate balloon busting in the evening. Balloon busters from 1915 on had employed the same tactic with varying degrees of success. The Great War was different from World War II. Allied coordination was poor, and the sharing of tactics and information was not frequent enough. Tactics that the French or British employed did not automatically get conveyed to the Americans.

What Frank and Joe *did* do was develop this tactic for the First Pursuit Group. Hartney confirms this in the series of articles written by John Knox. While not absolutely original, it was original as far as the AEF was concerned.

The Idea for the Advance Field

Much has been made about Frank coming up with the idea for the forward field where B Flight under Jerry Vasconcells was posted in late September. The Pruden diary clears that matter up effectively, indicating that it was Pruden and Vasconcells that proposed the concept to Grant and Hartney.

The confusion comes from Hartney's book *Up and at 'Em*, which suggests that the idea came from Frank. Given that Pruden's diary was written at the time and that Hartney's book was written in 1939, it is easy and logical to privilege Pruden's evidence.

Frank's Final Mission

A handful of armchair historians have attempted to turn Frank's death into a controversy much like the death of the Red Baron. In reality, there is no controversy, no great mystery. Some of this "controversy" was fueled by the affidavit that Royal Frey obtained in 1962 that seemed to contradict some of the events that were assumed as fact about Frank's demise.

There are certain undeniable facts about Frank's final mission. In reviewing them, they tell a story of bravery in facing death.

- Frank took off without Captain Grant's permission and narrowly avoided being placed under arrest by Lieutenant Vasconcells at the forward airfield.
- Frank was cocky on his last flight. He dropped a note telling a balloon company to watch the German balloon line so as to confirm his victories.
- He destroyed three balloons in a short span of minutes.
- Frank flew over Murvaux and was struck by ground fire.
- Frank brought his plane down and survived the landing.
- He got out of his airplane, with his automatic pistol, and managed to get some distance away from Spad Number 26.
- Frank may or may not have discharged his weapon.
- Frank died near the Milly creek as a result of a wound.

There is no doubt that the French civilians of Murvaux embellished their accounts immediately after the war to vilify the Germans and to celebrate the brave American aviator. This is confirmed both by the account in the original Murvaux affidavit and by veterans such as D'Olive that went to the village and met with locals who told a wide range of stories.

Matters were exacerbated by the fact that McCormick did not speak French very well. By the time Fred Zinn, fluent in French, arrived, the story had already morphed and changed. The additional points added by the French:

- Frank was attacked by eight Fokker aircraft.
- He successfully downed two aircraft.
- Prior to landing, Frank strafed the streets of the village, killing six Germans and wounding many more.
- Frank had a gun battle with the Germans on the ground which resulted in his death.
- Frank's body was abused by the Germans after his death and denied a Christian burial.

What drew historian Royal Frey to this mystery was his pursuit of resolving kill confirmations. But his account is weakened by the fact that decades had passed. One of the witnesses was four years old at the time that Frank died, bringing his recollections into question. Getting witnesses to any event to agree on it, even right after the event, is difficult. Frey gets concurrence, but decades later. What he did was admirable and added a level of clarity to the issue. For the most part, the affidavits he obtained in 1962 (there is more than one on file with the Lafayette Foundation), clear up some of the issues.

Frey's attempt to clarify matters, however, does lead to some problems. His attempt to deny Frank's strafing of the streets of the village denies Frank a part of his character—he was a pilot who liked emptying his guns before returning to base. Frank often strafed ground troops on his missions. By treating this as an event that happened earlier in the day, Frey poses himself a question that he cannot answer—who did strafe the streets of Murvaux on September 29? If not Frank, later in the day, then who? If the number of victims was wrong, wouldn't Fred Zinn have gotten the timing issue straightened out at the same time that he validated the number of dead?

Adding another layer of confusion is that Driggs, like Hall, modified his version of the original Murvaux affidavit, adding in some lines about the treatment of Frank's body that were not in the original document on file at Maxwell AFB's archives. Some newspaper accounts exaggerated even further. For example: "Frank Luke Dies Fighting Entire German Army."

Were all of the French "witnesses" positioned to see the entire series of events? Frank's plane went down some distance from the village. How would this have affected people's perceptions? In one account, the Germans kicked Frank's dead body. From a quarter of a mile away, would a German prodding an armed enemy to make sure he was dead with his foot appear like someone kicking a dead enemy? At best, the closest a witness could have been was 100 yards or so away from the crash site. At the worst, much farther.

Bernard Mangels's account, given in this book in detail from the letters he provided Royal Frey, is fraught with the same issues that Frey had to struggle with in dealing with the French civilians—blurred memories. Mangels was infuriated by the published accounts in American newspapers of how he treated Frank's body. Mangels was a Christian man and felt that he and his men had treated Frank fairly and that the French were altering their version of events to paint him in a bad light.[3]

The Williams diary, a good source of information on the 27th Squadron, is plagued with problems, as well. If one looks at the original document, it is obvious that additions were made and accounts were altered over the years. Williams, while he did not witness the last events of Frank's life, provides his own account of what happened, going so far as to assure any reader that Frank was not shot down but ran out of gas. He bases this claim on his own supposition that Frank was not topped off on September 29th before defying Grant and leaving Rembercourt.[4] A check of the Pruden diary, however, confirms that the advanced field crew gassed up Frank's Spad before he took off. Williams alters his accounts several times, making it difficult to completely rely on some passages.

Adding still more confusion is author Arch Whitehouse's account in *Hun Killer*. Whitehouse fictionalizes the final series of events in Frank's life, and tells of his having made his last stand in the graveyard of Murvaux. Since Whitehouse was a pilot from the AEF at the same time, many people look at this book as "history." It would be best classified as "historical fiction."

In the end, one has to look both at the two French versions of events and Bernard Mangels's version. Somewhere in the middle is the truth.

Checking with sources such as the *The Jasta War Chronology* allows us to invalidate some aspects of the original French version of events. There were no planes shot down near Murvaux that could be attributed to Frank, for example.

The account that I have provided in this book is what I assume to be the best possible version of events based on the data gathered. There are bound to be some who will disagree.

Regardless of what version or hybrid version of the events you, as the reader, wish to assemble, it does not diminish what Frank accomplished. His nomination for the Congressional Medal of Honor was started long before any details of his death were known. He had been hit, most likely from a ricochet, in the chest. The bullet may have been spinning when it hit him as a result of the ricochet. It tore through his lungs—that much was confirmed by the Frey affidavit. He brought down his airplane relatively intact, but it was still a crash landing. As his lungs filled with blood, he managed to climb out. What happened next ... does it really matter?

Other Balloons and Alleged or Bogus Victories

World War I aviation historians are fans of lists. In the years following the Great War, men compiled lists of victories, victims, etc. It is not surprising that there are balloon and aircraft victories that have not been confirmed on those lists.

When looking at Frank's cavalier approach to the chain of command and his placement as the number two American Ace, it is tempting to assign him some of the unclaimed victories. Even Major Hartney felt that Frank had more victories to his credit than have been acknowledged. Yet belief alone did not make it so.

While it is easy to look at a list of potential balloon victories and dates when Frank might have achieved them, and assign them—such approaches are sloppy historical research. Without corroboration in some form, any such effort is conjecture. Corroboration can come in a number of forms, such as written claims of victories or by individuals who witnessed (and documented) Frank scoring a kill.

A good example of a probable but unconfirmed victory is Frank's first kill claim, from August 16, 1918. Frank filed a claim for a victory. There was an airplane driven back to its aerodrome that day in the area where Frank claimed his kill. Hartney's version of events substantiates Frank's claim, as well. It is easy to marry the two stories and the information together. Because the aircraft was not downed on the field of battle, it most likely would not have counted as a true "victory" but it does remove some of the hint that Frank lied about the battle. It is possible that Frank's first "victory" was any number of German aircraft that may have dove for cover and appeared to have crashed from his perspective.

Frank meticulously filed combat reports and claims for his kills. He wrote Cliff Nelson on August 20, 1918, to tell him about his kill to claim a prize offered in San Diego (The Margarita Fisher Award) for the first aviator to graduate from Rockwell Field to down a German in battle. "Was over the lines alone the other day. Ran into a German formation, they did not see me so got into the sun and shot down the last man and then made a grand retreat for home with the whole bunch after me. Have not received it official yet but hope to real soon … . Do you know any San Diego boys with Huns to their credit? Have heard there were several prizes for the first San Diego boys to bring down Huns. Have you heard anything about it? If you have please let me know, for don't think there are any San Diego fellows with Huns to their credit."[5]

If he indeed had a kill prior to that, he most assuredly would have mentioned it in the letter since it would solidify his claim on that prize. He did not. Why? Most likely because he did not have a victory prior to August 16. That is why this version appears in this book. There is ample evidence from Frank's account of the battle, Hartney's corroboration of the account, and the German records of a downed aircraft at the location that Frank identified in his report to suggest that Frank scored a kill on the 16th.

Between August 17 and September 29, he could potentially have racked up uncredited kills. There were more than a dozen enemy aircraft, including balloons, were downed in that time not awarded to pilots in sectors within flying range of Frank's Spad XIII. These could have been lost because of anti-aircraft fire, mechanical failure, or destruction by combat. They may have been taken down by Frank—or they may not have been. Any attempt to tag these victories as Frank's would require tangible evidence, evidence that has not surfaced in ninety years.

The most serious error in Frank's combat record is a false victory sometimes credited to him for September 28, 1918. This appears on a number of lists as a verified kill. A check of the German field reports does not show an aircraft as missing or shot down that day that was not acconted for by other pilot claims. Likewise, none of the primary sources record any combat report filed by Frank referencing this aircraft (a Hannover CL). Why would there be a plane that he wouldn't claim? The short answer is, there wasn't. This is further proven by going through the daily and hourly records of the First Pursuit Group from the Air Force's own archival records. Each flight, mission, and combat claim for each year of the war is noted, and this document does not record Frank flying a mission involving any combat whatsoever against an aircraft on that date. This kill is simply an error that first appeared in the records in the 1960s and has been cited as fact since.

While pundits will try to add to Frank's victory list, this is impossible to do without credible evidence. Even Walter Williams, the unofficial historian for the 27th Squadron, was unable to attribute additional victories to Frank after the war.

We cherish our heroes and seek to make them more than they are, larger than life. This author would have loved nothing more than to enhance the image of Frank Luke, Jr., and to raise his victory total. That would not be fair, either to people who know Frank and his story or to those responsible for recording history.

Was There a Conspiracy by the Government Regarding Frank's Death?

It is possible for fertile minds to speculate that some of the "records" of the events of Frank's last flight were the product of a "conspiracy" by the Air Service to make his final mission seem even more heroic than it was. Some would say that Frank fled an arrest warrant on his last flight. Some would say that the exaggerations of the Murvaux affidavits are part of a deliberate effort to valorize Frank's final mission. As with most good conspiracy theories, the proponents cite the lack of firm evidence as proof of the cover-up.

There was a call to the advance airfield to place Frank under arrest ... at least that was the memory of the man who took the call half a century after the events. The words "under arrest" were most likely another way of saying "grounded." The authority to place an officer under arrest did not reside with the squadron, but with the air group.

Did Frank flee from an arrest warrant? To prove that, one would need evidence of a warrant and proof that Frank was aware of a warrant, and proof that Frank departed to avoid arrest. But this is all conjecture. Added to that, Frank Luke, the young man who fought hardened miners in Arizona and who had faced arrest as a youth, was not a man taken to running from confrontation. There is also no evidence, independently supported, that shows that he was aware that Grant had called down for him. Indeed, the Pruden diary and Hartney's account both suggest quite the opposite.

Are there conflicting versions of events for September 29, 1918? Yes. However interviews provided after the war explain much about these misunderstandings. Major Zinn, in his interview with Phoenix newspapers after the war, explains that the original investigation of the incident at Murvaux was done by an officer—McCormick—who did not speak French. Zinn clarified the testimony further, hardly the act of a government attempting to conspire what occurred.

Most of the overblown accounts of Frank's death came not from the government, but from newspaper and book accounts published after the war. "Luke

Dies Fighting Entire German Army" is a big claim. Often, armchair historians have confused these tabloid boasts with primary source accounts of what occurred. It is a common mistake, but does not support a conspiracy of any sort.

In the 1960s Air Force historian Royal Frey attempted to determine the contents of the note that Frank dropped on his last mission. His correspondence to four men who read the actual note produced four different versions of what the note said. This was a matter of a handful of words, yet their accounts varied. If these accounts didn't agree, why should the accounts of all the witnesses at Murvaux agree?

This author has attempted to cull from the best evidence the best *supportable* series of events. The most persuasive documentation is that from Bernard Mangels from the Lafayette Foundation's archives of Royal Frey's correspondence. But even there, Mangels's account has several errors in it that are contradicted by the Prussian Army reports from that day.

It is popular to cry "conspiracy" and claim that the proof is that the evidence is missing. None of us want to believe that such an energetic young man would die alone behind enemy lines. We all want to believe that greater forces must have been at work against Frank—as if what he faced that day was not enough. Wanting it and proving it, however, are two different things.

* * * *

I began this book to tell the rest of the world about the life of Frank Luke, Jr. I wanted to make sure that people knew him for how he lived and who he was, rather than how he died. For me, the story of Frank's life was never to be found in the village of Murvaux. He only flew over that little village in the last few minutes of his life. Chances are he didn't even know the name of the place where he was shot and eventually died. To him, it was probably not important.

The story of Frank Luke, Jr., was tied up with those of the people around him. I found one of those people, Marie (Rapson) Jackson, and gave her a voice once more, a voice that until now had been unheard. I learned about

Alfred Grant and his cold indifference and basked in the warmth of Harold Hartney. Fred Zinn's persistence in finding the men he had sent to their deaths was not lost on me. I discovered the bond of friendship between Frank and Joe Wehner, a bond that few of us ever find in life. One person, Ivan Roberts, evaded me even from beyond the grave, remaining officially missing in action.

Their stories have been the purview of military aviation buffs and self-proclaimed experts. These people stare at photos for months at a time to debate the time of day that a photograph from 1918 photo was taken at and what direction the wind was blowing at the time rather than getting to know the men themselves. It is easy to forget that these early aviators were men, mortal men. They had strengths, they had flaws. Most importantly, they had great stories to tell. I have simply been lucky enough to get to tell a few of these stories.

All the Great War pilots have flown into the setting sun of the western horizon, where all such pilots go. They count on us to remember them, to retell their stories. In reading *New England Aviators*, I came across a poem that touched me, and I knew it belonged in my book—the last tribute to the aviators of the Great War. It only seems fitting that this memory of those who have given their lives for our freedom be the final word in this book.

"Soldiers of the Wooden Cross"

CHARLES HENRY BRENT

Medals that adorn the uniform tell of courage and endurance and heroism that braved the worst for the cause. Their wearers live to hear the acclaim of their comrades. But there is another decoration, the commonest even though the most distinguished of all: the Wooden Cross that is awarded only to the men who have done the greatest thing that man—yes, even God—can do.

Yonder they lie, along that front where with face to the foe they counted not their lives dear unto themselves but bore the standard of liberty onward. Above their graves rise the sheltering arms of the rough-hewn cross, than which no fitter monument ever reared its form over mortal remains.

Our comrades they were. Our comrades they are. Death was powerless in the face of their bold daring to rob us of them or them of us. They are separated now from us, not by the gaping gulf of time but by a veil so thin that at times we almost see their figures through its waving folds. They live—live gloriously in the land of far distances. Death stripped them of nothing essential. In the permanent society of the world beyond this they think and speak and see and love. They are what they were, except so far as the river of death has washed away the dust of earth and left them cleaner and better by reason of this their last great adventure.

The same dauntless spirit moved them, one and all. There was something dearer than life. To it they gave themselves and their all, and won the decoration of the Wooden Cross.

These men and a myriad more are calling to us, calling to us, and bidding us to carry on. If we would still hold to their comradeship we must display in life the spirit they displayed in death. We must live for the things for which they died. That which we have achieved by victory we must weave into the fabric of the new world and the new age. The Wooden Cross of our dead comrades is for them a glorious decoration. For us it is the banner of our life that is to be. It challenges us to hold more precious than mortal life ideals of honor, justice, and righteousness. After all, the Cross that redeemed the world was a wooden cross, too, was it not? It was no toy or pretty bauble, but a thing of nails and pain and death—and yet a thing of glory.

Bibliography

Books

Allen, Stookie, *Men of Daring*. New York, 1933.

Andrews, C. F., *Profile 17—The Spad XIII C. 1*. Berkshire, 1971.

Archibald, Norman. *Heaven High, Hell Deep*. New York, 1935.

Bacon, H., M. Schrier, P. McGill, and G. Hellinga. *Aerospace: The Challenge*. Maxwell AFB, Alabama, 1989.

Barrett, William. *Sky Fighters of World War One*. Greenwich, Connecticut, 1961.

Bowen, Ezra, *Knights of the Air*. Alexandria, Virginia, 1980.

Bull, Stephen. *Aspects of War: Trench Warfare*. London, 2003.

Clark, Alan. *Aces High: The War in the Air 1914–1918*. London, 1973.

Connors, John. *Spad Fighters in Action, Squadron Books Aircraft Number 93*. Carrollton Texas, 1989.

Cooke, David C. *Sky Battle, 1914–1918: The Story of Aviation in World War I*. New York, 1970.

Driggs, Laurence La Tourette. *Heroes of Aviation*. Boston, 1918–1927.

Durkota, Alan E. *Medal of Honor, Volume 1: Aviators of World War One*. Stratford, Connecticut, 1998.

Dwiggins, Don. *Flying Daredevils of the Roaring Twenties*. London. 1969.

Esposito, Vincent J. *The West Point Atlas of American Wars: Volume II 1900–1953*. New York, 1959.

Farmer, James H. *America's Pioneer Aces*. Upland, California, 2003.

Fitzsimons, Bernard, *Tanks and Weapons of World War One*. London, 1973.

Fitzsimons, Bernard, ed. *Warplanes & Air Battles of World War I*. London. 1973.

Franks, Norman, and Greg Wyngarden. *Fokker D VII Aces of World War 1*. London 2003.

Franks, Norman, and Frank W. Bailey. *Over the Front*. London, 1992.

Franks, Norman, Frank Bailey, and Rick Duiven. *Casualties of the German Air Service*. London, 1992.

Franks, Norman, Frank Bailey, and Rick Duiven. *The Jasta War Chronology*. London, 1998.

Franks, Norman, Hal Giblin, Nigel McCrery. *Under the Guns of the Red Baron*. London, 1995.

Franks, Norman. *Who Downed the Aces in WWI?* London, 1996.

Freidel, Frank. *Over There*. New York, 1994.

Gaetjens, Charles J. *People & Legends of Ajo, Arizona*. Ajo, Arizona. 1992.

Graham, John W. *The Gold Star Mother Pilgrimages of the 1930s*. Jefferson, North Carolina, 2005.

Gregory, Barry. *Argonne 1918: The AEF in France*. New York, 1972.

Guttman, Jon. *Balloon-Busting Aces of WW1*. Oxford, 2005.

Guttman, Jon. *Spad XII/XIII Aces of World War 1*. Oxford, 2002.

Haiber, William, *Frank Luke: The September Rampage*. La Grangeville, NY, 1999.

Hall, Norman S. *The Balloon Buster*. New York, 1966.

Hall, Norman, and Charles Bernard Nordhoff, *The Lafayette Flying Corps, Volumes 1 and 2*. New York, 1920.

Hallion, Richard P. *Rise of the Fighter Aircraft 1914–1918*. New York, 1984.

Hanson, Neil. *Unknown Soldiers: The Story of the Missing of the First World War*. New York, 2006.

Hartney, Harold E. *Up and at 'Em*. New York, 1940.

Hirsch, Phil, and Joseph V. Mizrahi. *Fighting Eagles*. New York, 1956.

Hudson, James J. *Hostile Skies: A Combat History of the American Air Service in World War I*. New York, 1968.

Jackson, Robert. *Fighter Pilots of World War I*. New York, 1977.

Jeffers, Paul H. *Ace of Aces: The Life of Captain Eddie Rickenbacker*. New York, 2003.

Johnson, Don C. *History of Springville*. Springville, Utah, 2003.

Kosek, John, *A Bonfire in the Skies*. Oakland, California, 2000.

Kroll, H. D., Lieutenant. *Kelly Field in the Great War*. San Antonio, Texas, 1919.

Lewis, David W. *Eddie Rickenbacker: An American Hero in the Twentieth Century*. Baltimore, 2005.

Longstreet, Stephen. *Canvas Falcons*. New York, 1979.

Lowell, Lawrence A. *New England Aviators: 1914–1918*. New York, 1919.

Madsen, Brigham D. *The Shoshoni Frontier and the Bear River Massacre*. Salt Lake City, Utah, 1985.

Maitland, Lester J. *Knights of the Air*. New York, 1929.

Michelin and Cie. *The Americans in the Great War, Volume 3: Meuse-Argonne Battle (Illustrated Michelin Guides to the Battle-Fields 1914–1918)*. Reprint. London, 1919, 2000.

Mitchell, Billy. *Memoirs of World War I*. New York. 1960.

Morgan, Len, and R. P. Shannon. *Famous Aircraft: The Planes the Aces Flew, Volume I.* Dallas, Texas, 1964.

Morse, Edwin W. *America in the War: The Vanguard of American Volunteers in the Fighting Lines and in Humanitarian Service.* New York, 1919.

Murdock, John R. *Arizona Characters in Silhouette.* Arizona, 1939.

Musciano, Walter A. *Eagles of the Black Cross.* New York, 1965.

Normau, Aaron. *The Great Air War.* New York, 1929.

Palmer, Svetlana, and Wallis, Sarah. *A War in Words.* London, 2003.

Ralph, Wayne. *Barker VC: The Life, Death and Legend of Canada's Most Decorated War Hero.* Toronto, 1997.

Reynolds, Quentin. *They Fought for the Sky.* New York, 1958.

Rickenbacker, Edward V., and Laurence La Tourette Driggs. *Fighting the Flying Circus.* Chicago, 1997.

Rickenbacker, Edward V. *Rickenbacker.* Greenwich, Connecticut, 1967.

Robertson, Bruce. *Air Aces of the 1914–1918 War.* Letchworth, Hertfordshire. 1959.

Robertson, Linda R. *The Dream of Civilized Warfare: World War I Flying Aces and the American Imagination.* Minneapolis, 2003.

Roosevelt, Theodore. *Rank and File: True Stories of the Great War.* New York, 1928.

Shamburger, Page, and Joe Christy, *Command the Horizon.* New York, 1968.

Sloan, James J. *Wings of Honor.* Atglen, Pennsylvania, 1994.

Smith, Dean. *Arizona Highways Album: The Road to Statehood.* Phoenix, 1987.

Smithers, A. J. *Wonder Aces of the Air.* New York, 1980.

Springs, Elliot White. *War Birds: Diary of an Unknown Aviator.* New York, 1926.

Sterner, C. Douglas. *World War I: The Birth of Military Aviation.* Pueblo, Colorado, 2003.

Strachan, Hew. *The First World War.* London, 2003.

Thayer, Lucien H. *America's First Eagles: The Official History of the U.S. Air Service, A.E.F. (1917–1918).* San Jose, California, 1983.

The Blue Book of Aviation. Los Angeles, 1932.

The History of Arizona Family and Personal History. Volume 3. New York, 1958.

The Phoenician 1917: Yearbook of Union High School. Phoenix, Arizona, 1917.

Thetford, O. G., and Riding, E. J. *Aircraft of the 1914–1918 War.* London, 1946.

Treadwell, Terry C. *America's First Air War.* Shrewsbury, 2000.

VanWyngarden, Greg. *Jagdgeschwader Nr. II Geschwader "Berhold."* Oxford, 2005.

Vaughan, David K. *An American Pilot in the Skies of France: The Diaries and Letters of Percival T. Gates, 1917–1918.* Dayton, Ohio. 1992.

Walker, Dale L. *Mavericks: Ten Uncorralled Westerners.* Phoenix, 1989.

Westermann, Edward B. *Flak: German Anti-Aircraft Defenses 1914–1945.* Lawrence, Kansas, 2001.

Whitehouse, Arch. *Hun Killer.* New York, 1966.
Winter, Denis. *The First of the Few: Fighter Pilots of the First World War.* New York, 1982.

Official Publications

Annual Report of the Secretary of War to the President War Department Fiscal Year Ended June 30, 1923, Washington: Government Printing Office, 1923. 162–174.
Army General Staff. *The Infantry Aeroplane and the Infantry Balloon.* British translation of captured German document dated 1 Sept. 1917. Published by U.S. War Department, 26 Feb. 1918. pp. 15–23. UH150.1I5713.
Maurer, Maurer. *The U.S. Air Service in WWI. Volume III: The St. Mihiel Offensive.* Office of Air Force History, the Albert F. Simpson Historical Research Center, Maxwell AFB, Alabama, 1979.
Maurer, Maurer. *The U.S. Air Service in WWI. Volume IV: Postwar Review.* Office of Air Force History, the Albert F. Simpson Historical Research Center, Maxwell AFB, Alabama, 1979.
Notes and Rules for Pilots and Crews. War Office, Washington, D.C. 1917.
O'Connell, Jr. Charles. *First Fighter. A History of the America's First Team 1918–1983.* Office of TAC History, Headquarters, Tactical Air Command, Langley AFB, Virginia.
The National Aeronautical Collections. Smithsonian Institution National Air Museum, Ninth Edition, 1959. Publication 4255.
The Official Pictorial History of the AAF. Historical Office of the Army Air Forces. Washington, D.C.

Articles

"Balloon Platoon 148: Recollections of a Luftschiffer." *Der Angriff* (May 1981): 10–19.
"Flying with the Balloon Buster of Arizona." *Literary Digest* (August 18, 1928, Vol. XCVIII) 46, 48, 52, 54–55.
"Frank Luke—Balloon Ace." *St. Nicholas* (October 1920): 1094–1099.
"Frank Luke's Elgin (Watch) at U.S. Air Force Museum." *American Aviation Historical Society Journal* (Spring 1985): 23.
"Frank Luke's First Write-Up." *Arizona Magazine* (December 1, 1968): 16–19.
"French Invent New Type of Captive Balloon." *Scientific American* (December 16, 1916): 545.

"Insignia of the 27th Aero Squadron." *The Cross and Cockade Journal* (Summer 1960): 10.

"Interview with Charles R. D'Olive. Formerly Lt. Charles R. D'Olive, 94th Pursuit Squadron, U.S. Air Service." *The Cross and Cockade Journal* (Spring 1960): 3–17.

"Memorial to a Hero." *Arizona Days and Ways Magazine* (May 10, 1959): 29.

"My Most Thrilling Sky Flight." *Sky Fighters*. 107. From Marie Rapson family collection.

"Second Lieutenant Frank Luke Jr. U.S. Army Air Service" *The Annals* (March 2002): 22–23.

"The Role of the Airplane Mechanic." *Scientific American* (March 2, 1918): 184.

Aitken, Ken, "The Aces: Frank Luke." *Aeroplane Monthly* (September 1996): 35.

Bamford, Master Sergeant Hal. "In the Name of Congress ... The Mystery of an Airman." *The Airman.* (November 1958): 39–40.

Barrett, William E. "Frank Luke and the Bravest of the Brave." *Cavalier Magazine* (July 1960): 18–21, 70–79.

Beaubois, Henry "Un Hero Meconnu de la Grand Guerre ... Frank Luke L'Indompatable." *Forces Aériennes Francaises,* (April 1963): 505–520.

Bennett, Tech Sergeant William. "Medal of Honor: Frank Luke Jr." *Journal of the American Aviation Historical Society* (Fall 1975): 210–211.

Bennett, William J. "Research Projects: Frank Luke Jr." *American Aviation Historical Society Journal* (Summer 1970): 121–122.

Bissell, Paul. "Top Man for Luke." *Flying Aces* (October 1934): 12.

Bronnenkant, Lance. "Mentioned in Dispatches—A Frank Discussion." *Over the Front* (No. 1, 2002): 88–91.

Bronnenkant, Lance. "Mentioned in Dispatches—Frank Luke's Aircraft and Photographs Clarification." *Over the Front* (No. 4 2004): 407–409.

Brown, Carol Osman. "A Grand Old House." *Phoenix* (April 1977): 56–57, 82.

Driggs, Laurence La Tourette. "Two Boys of Twenty: The Marvelous Story of Frank Luke, the Greatest Balloon 'Strafer' in the American Army, and His Faithful Friend." *The Ladies' Home Journal* (August 1919): 29–30, 78, 82, 84.

Farris, Elbert W. "Exploring the Air Trails of WWI." *The Cross and Cockade Journal* (Autumn 1986): 284–287.

Fedders, Peter A. "German Air Losses and Victories 1917–1918." *Over the Front* (Winter 2004): 397–406.

Feeney, Bill. "In Their Honor." *Model Airplane News* (December 1961): 18, 38.

Flanagan, Brian P. "Review—Norman Hall's Balloon Buster: Frank Luke of Arizona." *The Cross and Cockade Journal* (Spring 1964): 89–90.

Franzi, Emil and Terri Solty Luke. "WWI Ace Frank Luke, an Enigmatic American Hero." *Arizona Highways* (February 1998): 14–23.

Fredette, Raymond H. Lt. Colonel. "Watch for Burning Balloons" *Air Force Magazine*. (September 1979): 78–82.

Frey, Royal D. "A.E.F Combat Airfields and Monuments in France." *Journal of the American Aviation Historical Society.* (Fall 1972): 195–200.

Frisbee, John L. "The Valor Series: A Man for His Time—The Pilot for Whom Luke AFB Was Named Is a Unique Figure in the History of Air Warfare." *Air Force Magazine* (January 1987).

Grosz, Peter M. "German Captive Balloon Organization." *The Cross and Cockade Journal.* (September 1982): 138–143.

Guttman, Jon. "France's Foreign Legion of the Air. Part 25 Fred W. Zinn—The Searcher ..." *Windsock International.* (July/August 1994): 20–23.

Guttman, Jon. "France's Foreign Legion of the Air." *Windsock International* (Autumn 1989): 15–17, 23.

Guttman, Jon. "Balloon Buster." *Aviation Heritage* (January 1992): 46–53.

Hall, Norman. "The Balloon Buster of Arizona." *Liberty Magazine* (January 14, 1928): 6–11.

Hall, Norman. "The Balloon Buster of Arizona." *Liberty Magazine* (January 21, 1928): 17–22.

Hall, Norman. "The Balloon Buster of Arizona." *Liberty Magazine* (January 28, 1928): 29–33.

Hall, Norman. "The Balloon Buster of Arizona." *Liberty Magazine* (February 11, 1928): 49–53.

Hall, Norman. "The Balloon Buster of Arizona." *Liberty Magazine* (February 18, 1928): 33–44.

Hall, Norman. "The Balloon Buster of Arizona." *Liberty Magazine* (February 25, 1928).

Hall, Norman. "The Balloon Buster of Arizona." *Liberty Magazine* (March 11, 1928).

Hall, Norman. "The Balloon Buster of Arizona." *Liberty Magazine* (March 17, 1928): 62–73.

Hall, Norman. "The Balloon Buster of Arizona." *Liberty Magazine* (March 24, 1928): 71–74.

Hide, David. "Half a Pair of Wings." *The Cross and Cockade Journal* (Fall 1996): 118–134.

Hylands, Dennis. "The Ace from Arizona." *Flypast Magazine* (August 1994): 30–31.

Jordan, Glenn H. "Frank Luke, Jr., Arizona Balloon Buster." *Military History of Texas and the Southwest* (1976): 5–10.

Keller, John W. Captain. "End of An Ace." *The American Legion Magazine* (February 1960): 11–12, 42–44.

Kilduff, Peter. "Balloon Buster." *Wings* (Part 77, 1978): 1524–1525.

Kloss, Walter E. "Joe Wehner, The Other Half of the Famous Balloon Busters." *Over the Front* (Summer 2004): 122–139.

Knight, Clayton. "A Portfolio of Vintage War Birds." *True Magazine* (September 1957): 68–73.

Kosek, John. "The Search For Frank Luke." *Over the Front* (Winter 1998): 332–343.

Kullgren, Thomas E. "The War Diaries and Letters of Walter L. Avery and Lansing C. Holden, Jr.—95th Aero Squadron." *Over the Front* (Fall 1986): 201–230.

Law, James C. Balloon Buster: The Epic Table of Frank Luke: World War I Ace Who Scored 18 Victories in 17 Days." *Royal Air Force Flying Review.* (July 1956): 37–38, 41–42.

Law, James. "They Called Him The Indestructible Balloon Buster."

Leiser, Edward L. "Victory Lists of the Leading Aces: A Study." *The Cross and Cockade Journal* (Winter 1973): 304–308.

Lewis, Jerry D. "A Long Journal … The First Pursuit Group." *Aerospace Historian* (1977): 34–39.

Lucas, Stephen and Alan D. Toelle "Ten Days: Lt. Charles B. Sands, 27th Aero Squadron" *Over the Front* (Summer 2004): 100–117.

Lyman, David. "2nd Lieutenant Frank Luke Jr. U.S. Army Air Service" *The Annals* (September 2002): 75–77.

Mahoney, Tom. "Alvin York and Frank Luke: Legendary WWI Heroes." *American Legion Magazine* (November 1968): 22–23, 50–53.

Miller, Joseph. "Lieutenant Frank Luke America's Heroic War Eagle." *Arizona Highways* (November 1939): 3–7, 25–27.

Miller, Jr., Thomas G. "Air Service Combat Organization." *The Cross and Cockade Journal* (Spring 1962): 1–5.

Miller, Jr., Thomas G. "Table of Organization: Pursuit Aviation." *The Cross and Cockade Journal* (Spring 1962): 37–42.

Noble, J. "Frank Luke Jr., The Balloon Terror: The Miner of Arizona Who Became America's Second War Ace." *Model Aircraft News* (February 1932): 40–43, 46.

O'Neal, Michael. "Lt. Zenos R. Miller, 27th Aero USAS." *Over the Front* (Fall 1996): 194-207.

"Obituaries, Gordon McAlister Jackson (1919)." *Shipmate Magazine* (December 1960): 19.

Ogilvie, Carl B. "The Career of Frank Luke." *Popular Aviation* (November 1932): 280, 282–332.

Parks, James J. "Jerry Cox Vasconcells, Colorado's Only AEF Ace." *Over the Front* (Winter 1988): 321–344.

Puglisi, William R. "The 27th Squadron's Black Day." *The Cross and Cockade Journal* (Autumn 1962): 229–237.
Skinner, Stephen. "Monument to Frank Luke Restored by International Coalition." *Over the Front* (Spring 2001): 87–88.
Stevens, Joseph E. "The Balloon Buster." *American History* (June 2002): 18.
Sufrin, Mark. "Frank Luke—The Great American Air Ace Shot Down 21 Planes in 30 Glorious Hours." *Men* (August 1962): 21–23, 72–77.
Tegler, John H. "A New Hampshire Pursuit Pilot: A Taped Interview with F.I. Ordway of the 27th Pursuit Squadron." *The Cross and Cockade Journal* (Autumn 1963): 217–238.
Tegler, John H. "An Ace with No Victories." *The Cross and Cockade Journal* (Summer 1962): 95–110.
Toelle, Allen D. "Frank Luke's Spad #21" *Over the Front* (Summer 2004): 118–121.
Urwin, Gregory J.W. "The Balloon Buster: The Story of Second Lieutenant Frank Luke Junior." *Air Classics* (December 1978): 15–16, 67–74.
Walker, Dale. "Frank Luke: WWI Balloon Buster." *Aviation Quarterly* (4th Quarter 1978): 370–381.
Wayne, Hugh H. "A Brief History of the 27th Aero Squadron—First Pursuit Group—A.E.F." *The Cross and Cockade Journal* (Summer 1960): 11–42. [Note: Includes documentation on ground crew activities written by Walter S. Williams.]

Newspapers

Arizona Daily Star. "C.A. Luke and Frank Luke Have Sold Their Canal Heading and Right of Way on the Gila Near Painted Rocks to the South Gila Canal Company for $25,000." July 28, 1893.
Boston Daily Globe. "South Lee Aviator Dies in German Prison Camp." January 29, 1919.
Denton Record-Chronicle. "Americans and French Deliver Attack; Capture 500 Near Chateau-Thierry." July 31, 1918.
Denton Record-Chronicle. "Americans Capture Much War Material." July 4, 1918.
Denton Record-Chronicle. "Aviation Attracted Denton Country Boys." July 30, 1919.
Denton Record-Chronicle. "Cadet Aviator Foote Faces Courtmartial on Recovery." February 8, 1918.
Denton Record-Chronicle. "Captain Alfred A. Grant, Twice Cited for Extraordinary Bravery in Air, Returns Home from Overseas Service." April 21, 1919.
Denton Record-Chronicle. "Denton Man Is Cited for Extraordinary Bravery." October 31, 1918.

Denton Record-Chronicle. "Funeral Services for Silas Grant at 10. A.M. Wednesday." February 5, 1918.

Denton Record-Chronicle. "Kaiser's First Denton Victim." February 9, 1918.

Denton Record-Chronicle. "Lieutenant Alfred A. Grant Is Cited for Extraordinary Heroism in Action and Is Awarded U.S. Distinguished Service Cross." Date Unknown.

Denton Record-Chronicle. "Officers Investigating Aeroplane Accident Here." February 9, 1918.

Denton Record-Chronicle. "Texas Aviator Is Made Ace." October 31, 1918.

Denton Record-Chronicle. "Silas Grant Killed When Airplane Falls Near Town." February 4, 1918.

Mohave County Miner. "Luke Party Massacre." March 2, 1912.

Montgomery Advertiser. "Aviators Are Given Honors." November 11, 1918.

Nevada State Journal. "Flying Circus Put on 20 'Big Shows.'" May 11, 1919.

Nevada State Journal. "Hero's Last Message Enroute to Fiancee." May 11, 1919.

New York Times. "A Poor Soldier and a Great Warrior." August 12, 1928.

New York Times. "A Stirring Book on America's World War Aces." April 21, 1940.

New York Times. "Frank Luke: Seventeen Days, Eighteen Huns." May 25, 1919.

Oakland Tribune. "Aero Squadron Did Great Work." April 9, 1919.

Out of Control. "Commanding Officer First Pursuit Group—Our C.O.'s Career." November 19, 1918.

Out of Control. "History of Organisation, Development and Growth of First Pursuit Group." December 13, 1918.

Out of Control. "Lt. Luke's Body Found?" November 7, 1918.

Phoenix Gazette. "Frank Luke Refused to Become Prisoner." September 8, 1978.

Phoenix Gazette. "Luke Dies; Once Built Own Town." July 31, 1968.

Phoenix Herald. "Charles Luke Appointed." February 6, 1888.

Phoenix Herald. "Principle Owner of the Archade Brewery." May 1, 1880.

Salisbury Daily Times. "Flaming Jet Crash in Berlin; Second Pilot 'Chutes to Safely At 30,000 Feet." October 7, 1955.

San Francisco Chronicle. "U.S. Flyer Destroys 11 Balloons." September 21, 1918.

Stars and Stripes. "First Air Depot of the A.E.F At Front Fast Winding Up." May 16, 1919.

Stars and Stripes. "Lieut. Luke Missing, One of Paired Aces. Flyer Does Not Return After Dropping Three Boche Machines." November 1, 1918.

Stars and Stripes. "Officer Who Sent Aviators to Front Now Seeks Missing. Graves of 70 Fliers Who Failed to Return Found by Captain Zinn." March 28, 1919.

The Arizona Gazette. "Aces Up!" February 22, 1928.

The Arizona Gazette. "Aces Up!" February 11, 1928.

The Arizona Gazette. "Aces Up!" February 13, 1928.
The Arizona Gazette. "Aces Up!" February 14, 1928.
The Arizona Gazette. "Aces Up!" February 15, 1928.
The Arizona Gazette. "Aces Up!" February 16, 1928.
The Arizona Gazette. "Aces Up!" February 17, 1928.
The Arizona Gazette. "Aces Up!" February 18, 1928.
The Arizona Gazette. "Aces Up!" February 19, 1928.
The Arizona Gazette. "Aces Up!" February 20, 1928.
The Arizona Gazette. "Aces Up!" February 22, 1928.
The Arizona Gazette. "Exposition." March 5, 1881.
The Arizona Gazette. "Frank Luke's Final Week's on Earth Were Thrilling." May 6, 1919.
The Arizona Gazette. "Official Communication Tells of How Frank Luke Battled to His Death on the Western Front."
The Arizona Gazette. "Proof That Lieut. Luke Died Fighting Entire Army. American Red Cross Cables Authentic Proof of Brave Manner in Which Lieut. Luke Met Death Defending U.S."
The Arizona Republic. "A.C. 'Pidge' Pinney, Prominent Sportsman and Merchant Dies." June 26, 1931.
The Arizona Republic. "Arizona Pioneer (Edwin Luke)." March 14, 1960.
The Arizona Republic. "Balloon Buster's Record Still Unequalled in Annals of War." July 30, 1975.
The Arizona Republic. "Ex-Phoenix Clerk Dies in Coast City." April 15, 1953.
The Arizona Republic. "Floyd Craver Is Killed Under Auto Truck at Ajo." December 16, 1916.
The Arizona Republic. "Frank Luke Jr. Gained Early Reputation as a Football Hero." July 28, 1975.
The Arizona Republic. "Frank Luke: War Hero—Arizonan Also a Family Legend." January 6, 2006.
The Arizona Republic. "Frank Luke's Buddies to Hold Reunion Here." September 18, 1970.
The Arizona Republic. "Hall of Fame Will Induct Frank Luke." October 21, 1975.
The Arizona Republic. "Hero of Arizonian Shines Through Years." March 1941.
The Arizona Republic. "Librarian's Book Recounts Life of Frank Luke." December 6, 1976.
The Arizona Republic. "Luke Remembered." May 10, 1965.
The Arizona Republic. "Luke the Balloon Buster." May 2, 1965.
The Arizona Republic. "Luke Will Celebrate Golden Anniversary." December 30, 1934.

The Arizona Republic. "Nonconformist Frank Luke Was the Despair of His Officers." July 29, 1975.

The Arizona Republic. "WWI Vets Recall Flying Days." October 17, 1970.

The Arizona Republic. "Charles Luke Services Tomorrow." August 1, 1968.

The Arizona Republican. (No Title) October 2, 1896.

The Arizona Republican. "He Lived and Died in 43 Blazing Days of Glory." February 19, 1919.

The Arizona Republican. "Arizona Honors War Dead. Unveiling of Frank Luke Memorial High Light of Celebration." November 12, 1930.

The Arizona Republican. "City and County in Brief." May 20, 1897.

The Arizona Republican. "Frank Luke Jr.—Arizona's Great Ace. Colonel Theodore Roosevelt Recounts Thrilling Exploits of Another Hero of the Service." August 21, 1927.

The Arizona Republican. "Frank Luke Jr. Gets Airplane to His Credit." September 20, 1918.

The Arizona Republican. "Frank Luke Jr. Is Now Ranked as Ace of Air." September 21, 1918.

The Arizona Republican. "Frank Luke Jr. Sets High Record; Balloons Harder to Down Even Than Airplane." September 19, 1918.

The Arizona Republican. "Frank Luke Jr., Arizona's Great Ace." August 21, 1927.

The Arizona Republican. "Frank Luke Killed in Action." November 26, 1918.

The Arizona Republican. "Lieutenant Frank Luke Reaps New Glory on French Line." October 1, 1918.

The Arizona Republican. "Local Briefs." August 16, 1893.

The Arizona Republican. "Local Briefs." July 16, 1893.

The Arizona Republican. "Local Briefs." October 21, 1893.

The Arizona Republican. "Personal Mentions." December 19, 1898.

The Arizona Republican. "Saved a Baby's Life: Little Francis Lount Narrowly Escapes a Horrible Death." July 26, 1894.

The Arizona Republican. "Statehood Meeting." October 21, 1891.

The Arizona Republican. "Statue at Capital to Immortalize Heroic Deeds of Arizona Ace." March 5, 1929.

The Arizona Republican. "Statue at Capitol to Immortalize Deeds of Arizona Ace." March 5, 1929.

The Arizona Republican. "Statue Will Be Unveiled. Celebrants to Witness Special Tribute to Frank Luke Jr." November 11, 1930.

The Arizona Republican. "Tribute Paid in Verse to Frank Luke." November 12, 1930.

The Arizona Republican. "Waiting for Luke During the Night the Famous Boy Aviator Did Not Return." November 1, 1918.

The Arizona Republican. "Hero Medal Has Been Awarded to Frank Luke." April 14, 1919.

The Arizona Republican. "Phoenix 1895—This Was News 75 Years Ago in Phoenix." February 9, 1970.

The Berkshire County Eagle. "Ascension Farm School Sold for All-Year Resort." January 13, 1947.

The Berkshire County Eagle. "Died in Hospital." February 4, 1919.

The Berkshire County Eagle. "Former Farm School Head Honored at Farewell Party. T. Lee Roberts Retired." January 15, 1940.

The Berkshire County Eagle. "Still Carrying On." August 27, 1947.

The Berkshire Eagle. "Mystery of the Berkshire Ace." November 11, 2006.

The Berkshire Evening Eagle. "'Pop' Roberts Dies at 77." October 30, 1947.

The Berkshire Gleaner. "Downs Nine Balloons." November 8, 1918.

The Berkshire Gleaner. "South Lee." August 23, 1918.

The Berkshire Gleaner. "South Lee." March 1, 1918.

The Berkshire Gleaner. "South Lee." November 8, 1918.

The Berkshire Gleaner. "With the Colors." August 20, 1918.

The Chicago Daily Tribune. "Lieut. Luke, The Balloon Ace, Buried Like Dog. Captain Tells of Germans Robbing Body After the Death of Air Hero."

The Denver Post—Empire Magazine. "Colorado's Lone World War Ace: The Jerry Vasconcells Story."

The Denver Post. "Yank Fliers Vanquish Huns in Many Battles and Lead Doughboys Into Verdun Gain." September 29, 1918.

The Detroit Free Press. "'Mad Yankee Ace,' Fights as Lone Hawk Has 18 Victories." November 10, 1918.

The Enquirer and News. "Fred Zinn, 68, Dies; Had Many Careers." October 4, 1960.

The Enquirer and News. "Mainly About Folks" October 12, 1941.

The Fort Wayne News and Sentinel. "Wins Air Victories on Thimbles of Gasoline: American Aviator Gets Three Enemy Balloons and an Airplane." September 20, 1918.

The Fort Wayne News and Sentinel. "Young Americans Starring In Air." October 9, 1918.

The Los Angeles Express. "Heroic Feats of Americas Second Ace Told: Officer Who Inspired Luke's Flight to War Glory is LA Visitor." February 21, 1928.

The Oakland Tribune. "Aces Up." January 25, 1928.

The Oakland Tribune. "Tears for a Comrade." August 20, 1962.

The Oxnard Daily Courier. "American Aviators' Record Day." August 2, 1918.

The Paper. "Now and Then." April 28, 1973.

The Phoenix Gazette. "Hall of Fame Honors Due Frank Luke Jr." October 21, 1975.
The Prescott Courier. [No title.] October 11, 1885.
The Rocky Mountain News. "An Arizona War Eagle" July 24, 1927.
The Rocky Mountain News. "Colorado Sported World War I Ace." March 7, 1993.
The Rocky Mountain News. "Denver War Birds." May 29, 1927.
The San Diego Union. "Commanding Officer's Duties Are Increased." October 6, 1918.
The San Diego Union. "Daring Aviator Missing Since October 20: Lieut. Frank Luke Fails to Return From Night Bombing Expedition." October 28, 1918.
The San Diego Union. "Frank Luke, U.S. Ace, May Be an Arizona Boy but San Diego Too Has a Real Claim on Him." September 24, 1918.
The San Diego Union. "Planes Will Fly to Phoenix in Honor of Ace." June 13, 1919.
The San Francisco Examiner. "American Night Flyer Downs 3 Enemy Balloons." October 3, 1918.
The San Francisco Examiner. "U.S. Flyer Destroys 11 Balloons." September 21, 1918.
The Southwesterner. "Frank Luke Was a Loner From Phoenix Who Loved to Fight His Own Way—and He Proved It Right." December 1964.
The Syracuse Herald, Monday. "Luke Downed 25 German Aircraft in 10 Day Period: Hun Gasbags Are the Special Hobby of 'The Nut.'" October 28, 1918.
The Tucson Daily Citizen. "Arizona Album: Phoenix' Luke Filed Named For Him." July 26, 1963.
Wichita Daily Times. "Denton Airman Decorated with Service Cross." October 29, 1918.
Wisconsin State Journal. "Old Flying Heroes Bid Farewell to a Comrade." August 20, 1962.

Archival Resources

National Museum of the United States Air Force
Luke Archival Collection: 1974–D09
Document: Officers Personnel Report, Frank Luke, April 1918
Telegram: Frank Luke to Mother, March 25, 1918
Letter: Frank Luke to sister Anna, February 13, 1917
Newspaper Article (unknown press): "Lieutenant Frank Luke, New Ace, Has Got Six Kills Since September 2"
Certificate: Royal Italian Army Cross of Military Valor, December 9, 1921

Luke Archival Collection: 1964–D06
Laminate Flying Map used by Frank Luke

Luke Archival Collection: 1980-D08
Senior Class Book

Smithsonian National Air and Space Museum Archives Division
Biographical Technical File CL-915000-01
Assorted articles and documentation relating to Frank Luke, Jr.

Archives—Aeronautics Division
A19500169000AER01
A19500169000AER02
Aircraft material (fabric) cut from airplanes by Frank Luke, Jr.

National Archives and Records Administration
Record Group 120 (Records of the American Expeditionary Forces) Modern Military Records Unit (NWCTM)
Gorrell's History of the AEF Air Services 1917–1919
Series C Tactical Units—Volume 7
Series E Squadron Histories, Volumes 6 and 27
Series I Orly Records. Volume 21
Series M Miscellaneous Volumes 11–12, 17–18
Series N First Army Volumes 2–5

Signal Corps Photographs—Records Group 65

Records Group 92
Burial Records
   Frank Luke, Jr.
   Ivan A. Roberts
   Joseph Wehner

Records Group 165
Prussian 7th Army War Diary—1918

Nachrichtenblatt der Luftftreittrafte (Air Intelligence Reports)

Prussian 5th Army War Diary—September 23–October 31, 1918
Addendum: Prussian 5th Army War Diary
Addendum: Prussian 5th Army War Diary—Orders to Balloon and Jasta Units 1918

Records Group 65
Investigative Case Files of the Bureau of Investigation, 1908–1922
Case File on Lieutenant Joseph Fritz Wehner

Maps:
Prussian 7th Army Placement and Reserve Area (Murvaux, Dun, to Sivry)
Placement of Prussian 5th Army (Including Air and Balloon Elements)

U.S. Census Data:
1920
1930
1940
1950

Military Records and Pension Files:
Lorenz Luke
Charles Luke

National Personnel Records Center
Military Records Request—Frank Luke, Jr. While detailed records were not available due to a fire at the facility, some materials on Frank Luke's burial were provided.

Air Force Historical Research Agency
Microfilm30531 Index 1383. Diary of Corporal Walter S. Williams, 27th Squadron, U.S. Air Service, AEF. Diary notes covering squadron history including observations regarding Frank Luke, Jr.
Microfilm B0036 Alford, James S. Major. *The History of the 1st Fighter Group, Volume 1—The 1st Pursuit Group in World War I. Chronology of the First Pursuit Group, 1918.* Air University Archives, Maxwell AFB, Alabama, 1959.

Library of Congress
Manuscript Division, the Billy Mitchell Collection. Mitchell's journal manuscript of the events during the Great War including details of his witnessing of Frank Luke in combat.

Arizona State Library, Archives and Public Records
History and Archives Division
MG-64 Frank Luke Junior Collection
Series 1 Correspondence from Frank, Jr., to his mother
Series 2 Correspondence from Frank, Jr., to his father
Series 3 Correspondence from Frank, Jr., to his sister Eva
Series 4 Correspondence to Frank, Jr., from family
Series 5 Miscellaneous correspondence
Series 6 Ephemera

Vertical File Frank Luke Junior
Vertical File Frank Luke Senior
Vertical File Charles Augustus Luke
- Alum Springs Massacre in Knights Canyon near Mineral Park. Note from John Riggs and A. M. McDuffie, September 27, 1911.
- History. Luke, Charles Augustus
Vertical File Charles Luke
Vertical File Edwin Luke

RG6 1879-1898 28:406 File Record group on Adolph Liebnow

Massachusetts Aviation Society
Information on Joseph Wehner

Phoenix Museum of History
General background information on Phoenix history

Missouri Historical Society
Joe Bronz Album: World War I

United States Army War College and Carlisle Barracks
U.S. Army Heritage and Education Center
U.S. Army Military History Institute
The United States Army in the World War 1917–1919. Historical Division, U.S. Army, Washington, D.C., 1948.
Articles on Experiences and Recommendations by Skilled Pilots of the 27th Aero Squadron.

Other assorted collections and translations

Willard Library Battle Creek
Source Material on Frederick Zinn

Arizona State University
Department of Archives and Special Collections
Arizona Transcript Collection
The Hayden Collection
   The George Luhr Oral History Transcript
   Assorted Articles and Letters

National Aviation Hall of Fame
Inductee Information 1975, Frank Luke Junior

Phoenix Public Library
Burton Barr Central Library, Arizona History Room
Union High School Material
Vertical Files Frank Luke Junior
Vertical File Frank Luke Senior
Vertical File Charles Luke

San Diego High Schools Alumni Archives
Student Records, Marie Rapson, Yearbook collection, 1916–1919

Ajo Historical Society
Collections—Mining Camps—1915–1917
Local Histories and Personalities

Ajo Copper News Archives
Archives 1916–1918

University of New Mexico Archives
Periodical Archives

Wings Over the Rockies Museum
Museum Archives and Library

The Lafayette Foundation
Personal Collections of Doctor Parks
Personal Collection of Royal Frey
Personal Connection of 27th Balloon Association

United States Air Force Academy Library
Walter Williams Collection
John Sherry Collection

United States Military Academy at West Point
Library, Archives Division
Records of Enrollees, U.S. Military Academy

Denton Public Library System
Emily Fowler Library
Genealogy/Special Collections
File on Alfred Grant
Denton High School Yearbooks 1910–1912 (The Broncos)

Wurttembergische Landesbibliother Bibliothek Fűr Zeitgeschichte—Stuttgart Germany
Archival Collection

San Diego Aerospace Museum
San Diego Flying Days
Vertical File—Frank Luke Jr.

The National Archives (U.K.)
RFC Casualty Lists September-November 1918

The San Francisco Public Library
Archives of *San Francisco Chronicle* and *San Francisco Examiner*

Lee Library Association, Lee Massachusetts
Archives of the Berkshire Gleaner—Articles on Ivan Roberts

Massachusetts National Guard Museum Archives
World War I Records for Ivan Roberts and Joseph Wehner

Berkshire County Historical Society
"See All the People." By Florence Conslati (Reference to Ivan Roberts)

Oklahoma Historical Society
US Census Data, 1930, Tulsa
1929, 1930, 1931 Tulsa City Directory

Archives—San Diego Tribune

Joel D. Valdez Main Library—Ajo, Arizona
Historical files—Frank Luke, Jr.

Ministère de la Défense France
French Military Archives
Squadron Records

University of Texas at Dallas, the George H. Williams WWI Aviation Library, Eugene McDermott Library, Special Collections Department
Records and Photographs Regarding Leutnant Buchner and Leutnant von Hantelmann
File Records on Frank Luke, Jr.

Wicomico County Public Library
Materials Relating to the Death of Lt. Commander Donald Gordon Jackson, USN

Joel D. Valdez Main Library, Tucson, Arizona
Reference materials relating to Ajo Arizona history

Sharlot Hall Museum
Love Collection

The Library of the College of Mary Washington, Fredericksburg Campus

The United States Naval Academy, Nimitz Library
Special Collections and Archives Division
William W. Jeffries Memorial Archives
Lucky Bag (1919)

Berkshire Athenaeum
Historical Information on Ivan A. Roberts

DUP (Daughters of Utah Pioneers) Museum & Historical Society
Springville Historical Society
Information on the Battle of Spanish Forks

The Comité de la Croix Rouge
Central Tracing Agency
Records for Joseph Wehner, Frank Luke, and Ivan Roberts

University of Massachusetts
W. E. B. Du Bois Library
Special Collections and University Archives
"Massachusetts Agricultural College in the War," *The M.A.C. Bulletin*, Vol. XIII,
May 1921, No. 4, pp. 60–61 Ivan Andrew Roberts—Class of 1920
Massachusetts Agricultural College War Service Records—Ivan Andrew Roberts
Letters from Thomas Lee Roberts
Letter from Captain Alfred Grant to Thomas Lee Roberts

The Museum of Flight
Dahlberg Center for Military Aviation History
The Joseph Wehner Collection

Belchertown Historical Association
The Stone House Museum, Belchertown, Massachusetts
Materials on Dorothy Thompson and Ivan Roberts

The Museum of Flight
Dahlberg Center for Military Aviation History
Display and Letters of Joseph Wehner
Files on Frank Luke, Jr.

Phillips Exeter Academy
Archives
Materials on Joseph Wehner

Notes to Chapters

Abbreviations Used in the Notes

NARA   National Archives Records Administration

Prologue

1   *The Arizona Republican.* "Arizona Honors War Dead. Unveiling of Frank Luke Memorial High Light of Celebration." November 12, 1930. This is part of a speech by Governor Phillips dedicating the statue of Frank Luke in front of the State Capitol on the previous day, Armistice Day 1930. Several sources erroneously place Eddie Rickenbacker at the dedication as a speaker. This is a misconception. Months earlier, Mr. Rickenbacker was interviewed by the *New York Times* and provided several generous quotes regarding Frank Luke. These quote are often associated with the dedication of the statue.

2   Lafayette Foundation. Royal Frey Collection. Also see Hall, *The Balloon Buster*, p. 108. Whitehouse. *Hun Killer*, p. 173. Note: There are three versions of this account that have seen print. The Arch Whitehouse account indicated that Captain Grant swore to give Luke the "Legion of Honor." Other accounts, including those printed in the *New York Times*, indicated that he claimed Luke was going to be given "The Medal of Honor." It is most likely that Grant would have recommended him for the Distinguished Service Cross at this point, not the Medal of Honor.

3   Annual Report of the Secretary of War to the President War Department Fiscal Year Ended June 30, 1923, Washington, D.C.: Government Printing Office, 1923. pp. 162–174 (War Decorations) and Hall, *The Balloon Buster*, p. 118. While Captain Rickenbacker's documentation pre-dates Luke's, he did not receive the medal until 1930. The other two Army Air Service aviators to receive their medals did so

in 1922. This count does not reflect the Navy and Marine aviators who received the medal as well.

⁴ Jordan, Glenn H. "Frank Luke, Jr., Arizona Balloon Buster." *Military History of Texas and the Southwest* (1976): 10.

Frank's numerous nicknames come from a variety of sources and articles listed in the bibliography of this book.

Chapter One

Note: *The opening quotation is courtesy of the Arizona State Library, Archives and Public Records, History and Archives Division MG-64 Frank Luke Junior Collection, Series 1.*

¹ Hartney. *Up and at 'Em.* p. 183.

² Reynolds. *They Fought for the Sky.* p. 216. Oddly enough, this is the only account I have found that directly mentions the major's presence on the flight, but it does match some of National Archives information, which acknowledges that he did fly a mission that day.

³ Hartney. *Up and at 'Em.* p. 245.

⁴ Flight Operations Report, American Expeditionary Forces Headquarters, 27th Squadron, S.C., Operations Office, August 16, 1918.

⁵ Details on the Spad XIII aircraft construction and specifications come from two sources: Andrews, *Profile 17—The Spad XIII C.1.*, and Connors, *Spad Fighters in Action, Squadron Books Aircraft Number 93.*

⁶ Headquarters, 27th Squadron S.C., July 24, 1918, General Orders, Major Harold Hartney, Arizona State Library, Archives and Public Records, History and Archives Division, MG-64 Frank Luke Junior Collection. This document, provided to the Arizona Archives by Lieutenant Martin after the war, was a set of orders apparently posted when the Spad XIIIs were provided to the 27th Squadron. This remarkable document provides additional details such as the startup procedure for the Spad.

⁷ Flight Operations Report, American Expeditionary Forces Headquarters, 27th Squadron, S.C., Operations Office, August 16, 1918.

⁸ NARA Combat Report, August 16, 1918. Lieutenant Luke Reports.

⁹ Ibid. The details of this engagement were drawn from a wide range of sources, the primary one being Luke's own combat report and the details provided in *Hartney's Up and at 'Em*, pp. 245–247. Hartney's version had him engaging a formation of enemy aircraft and forcing one of them to fall behind. This happens to mesh well

with Luke's account in his combat report. Details of the combat report from the National Archives are as follows:

Lieutenant Luke reports:
My machine was not ready so left an hour after formation, expecting to pick them up on the lines, but could not find formation. Saw Hun formation and followed, getting above into the sun. The formation was string out leaving one machine way into the rear. Being way above the formation I cut my motor and dove down on the rear man, keeping the sun direction behind. Opened fire at about 100 fee(t), keeping both guns on him until within a few feet of them, then zoomed away. When I next saw him he was on his back, but looked as if he was going to come out of it so I dove again holding both guns on him. Instead of coming out of it, he sideslipped off the opposite side much like a falling leaf and went down on his back. My last dive carried me out of reach of other machine that turned about. They gave chase for about five minutes and turned back for I was leading them. My last look at the plan shot down convinced me he struck the ground for he was still on his back about 1500 meters below. On coming home about our lines saw four E.A., started to get into the sun and above but they saw me and dove towards me. I peaked for home. Three turned back and the other came on. I kept out of range by peaking slightly, and he followed nearly to Coincy where he saw one of the 95th boys and turned about. The 95th man could have brought down this E.A. if he had realized quick enough that it was an E.A. The machine was brought down North East of Soissons in the vicinity of Joui and Vailly. Do not know the exact location as this being my first combat did not notice closely but know it was some distance within German territory, for archies followed me for about ten minutes on my way back. My motor was fixed at Coincy and filled with gas and oil. Also found out that our formation had been held up by the Salmson that it was to escort and had just started. So left the ground to find them. Flew at about 5000 meters from Soissons past Fismes, but did not see the formation. Saw one Salmson but no enemy E.A. Returned Home.

[10] Flight Operations Report, American Expeditionary Forces Headquarters, 27th Squadron, S.C., Operations Office, August 16, 1918.

[11] Hartney. *Up and at 'Em.* p. 246.

[12] Ibid.

[13] Hartney. *Up and at 'Em.* p. 246. Reynolds. *They Fought for the Sky.* p. 217. While Reynolds' account was probably based on Hartney's written word, Hartney's own words only appear in his account in *Up and at 'Em.*

[14] Hall. *The Balloon Buster.* p. 68.

[15] Franks, Bailey Duiven. *Casualties of the German Air Service.* pp. 297 and 374. Co-author Rick Duiven provided insights as to how to interpret the data and

to narrow this list considerably. Leutnant Alex Jagenberg was recorded as dead at Noyon, which is in the Soissons valley within a dozen kilometers of the vicinity that Frank's combat report references. Oddly enough, after the war when kill-counts for pilots were "modified" to inflate some records—no one seemed to associate this kill to Frank's record. Leutnant Jagenberg was listed as an observer from the town of Solingen and was twenty-seven years old.

There are a myriad of possible reasons why this kill never ended up on Luke's record. There may not have been witnesses who saw the aircraft get shot down. It is possible that some other pilot or ground unit claimed this kill or was, in reality, responsible for it. The proximity of Jagenberg's downing to the region Luke outlined in his August 16 combat report, however, makes it seem likely that Leutnant Jagenberg was Luke's first true combat kill.

[16] Whitehouse. *Hun Killer.* p. 182.

[17] Driggs *Heroes of Aviation.* p. 275.

[18] Rickenbacker and Driggs. *Fighting the Flying Circus.* pp. ix–x. The 1967 reprint of this book, ghost-written for Rickenbacker by Driggs just after the war, painstakingly makes notations of numerous mistakes and blatant additions to Eddie Rickenbacker's exploits. This annotated version spells out how Driggs altered the Rickenbacker book to help inflate sales and stir anti-German sentiments among readers.

Driggs only once in the telling of the Frank Luke story mentions that Luke allegedly lied about his first combat action. In his widely read article on Luke and Wehner, he never mentions this. Given the historical significance of such a lie, if it happened, one would think that Driggs would have mentioned this often. (Driggs. "Two Boys of Twenty: The Marvelous Story of Frank Luke, the Greatest Balloon 'Strafer' in the American Army, and His Faithful Friend." *The Ladies' Home Journal.* pp. 29–30, 78, 82, 84.)

[19] Walker, Dale. "Frank Luke: WWI Balloon Buster." *Aviation Quarterly.* p. 373.

Chapter Two

[1] The background of the early Luke family and Charles Luke comes from a variety of sources. Census data was used, and the military records of Charles Luke provided a wealth of information on his career. The book *History of Springville* (Johnson, Don C. *History of Springville.* Springville, Utah, 2003. pp. 61–67) provided by the DUP Museum in Springville was useful in recreating the engagement at Spanish Forks. The information on the massacre at Bear River comes from Brigham D. Madsen's *The Shoshoni Frontier and the Bear River Massacre.*

[2] The material on Charles Augustus Luke's background comes from the Arizona State Library, Archives and Public Records, Vertical File Charles Augustus

Luke. References were cross-checked with newspaper accounts. The Luke Party Massacre is documented as the Alum Springs Massacre in Knights Canyon near Mineral Park. In the files is a note from John Riggs and A. M. McDuffie, from September 27, 1911, detailing the events. Later versions of Charlie's version appear in his vertical file. A further version can be found in *Mohave County Miner*. "Luke Party Massacre." March 2, 1912.

3 Lorenz Luke's (aka Frederick Russell's) records were obtained from the National Archives. His pension file provides a great deal of information on his service with the 14th New York Cavalry Regiment. It does not reference his re-enlistment under his natural name in the 7th New York Infantry. It is most likely that Lorenz was enlisting the second time to obtain the bounty and did not want to expose that fact in later years when applying for his pension.

4 *The Arizona Republican*, July 18, 1893.

5 *The Arizona Republican*, October 21, 1893. Also an article on August 16, 1893, which refers to Frank Luke's and R. E. Kirkland's "famous silver lode."

6 *The Arizona Republican*, November 8, 1891.

7 Federal Census records 1900, 1920, Phoenix, Arizona. The history of the Luke family is compiled from a number of sources including: Hall. *The Balloon Buster*. pp. 4–5; Haiber. *Frank Luke—The September Rampage*. pp. 17–27; Whitehouse. *Hun Killer*. pp. 27–28. Also research with Arizona State Library, Archives and Public Records, the Phoenix Public Library, and *The History of Arizona Family and Personal History. Volume 3*.

8 Hall. *The Balloon Buster*. pp. 7–8. This account was of the few that were done in the book where the material was researched through discussions with the family and friends of Frank in 1927 during Hall's visit to Phoenix. The Luke family, in a later newspaper article, substantiated that the stories regarding Frank's childhood in the book were, for the most part, accurate.

9 Smith *Arizona Highways Album—The Road to Statehood*. pp. 1–38.

10 Per census and draft records at the National Archives and Records Administration; William G. Elder enlisted in the U.S. Army. Furthermore, he was a baseball player in high school, and owned and personally managed several construction businesses. According to *The Phoenician 1917—Yearbook of Union High School*, Elder was athletic enough to be a shortstop on the baseball team. Norman Hall created the myth of Bill Elder being a hunchback and provided the contrast to Frank who was his constant defender. Whatever impairments Mr. Elder had, they were not enough for the Army to outright reject him nor were they enough to prevent him from having a very full and active life. It is difficult to imagine the Army taking a hunchbacked youth into the service. While Hall's account adds to the illusion surrounding Frank, it is not an accurate depiction

of Mr. Elder. Bill Elder takes on the name of "Will" Elder in the Whitehouse version of the story. The Luke family has indicated they tend to place more confidence in the Normal Hall version of events—though they are similar. Frank's letters home to Bill were addressed "Bill" and Hall refers to him as "Bill."

11 Hall. *The Balloon Buster*. pp. 21–22. Whitehouse. *Hun Killer*. pp. 30–34. This story is relatively consistent in each telling of it in numerous articles etc. Note: Hall. *The Balloon Buster*. pp. 17–19. Hall's recounting of this story was based on his trip to Phoenix after the war, meeting with Bill Elder and members of the Luke family. This is further substantiated in Joseph Miller's "Lieutenant Frank Luke, America's Heroic War Eagle." *Arizona Highways* (November 1939): 3–7, 25–27. This account was based not on Hall's version of events but an interview with the Luke family in 1939.

12 Hall. *The Balloon Buster*. pp. 33–34.

13 *The Arizona Republican*. "Frank Luke, Jr., Gets Airplane to His Credit" September 20, 1918. Also validated in *The Phoenician 1917—Yearbook of Union High School*, which has a photograph of Frank shaving one of the victim's heads.

14 *The Arizona Republic*, "Frank Luke Jr. Gained a Reputation as a Football hero, by Lowell Parker," July 28, 1975. The description of the incident itself was drawn from a wide range of sources and articles on the subject. Apparently, the crowd that had gathered was quite large, photographs were taken of the incident, and it was quite the local stir for a day or so in Phoenix.

15 Ibid.

16 Norman Hall, "The Balloon Buster of Arizona," *Liberty Magazine*, January 28, 1928, p. 34.

17 Census and city directory records show that Charles Luke and his wife Eunice owned a house in Ajo, and Frank is known to have worked in Charles's hardware store, which was a branch of the Palace Hardware store in Phoenix, *The Arizona Republic*. "Charles Luke Services Tomorrow." August 1, 1968.

This, combined with information from discussions with John Luke, makes it doubtful that a close family like the Luke's would have had Frank living in a tent when he could have easily stayed with his brother's family. This is further substantiated by letters written by Frank in 1915–16 to his mother. Arizona State Library, Archives and Public Records, MG-64 Frank Luke Junior Collection, Series 1.

18 Letter to Mr. Frank Luke, Sr., from Herbert Strickland, the Acquisition Mining Company of Phoenix, Arizona, November 18, 1918. At this period Frank Luke, Jr., was still missing in action, but some details of his death were reaching

a variety of source. At this point Mr. Strickland was unaware of Frank's fate. The last line of the letter was, "My son Rooney is much concerned for his good friend Frank Luke." This letter was one of many that were sent to the Luke family when newspaper articles ran regarding Frank's feats in France.

[19] Draft Card data, National Archives. There were three men named Breen who were the right age to be the infamous "Irishman Breen," from the legends of Frank's youth. Maurice Breen was younger than Frank, and hence did not fit the story—supposedly Frank fought a slightly older man. There is another James Breen in addition to James Joseph Breen, but James Joseph listed his occupation as "miner," whereas James Breen of Douglas, Arizona, regarded himself as, "unemployed," hardly the tough miner experienced in the Colorado, New Mexico, and Arizona mines portrayed in the Norman Hall accounts.

[20] Hall. *The Balloon Buster*. pp. 24–25.

[21] Hall. *The Balloon Buster*. pp. 28–30. It is important to note that Floyd Craver was never interviewed directly by Norman Hall for his work in 1928 (reprinted in book form in 1966). Craver was killed shortly after the war in a truck accident. It was further validated by Frank's own letters and the article on Craver's death, *The Arizona Republic*. "Floyd Craver is Killed Under Auto Truck at Ajo." December 16, 1916. This detailed his experience as a cartoonist.

[22] Death certificate, Floyd Craver, Arizona State Board of Health. It is important to note that Norman Hall's account has Craver dying earlier in the year, which then served as the impetus for Frank to close the dance hall. The archival evidence indicates differently and is what is presented here. Further information is taken from *The Arizona Republic*. "Floyd Craver is Killed Under Auto Truck at Ajo." December 16, 1916.

[23] Arizona State Library, Archives and Public Records, History and Archives Division. MG-64 Frank Luke Junior Collection, Series 1.

[24] Roosevelt, *Rank and File—True Stories of the Great War*. There is a note in this book stating that Frank's father, Frank, Sr., had been pressed into military service in pursuit of Geronimo as a militiaman. Chances are he did take up a rifle in defense of his home and town, but not as a true member of a formalized military effort. A check of the National Archives records turns up Frank Lukes of approximately the right age, both of whom served in the Civil War, neither of whom ended up in Arizona.

[25] Gaetjeas, *People & Legends of Ajo, Arizona*. Page 35.
Note: The family history and Frank's enlistment were confirmed with materials in Arizona State Library, Archives and Public Records, MG-64 Frank Luke Junior Collection.

Chapter Three

Note: *The opening quotation in the chapter comes from Kelly Field in* The Great War, *San Antonio, Texas, 1919. p. 22.*

1. Hudson. *Hostile Skies, a Combat History of the American Air Service in WWI.* pp. 2–3. The overall history of the Air Service comes from a variety of sources, including *Wings of Honor* and James Hudson's *Hostile Skies.*
2. Hartney. *Up and at 'Em.* p. 21.
3. Franks, Bailey, and Duiven. *The Jasta War Chronology.* p. 31. Numerous books printed in the 1920s substantiate Hartney's claim that the Red Baron shot him down. Most of those accounts are not based on archival evidence, but were built off of newspaper accounts or other inaccurate accounts.
4. Hartney. *Up and at 'Em,* 1940. p. 87.
5. Ibid.
6. Hudson. *Hostile Skies, a Combat History of the American Air Service in WWI.* p. 7.
7. Hudson. *Hostile Skies, a Combat History of the American Air Service in WWI.* p. 29.
8. *Denton Record-Chronicle.* "Funeral Services for Silas Grant at 10 A.M. Wednesday." February 5, 1918, and *Denton Record-Chronicle.* "Kaiser's First Denton Victim." February 9, 1918, and *Denton Record-Chronicle.* "Officers Investigating Aeroplane Accident Here." February 9, 1918, and *Denton Record-Chronicle.* "Silas Grant Killed When Airplane Falls Near Town." February 4, 1918. Note: The accounts of Alfred Grant and his visits to his house were covered both in the article by Dr. Parks on the flying career of Jerry Cox Vasconcells and the newspaper accounts of Grant's progress in the war and the death of his brother, Silas. Even decades after the war, Jerry Vasconcells was convinced that Grant was a West Point graduate.
9. James J. Parks. "Jerry Cox Vasconcells, Colorado's Only AEF Ace." *Over the Front* (Winter 1988): 321–344.
10. *Denton Record-Chronicle.* "Kaiser's First Denton Victim." February 9, 1918.
11. Sloan. *Wings of Honor.* pp. 53–57. Also James Norman Hall and Charles Bernard Nordhoff, *The Lafayette Flying Corps, Volumes 1 and 2.* 1920. pp. 513–515.

Chapter Four

1. Arizona State Library, Archives and Public Records, History and Archives Division. MG-64 Frank Luke Junior Collection.
2. Ibid.
3. Arizona State Library, Archives and Public Records, History and Archives Division. MG-64 Frank Luke Junior Collection. Letter to Frank's mother on November 11, 1917.

4 Lafayette Foundation. Letter to Mr. Merle Rice, Regarding History of the 27th Squadron, May 8, 1970.

5 Arizona State Library, Archives and Public Records, History and Archives Division. MG-64 Frank Luke Junior Collection.

6 Harry Starkey Aldrich. "Frank Luke—Balloon Ace." *St. Nicholas* (October 1920): 1094.

7 Hall. *The Balloon Buster.* pp. 43–44.

8 United States Air Force Academy SMS 231 John Sherry Collection.

9 *The San Diego Union.* "Frank Luke, U.S. Ace, May Be an Arizona Boy but San Diego Too Has a Real Claim on Him." September 24, 1918.

10 Hall. *The Balloon Buster.* p. 45.

11 Arizona State Library, Archives and Public Records, History and Archives Division. MG-64 Frank Luke Junior Collection. Taken from letter to Frank's mother January 10, 1918.

12 Interviews with Douglas Jackson regarding stories his mother, Marie, regarding Frank Luke.

13 San Diego Aerospace Museum, San Diego Flying Days, October 1918.

14 National Museum of the United States Air Force, Luke Archival Collection: 1974-D09.

15 National Museum of the United States Air Force, Luke Archival Collection: 1974-D09. Personnel Report: Frank Luke Jr.

16 "Frank Luke, Jr., War Hero Arizonan Also a Family Legend." David Madrid, *The Arizona Republic.* January 6, 2006. This incident was also discussed in detail in *Phoenix Magazine*, April 1977, "A Grand Old House."

17 Arizona State Library, Archives and Public Records, History and Archives Division. MG-64 Frank Luke Junior Collection. Excerpt from a letter to Frank's mother, February 19, 1918.

18 Marie Jackson Collection. Letter from Frank to Marie.

19 Arizona State Library, Archives and Public Records, History and Archives Division. MG-64 Frank Luke Junior Collection. Excerpt from a letter to Frank's mother.

20 Lafayette Foundation. Letter from Jessie Saunders to Royal Frey, December 10, 1963.

21 Parks, James J. "Jerry Cox Vasconcells, Colorado's Only AEF Ace." *Over the Front* (Winter 1988): p. 325.

22 United States Air Force Academy SMS 231 John Sherry Collection.

23 San Diego High Schools Alumni Archives, Student Records, Marie Rapson, Yearbook collection, 1916–1919.

Chapter Five

Note: Opening quotation taken from a letter to Joe's sister Hazel in the Joseph Wehner Collection, the Museum of Flight, Dahlberg Center for Military Aviation History.

[1] James J. Sloan. *Wings of Honor.* p. 164.
[2] Tegler, John H. "An Ace with No Victories." *The Cross and Cockade Journal* (Summer 1962): 96.
[3] Richard P. Hallion, *Rise of the Fighter Aircraft 1914–1918.* p. 164.
[4] Hartney. *Up and at 'Em.* p. 126.
[5] Hall. *The Balloon Buster.* p. 50.
[6] Harry Starkey Aldrich, "Frank Luke—Balloon Ace." *St. Nicholas* (October 1920): p. 1094.
[7] Marie Jackson Collection. Letter from Frank to Cora Rapson.
[8] Arizona State Library, Archives and Public Records, History and Archives Division. MG-64 Frank Luke Junior Collection.
[9] Hall. *The Balloon Buster.* p. 52.
[10] Arizona State Library, Archives and Public Records, History and Archives Division. MG-64 Frank Luke Junior Collection. Excerpt of letter from Frank to his mother, April 9, 1918.
[11] Hall. *The Balloon Buster.* p. 54–55.
[12] Arizona State Library, Archives and Public Records, History and Archives Division. MG-64 Frank Luke Junior Collection. Excerpt of a letter from Frank to his mother, May 11, 1918.
[13] Marie Jackson Collection.
[14] Arizona State Library, Archives and Public Records, History and Archives Division. MG-64 Frank Luke Junior Collection.
[15] Arizona State Library, Archives and Public Records, History and Archives Division. MG-64 Frank Luke Junior Collection. Excerpt from a letter from Frank to his mother on July 5, 1918.
[16] Arizona State Library, Archives and Public Records, History and Archives Division. MG-64 Frank Luke Junior Collection.
[17] Air Force Historical Research Agency, Microfilm 30531 Index 1383. Diary of Corporal Walter S. Williams, 27th Squadron, US Air Service, AEF Diary of Walter Williams. Henceforth referred to as the Williams Diary.
[18] NARA. Gorrell's, History of the 27th Squadron.
[19] Bernard Kelly, *The Denver Post—Empire Magazine.* "Colorado's Lone World War Ace: The Jerry Vasconcells Story." p. 6.
[20] Hartney. *Up and at 'Em.* p. 174.

[21] University of Massachusetts. W. E. B. Du Bois Library, Special Collections and University Archives. Massachusetts Agricultural College War Service Records—Ivan Andrew Roberts.

[22] NARA. Zinn's responsibilities are spelled out in Gorrell's. While there is no specific reference to him sending Wehner and Luke to the front, it was his responsibility to do so—and one of the reasons he remained after the war to search for the men he had sent out to their deaths.

[23] Archibald. *Heaven High, Hell Deep.* pp. 100–102.

[24] Phillips Exeter Academy. Student records for Joseph Wehner. Joe's grades dropped to four Cs, one D and one E. Though a D at Exeter was still considered a passing grade, Joe stayed in a scholarship dorm, Abbot Hall. His grades may have been so low that he was forced to move on.

[25] The Museum of Flight. Dahlberg Center for Military Aviation History, the Joseph Wehner Collection. Excerpt from a letter from Berlin on August 29, 1916, to Joe's sister Hazel.

[26] Kloss "Joe Wehner, the Other Half of the Famous Balloon Busters." *Over the Front.* pp. 122–126. This article provides the basis of much of the material on Joseph Wehner's background. Additional information was obtained from Phillips Exeter Academy Yearbook, 1916.

[27] NARA. Records Group 65, Justice Department Field Reports, Joseph Fritz Wehner.

[28] Courtesy of Walter Kloss, from the Wehner family collection of Joe's correspondence.

Chapter Six

Note: Opening quotation is from an article in The Cross and Cockade Journal *(Spring 1960): p. 6.*

[1] Hartney. *Up and at 'Em.* pp. 175–176.

[2] Hartney. *Up and at 'Em.* p. 240.

[3] Williams Diary. This was found in the postscript section where Walter Williams was attempting to write a formal history of the Fighting Eagles.

[4] NARA. Combat Report from Donald Hudson.

Per Lieutenant Donaldson's report of the engagement:
Protection for photographic machine. Met Salmson at 7 h 50 and went with Salmson into the lines going north. We made three circuits around Oulchy going into Germany and coming back over our lines in big circles. As we went in for the

fourth time. We were about half a mile from the Salmson and seven Huns came down on us from above. One got on my tail and I dived and he followed at about 2000 meters. I fell with a spin and he left me. We were about 4000 meters when the fight started. After shaking the Hun I looked around but could see none of the rest of the formation so came back over the lines. Came back at an altitude of 1000 meters and was archied with blast archied for about 4 or 5 minutes. The scrap started about 8 h 45 behind the German lines. The Huns came upon us at about 200 meters above us and to our left about that far, coming straight towards us head on. They turned and dove on our tails. I first pulled up and fired at them as they went out when the one got on my tail I dove and he followed. One gun hammed and I could not fix it at all. I landed at our Airdrome at 9 hr 05.

5 Hartney. *Up and at 'Em.* pp. 241–43. This description is quoted as presented in the Hartney version of events. However in cross-referencing this with Frank's and Bailey's, *Over the Front,* Hartney seems to have described a crash scene that simply was not possible. The two planes that Donald Hudson had hit crashed a short distance apart. They did not collide. It is entirely possible that given the position of the wreck and the condition of the site, that it appeared that there were two aircraft in the wreckage, but there was most certainly only one.

6 Hartney. *Up and at 'Em.* pp. 243–44. The date that Hartney uses in his account, written decades after the events, was August 1. The account had to have taken place on or about August 3. This is substantiated with the account in the article by Tom Mahoney. "Alvin York and Frank Luke: Legendary WWI Heroes." *American Legion Magazine* (November 1968): 22–23, 50–53.

7 Missouri Historical Society, Joe Bronz Album.

8 Archibald. *Heaven High, Hell Deep.* pp. 123–124.

9 Guttman. *Spad XII/XIII Aces of World War One.* p. 7.

10 United States Air Force Academy SMS 231 John Sherry Collection.

11 Williams Diary. This event is also covered Hudson's *Hostile Skies, a Combat History of the American Air Service in WWI.* The biggest discrepancy is that the date of the change of command in one account is August 20 and in the other it is August 22. Ironically, Hudson references the Williams diary extensively. The discrepancy could be because the formal document outlining the change of command could have been typed up two days after the fact.

12 The details of the Liberty Parties come from NARA, Gorrell's Reports in the section on the History of the 27th Squadron. The Williams Diary serves as a source for the sounding of reveille as part of the Grant regime of command. Needless to say, this army formality did not sit well with the enlisted ranks.

13 The Lafayette Foundation. Letter to Cliff Nelson.

14 Missouri Historical Society, Joe Bronz Album.

[15] NARA, Gorrell's. All of these accounts are detailed in mission reports.

[16] Williams Diary. Entry for September 5.

[17] Harry Starkey Aldrich, "Frank Luke—Balloon Ace." *St. Nicholas* (October 1920): 1095.

[18] Lafayette Foundation. The Wartime Diary of Russell Godine Pruden, Captain, Air Service, U.S. Army, July 16, 1917–March 31, 1919. Adjutant, 27th Squadron, AEF.

[19] Arizona State Library, Archives and Public Records, History and Archives Division. MG-64 Frank Luke Junior Collection.

[20] There are numerous sources, including the Williams Diary and supportive letters that outline when Frank may have gone to the Les Cigognes squadron on his informal visits. Having reviewed the records of the Ministére de la Defénse there are no references to Frank visiting the squadron, but that is not surprising since such a minor occurence would hardly be worth noting in official records.

Chapter Seven

Note: The opening quotation from Rickenbacker comes from his address to the Rotary Club in Phoenix, as reprinted in the Arizona Republic *the following day under the heading "Tribute to the Record of Phoenician."*

[1] Guttman, *Spad XII/XIII Aces of World War One*. p. 68.

[2] Barrett. *Sky Fighters of World War One*. p. 122.

[3] Westermann. *Flak: German Anti-Aircraft Defenses 1914–1945*. Chapter One, "The Great War and Ground-Based Air Defense, 1914–1918," serves as the basis for much of this section. Also reference "Balloon Platoon 148: Recollections of a Luftschiffer." *Der Angriff.* pp. 10–19. Also the book by Bernard Fitzsimons. *Tanks and Weapons of World War One*. pp. 148–149.

[4] Archibald. *Heaven High, Hell Deep*. pp. 186–188.

[5] Guttman. *Balloon Busting Aces of World War 1*. pp. 12–15.

[6] Connors. *Spad Fighters in Action, Squadron Books Aircraft Number 93*; Guttman. *Spad XII/XIII Aces of World War One*. pp. 1–12.

[7] Williams Diary. History of the 27th Squadron, Origins of the Emblem.

[8] Williams Diary. Entry for September 11.

Chapter Eight

Note: Opening quotation courtesy of the Marie Jackson Collection. Sausage Hunting Has Thrills for Group of Birdmen, *by George Seldes.*

[1] Library of Congress. the William Mitchell Collection. Billy Mitchell's diary describes this incident.

2 The Lafayette Foundation. Letter from W. B. Wannamaker to Royal Frey. It is important to note that Wannamaker heard of the story in the POW camp from fellow captured pilots McElvain and Whiton who were witnesses to this. A separate note from McElvain substantiates this account.

3 Kosek. "The Search For Frank Luke." *Over the Front*. p. 335. Also confirmed in Jon Guttman's *Spad XII/XIII Aces of World War One*.

4 NARA. Records Prussian 5th Army War Diary—September 9–12, 1918. Also, references to the American build-up are in the Prussian 5th Army War Diary for the same dates. The Germans were pressing their balloons into service despite the bad weather because they knew an offensive was about to erupt.

5 NARA. Gorrell's. Combat Report from Frank Luke:

Lt. Frank Luke reports:
Saw 3 E.A. near Lavigneulle and gave chase following them directly east towards Pont-a-Moussen where they disappeared towards Metz. Saw enemy balloon at Marienville. Destroyed it after three passes at it. Each within a few yards of the balloon. The third pass was made when the balloon was very near the ground. Both guns stopped so pulled off to one side. Fixed left gun and turned about to make one final effort to burn it, but saw it had started the next instant it burst into great flames and dropped on to the winch, destroying it. The observer Joseph M. Fox who saw the burning said he though several were killed when it burst into flames so near the ground. There was a good field near our balloons, so landed for confirmation. Left field and started back when my motor began cutting out. Returned to same field and there found out my motor could not be fixed, so returned by motor cycle. Attached you will find confirmation from Lt. Fox and Lt. Smith. Both saw burning.

6 Guttman. "Balloon Buster." *Aviation Heritage*. p. 50. Klemm is mentioned as a "jumper" in the NARA holdings for the Records Prussian 5th Army War Diary—September 12, 1918.

7 The Lafayette Foundation, the Royal Frey Collection substantiates this account, as do the post-war writings of Harold Hartney. The Craig Herbert letter to Royal Frey on June 27, 1952, states, "As I recall Frank Luke landed in a shell-torn field near our balloon, either once or twice, narrowly escaping death from low hanging 'phone wires. On one such occasion it sees he was forced down disabled by either anti-aircraft fire or bullets. He borrowed a blanket and slept by the plane overnight. Unable to fly off again we sent him to the rear in the sidecar of one of our motorcycles. This was around September 12th—we were located somewhere north of Griscourt—we confirmed that Luke had just burned a balloon—in fact it was the only German balloon up that day."

A subsequent letter written a year later in the holdings of the U.S. Air Force Historical Association by Mr. Herbert states that he was responsible for giving Frank the tactics for dealing with the balloons. This letter, full of errors (including that Frank spent two nights with the balloon company), is largely disregarded.
8 Driggs. *Heroes of Aviation.* p. 280. Normally I discount Driggs's accounts. I did check with the NARA holdings for the U.S. Signal Corps and found a reference to his being present at the First Pursuit Group on this day—that is if his itinerary held. If that was the case, he may have indeed witnessed this or obtained his quote from a witness.

Chapter Nine

Note: *Opening quotation courtesy of the Marie Jackson Collection.*

1 Hartney. *Up and at 'Em.* p. 249. Hartney's book relates a long dialogue with Lieu-tenants Clapp and Grant discussing how if Luke does not get a balloon at Boinville he will get transferred out of the squadron. This makes little sense in light of the events that had taken place earlier on the 12th. Given that Hartney's account was written many years later and that his earlier newspaper accounts do not relate this discussion, I have omitted it here.
2 NARA Prussian 5th Army War Diary. Kommandeur der Luftschiffer H. Qu., den 14. 9. 1918. 5. Armee. Ballonzentrale. Nr. I. 1987/18. Tagesmeldung.
3 NARA. Gorrell's. Combat Reports for Dawson, Lennon and Luke.

Combat Report   September 14, 1918
Lt. Leo H. Dawson reports:
I left the formation over Moranville and attacked an enemy balloon near Boinville, while diving at it three times and empting both guns. Tracers entered it in great numbers. The observer jumped and the balloon was hauled down in a very flabby condition. White flaming balls were fired at me. Lieutenant Luke was below the balloon firing at the Archie battery. I left after the balloon had struck the ground it was not sent up again, at the time I left, twenty minutes later. From what I could observe it was very badly shot up. Confirmation requested.

Combat Report   September 14, 1918
Lt. T.F. Lennon reports:
Followed Lt. Luke and Dawson. Saw them attack enemy balloon in vicinity of Boinville. Observed that the observer jumped and enemy archie began to burst. The balloon flattened out and went to the ground. I dove on it and fired 50 rounds from each gun. The last I saw of the balloon it was on the ground in a very flabby condition. Confirmation requested.

Combat Report   September 14, 1918
Lt. Frank Luke reports:
Left formation at Abucourt and attacked an enemy balloon near Boinville. Dove at it six times at close range. Had two stoppages with left gun which carried incendiary bullets, and after fixing both, continued the attack. After about 75 rounds being left in the right gun, I attacked an archie battery at the base of balloon. Am sure that my fire took effect as the crew scattered. After my first attack on balloon, the observer jumped. The last I saw of the balloon, it was on the ground in a very flabby condition. Confirmation requested.

[4] Rickenbacker and Driggs. *Fighting the Flying Circus*. pp. 290–291.

[5] Thayer. *America's First Eagles. The Official History of the U.S. Air Service, A.E.F. (1917–1918)*. p. 3. Note: This set of wings, attributed as Frank Luke's, is on display at the Museum of Flight in Seattle, Washington.

[6] Kloss. "Joe Wehner, the Other Half of the Famous Balloon Busters." *Over the Front*. p. 137.

[7] *The Arizona Republican*. "Waiting for Luke During the Night the Famous Boy Aviator Did Not Return." November 1, 1918.

[8] Marie Jackson Collection. Article from *Sky Fighters*, 1935, a print of a letter from Joe Wehner. Several of the minor facts presented in the preface of the article have confirmed that this was written, indeed, by Joe Wehner, though never for publication purposes.

[9] NARA. Gorrell's. Combat Report, Frank Luke.

Combat Report   September 14, 1918
Lt. Frank Luke reports:
I and Lt. Wehner were to leave with formation, dropping out at Buzy to attack enemy balloon. By orders of the C.O. on arriving at Buzy left formation and brought down enemy balloon in flames. While fixing my gun so I could attack another nearby balloon, eight enemy Fokkers dropped down on me. Dove and pulled away from them. They scored several good shots on my plane. I saw Lt. Wehner drive through enemy formation and attack two enemy planes on my tail, but as my guns were jammed did not turn, as I was not sure it was an allied plane until he joined me later. You will find attached confirmation of balloon.

The confirmation of Ballonzug 14 being posted at Buzy was done through NARA holdings for the Prussian 5th Army War Diary.

[10] Williams Diary. Entry for September 14. Note: Evidence in the Jasta War Chronology suggests that there is a chance Wehner only inflicted enough damage to force the Germans to withdraw and did not shoot them down. There simply are no missing unaccounted-for aircraft that Wehner can get the confirmation on.

[11] Cooke. *Sky Battle, 1914–1918—The Story of Aviation in World War I.* p. 259.
[12] Hartney. *Up and at 'Em.* pp. 250–252.
[13] NARA. Prussian 5th Army War Diary—September 14, 1918. Combat Reports for the evening list the losses.

Chapter Ten

[1] NARA. Gorrell's. Combat Report for Hoover, Clapp, Wehner, and Luke.

Combat Report   September 15, 1918
Lt. W.J. Hoover and Lt. Frank Luke report:
Patrol to attack balloon at Etain. Only three machines left of patrol by the time we reached Etain. Then Lieut. Clapp dropped out on account of engine trouble. Balloon was pulled down. Archie very accurate above balloon. We were followed the entire time by six Fokkers. They had at least 500 meters altitude on us, but did not attack.

Combat Report   September 15, 1918
Lt. W.J. Hoover reports:
Flew to Mars-le-Tour. No balloon up, so patrolled to Etain for another. Lt. Luke left the formation to attack the balloon south of Boinville. Saw the balloon go up in flames and drop just south of Boinville. Patrolled the lines three times, followed up and down by 7 Fokkers, higher and in Germany. On the way back I saw the wood North of Three Fingered Lake being heavily shelled, also the town of Fresnes and other little towns near this place along the ridge. I did not notice any movement of troops.

Combat Report   September 15, 1918
Lt. K.S. Clapp reports:
Owing to darkness, only artillery action could be observed. Could not observe any troop movements. Saw a little artillery action E. of Verdun but it was not excessive. There was much greater activity in the direction of Conflans. Lieut. Wehner of this patrol fired about 100 rounds at an enemy battery, which was in action.

Combat Report   September 15, 1918
Lt. Frank Luke reports:
I left formation and attacked an enemy balloon near Boinville in accordance with instructions and destroyed it. I fired 125 rounds. I then attacked another balloon near Bois d'Hingry, and fired 50 rounds into it. Two confirmations requested.

Combat Report   September 15, 1918

Lt. J.F. Wehner Reports:

Left airdrome after formation expecting to pick them up on the front. I was instructed to attack enemy balloons with Lt. Luke, so I stayed at a low altitude. Saw formation coming North so I flew towards the Hun lines to pick up a balloon. Attacked at Hun balloon N.E. of Verdun and S.W. of Spincourt, at about 17 h 10 bringing it down. I was forced to pull off immediately as a formation of five Hun planes were trying to cut me off and my guns were empty. The Hun planes were both Fokker and Albatross. I maneuvered down towards Chambley where the Huns left me, after seeing a formation of French Spads approaching. I fired approximately 100 rounds in to balloon.

Also used was the recommendation for Frank's Distinguished Service Cross from Microfilm B0036. Alford, James S. Major. *The History of the 1st Fighter Group, Volume 1—The 1st Pursuit Group in World War I. Chronology of the First Pursuit Group, 1918.* Air University Archives.

[2] NARA Gorrell's. Combat Report for Joseph Wehner.

Combat Report   September 15, 1918

Lt. J.F. Wehner reports:

Left airdrome 15 minutes after the patrol and few East expecting to pick them up near Verdun. I did not see the formation so I flew towards a Hun balloon at Etain which Lt. Luke and I were detailed to straff (sp). When about a mile away I saw the balloon go up in flames, so I headed towards a second balloon further south, flying at an altitude of 1500 meters. There was considerable A.A. fire near the place where the balloon had burned. Changed my direction hoping to pick up Lt. Luke. Saw him near Rouvres heading back to our lines pursued by seven or eight planes of the Fokker and Albatross type. Peaked at them opening up with both guns. Shot at several in the rear of the Hun formation. Brought down a Fokker near Waroq, which was on Lt. Luke's tail. It fell off into a spiral, sideslip and then spun into the ground, crashing. I then shot at an Albatross also on Lt. Luke's tail. It turned and started towards the ground in a steep dive. The rest of the Hun planes pursued us to our lines then turned back. Two confirmations requested.

[3] Note. Joe's machine guns were empty at this point.

[4] *New York Times.* "Frank Luke: Seventeen Days, Eighteen Huns." May 25, 1919. This report is important because it was given by Major Hartney just a few months after the war and is believed to be a more accurate account than that provided in *Up and at 'Em* decades later.

[5] Tegler "A New Hampshire Pursuit Pilot: A Taped Interview with F. I. Ordway of the 27th Pursuit Squadron." *The Cross and Cockade Journal.* p. 228.

[6] *The Rocky Mountain News.* "An Arizona War Eagle." July 24, 1927.

[7] Library of Congress. The William Mitchell Collection. Billy Mitchell's diary describes his request to have balloons taken out and how Hartney behaved. A counter-perspective is offered by Hartney in *Up and at 'Em.* This is a distillation of these two accounts. Note: The Americans did not invent this tactic but because intelligence was erratically shared among the Allies, it was new to them.

[8] Hartney. *Up and at 'Em.* pp. 253–255.

[9] Marie Jackson Collection. Hartney is quoted in *The Arizona Republican.* "Official Communication Tells of How Frank Battled to His Death on the Western Front." It is also retold in *New York Times.* "Frank Luke: Seventeen Days, Eighteen Huns." May 25, 1919.

[10] The Lafayette Foundation. Letter to Royal Frey from Bernard Mangels, August 11, 1963.

[11] NARA Gorrell's. Combat Report for Frank Luke.

Combat Report   **September 15, 1918**

Lt. Frank Luke reports:

Patrolled to observe enemy activity. Left a little after formation expecting to find it on the lines. On arriving there I could not find formation, but saw artillery firing on both sides, also saw ma light about 500 meters. At first I thought it was an observation machine, but on nearing it, I found it was a Hun balloon, so I attacked and destroyed it. I was archied with white fire and machine guns were very active. Returned very low. Saw thousands of small lights in the woods north of Verdun. On account of darkness coming on I lost my way and landed in a French wheat field at Agers at about 21 h 30. Balloon went down in flames at 19 h 30.

[12] Recommendation for Frank's Distinguished Service Cross from Microfilm B0036. Alford, James S. Major. *The History of the 1st Fighter Group, Volume 1—The 1st Pursuit Group in World War I. Chronology of the First Pursuit Group, 1918.* Air University Archives.

"On September 15, this officer attacked a balloon in the vicinity of Boinville and destroyed it. This combat was confirmed by officers of this Group in the vicinity at that time . At 18 h 50 a call was made by the chief of Air Services to this squadron, requesting planes to get data on a counterattack in progress near Chatillon-sous-les-Cotes. Lieutenant Luke answered this call. He became lost in the darkness north of Verdun but discovered a German balloon using a light signal. He attacked this balloon in the dark but was successful in destroying it. Confirmation of this attack is being forwarded by the French."

[13] Williams Diary, entry for September 15. Also used was material from the Lafayette Foundation. The Wartime Diary of Russell Godine Pruden,

Captain, Air Service, U.S. Army, July 16, 1917–March 31, 1919. Adjutant, 27th Squadron, AEF.

[14] NARA. Prussian 5th Army War Diary—September 15, 1918. Combat Reports for the evening list the losses. Also the entries corresponding to this date from Nachrichtenblatt der Luftftreittrafte.

[15] Guttman. "Balloon Buster." *Aviation Heritage*. p. 50.

Chapter Eleven

[1] Williams Diary, entry for September 16. Also used was material from the Lafayette Foundation. The Wartime Diary of Russell Godine Pruden, Captain, Air Service, U.S. Army, July 16, 1917–March 31, 1919. Adjutant, 27th Squadron, A.E.F.

[2] Marie Jackson Collection. Hartney's quotation is from *The Arizona Republican*, "Official Communication Tells of How Frank Battled to His Death on the Western Front." It is also retold in *New York Times*. "Frank Luke: Seventeen Days, Eighteen Huns." May 25, 1919.

[3] Library of Congress. The William Mitchell Collection. Billy Mitchell's diary.

[4] Hartney. *Up and at 'Em.* p. 256.

[5] Rickenbacker and Driggs. *Fighting the Flying Circus.* Page 286.

[6] NARA. Gorrell's. Combat Reports for Wehner and Luke.

Combat Report   **September 16, 1918**
Lt. F.F. Wehner reports:
Patrol to strafe balloons. Flew North-East passing over Verdun and attacked a balloon in the vicinity of Reville with Lt. Luke at 19 h 05. We each fired one burst when I observed that it instantly caught fight. The observer jumped but was burned by the flaming balloon before reaching the ground. I headed towards the Meuse river trying to pick up another balloon but could not locate one so headed towards Verdun. On the way back saw a fire in the vicinity of Remagne which evidently was Lt. Luke's second balloon. While waiting for Lt. Luke near Verdun saw red flare near Mangiennes thinking it was our pre-arranged signal from Lt. Luke, I headed in that direction. Saw balloon just above the tree tops near Mangiennes and brought it down in flames with one burst at 19 h 35. Anti-aircraft very active. Two confirmations requested.

Combat Report   **September 16, 1918**
Lt. Frank Luke reports:
Patrol to strafe balloons—Everything very carefully arranged. Lt. Wehner and I left airdrome passing over Verdun. We attacked balloon in vicinity of Reville at

19 h 03. Both Lt. Wehner and I shot a burst into it. It burst into flames and fell on observer who had jumped a few seconds before. We started for another balloon in the vicinity of Remagne. I attacked and destroyed it. It burst into flames on the ground burning winch. The anti-aircraft guns were very active scoring several good hits on my plane. The last I saw of Lt. Wehner he was going in a south-easterly direction after the first balloon went down. I shot at supply trains on my way back. Two confirmations requested.

7 Hartney. *Up and at 'Em.* p. 260.

8 Hartney. *Up and at 'Em.* p. 260. *Note:* Hartney has the day wrong in his recounting of this demonstration. All other accounts point to September 16, but Hartney incorrectly lists it as September 15.

9 NARA Prussian 5th Army War Diary. Kommandeur der Flieger 5. Armee Ia Nr. 15330. H. Qu., den 16. 9. 1918. 1. Abendmeldung.

10 Ibid.

11 Guttman. "Balloon Buster." *Aviation Heritage.* p. 50.

Chapter Twelve

Note: Opening quotation taken from a letter in the Joseph Wehner Collection, the Museum of Flight, Dahlberg Center for Military Aviation History.

1 Williams Diary. September 17.

2 Lafayette Foundation. The Wartime Diary of Russell Godine Pruden, Captain, Air Service, U.S. Army, July 16, 1917–March 31, 1919. Adjutant, 27th Squadron, AEF.

3 *New York Times.* "Frank Luke: Seventeen Days, Eighteen Huns." May 25, 1919.

4 NARA. Nachrichtenblatt der Luftftreittrafte. Activity of the Airforces; Daily Reports for the week from 18th till 24th September 1918.

5 Wyngarden. *Jagdgeschwader Nr. II Geschwader 'Berhold'.* p. 34; Franks and Wyngarden. *Fokker D.VII Aces of World War 1.* p. 67.

6 NARA. Gorrell's. Combat Report by Frank Luke.

Combat Report
Lt. Wehner and I left the airdrome at 16 h 00 to spot enemy balloons. Over St. Mihiel we saw two German balloons near Labeuville. We maneuvered in the clouds and dropped down, burning both. We were then attacked by a number of E.A. The main formation attacking Lt. Wehner who was above and on one side. I started climbing to join the fight when two E.A. attacked me from the rear. I turned on them, opening with both guns on the leader. We came head on until a few yards within each other when my opponent turned on one side in a nose dive, and I saw him crash

on the ground. I then turned on the second, shot a short burst and he turned and went into a dive. I saw a number of E.A. above, but could not find Lt. Wehner, so turned and made for our lines. The above fight occurred in the vicinity of St. Hilaire. On reaching our balloon lines, flew east. Saw archie on our side, flew towards it and found an enemy observation machine. I gave chase with some other Spads, and we got him off from his lines, and after a short encounter he crashed within our lines, southeast of Verdun. Lt. Wehner is entitled to share in the victories over both balloons. Confirmation requested, two balloons and three planes.

The location of Rattentaut was determined from reviewing the Signal Corps photo descriptions of the location. These were from NARA Signal Corps Photographs—Records Group 65.

[7] Guttman. "France's Foreign Legion of the Air." *Windsock International.* p. 16.

"On September 18, Gaudermen and I encountered a German photographic plane whose pilot evidently had orders to get pictures. The pilot was very sharp .... we spent two hours stalking that two-seater, which just kept turning away whenever we presented a threat, then would return to his work when we seemed to give up. After three attempts we finally cut him off. At the same time, an American Spad came up under his tail, also shooting, and landed where the German fell. Gaudermen and I were credited with this 'plane as was the American, 2/Lt. Frank Luke Jr. of the 27th Aero Squadron, who was to go one to become one of the leading American aces."

[8] NARA. Records Group 92, Burial Records. Joseph Fritz Wehner.

[9] Thayer. *America's First Eagles. The Official History of the U.S. Air Service, A.E.F. (1917-1918).* p. 3.; Kloss. "Joe Wehner, the Other Half of the Famous Balloon Busters." *Over the Front.* p. 137.

[10] Smithsonian. A19500169000AER01 and A19500169000AER02. Aircraft material (fabric) cut from airplanes by Frank Luke, Jr. Once on display at the National Aeronautical Museum (precursor to the Air and Space Museum) two large pieces of the plane that Frank shot down on September 16 have been placed in storage since the 1960s. Another piece of the Halberstadt used to be on display in the Arizona State Capitol, as well, and is most likely the one that Frank cut himself.

[11] *The Arizona Republic.* "Luke Remembered." May 10, 1965.

Chapter Thirteen

Note: Opening quotation taken from Marie Jackson Collection.

[1] Hartney. *Up and at 'Em,* 1940. Page 266.

[2] NARA. Gorrell's. Combat Report, Frank Luke Jr., September 18, 1918.

3 Arizona State University, Department of Archives and Special Collections. Historical Summary: Frank Luke Jr. Arizona's Great Ace.
4 Rickenbacker and Driggs. *Fighting the Flying Circus.* p. 296. Other accounts have Frank bragging that he was going to avenge the loss of Wehner. When traced, however, none of these accounts can be attributed to a witness who was present at the affair.
5 *The Arizona Republican.* "Frank Luke Jr. Sets High Record; Balloons Harder to Down Even Than Airplane." September 19, 1918.
6 *The Arizona Republican.* "Frank Luke Jr. Is Now Ranked as Ace of Air." September 21, 1918.
7 *The Arizona Gazette.* "Aces Up!" February 17, 1928.
8 *The Arizona Republican.* "Frank Luke Jr. Is Now Ranked As Ace of Air." September 21, 1918.
9 Arizona State Library, Archives and Public Records, History and Archives Division. MG-64 Frank Luke Junior Collection, Series 1.
10 Franzi and Luke. "WWI Ace Frank Luke, An Enigmatic American Hero." *Arizona Highways.* p. 22.
11 Williams Diary. September 23.
12 Lafayette Foundation. The Wartime Diary of Russell Godine Pruden, Captain, Air Service, U.S. Army, July 16, 1917–March 31, 1919. Adjutant, 27th Squadron, AEF. Also substantiated by comments in the Williams Diary entry on September 24.

Chapter Fourteen

1 The background material on Ivan Roberts comes from a wide range of sources. The most useful source was the University of Massachusetts, W.E.B. Du Bois Library, Special Collections and University Archives. "Massachusetts Agricultural College in the War," *The M.A.C. Bulletin,* Vol. XIII, May 1921, No. 4, pp. 60–61 Ivan Andrew Roberts—Class of 1920; as well as Massachusetts Agricultural College War Service Records—Ivan Andrew Roberts; and the letters from Thomas Lee Roberts. Also used in this was NARA Records Group 92, Burial Records, Ivan A. Roberts. Numerous newspaper accounts from Ivan's hometown were used to reconstruct his career.
2 Williams Diary. September 25.
3 NARA Gorrell's Battle Order Number Eight and Daily Combat Orders.
4 Wyngarden. *Jagdgeschwader Nr. II Geschwader 'Berhold'.* p. 93.
5 Franks and Wyngarden. *Fokker D VII Aces of World War 1.* pp. 55–59.
6 Kenney. A Flier's Journal. pp. 54–55.
7 Williams Diary. September 26.

[8] The Lafayette Foundation. The serial number information is pulled from Frederick Zinn's notes compiled by Royal Frey.

[9] NARA, Gorrell's Combat Report of Luke, White, Nicholson, and Hoover.

Frank Luke reports:

On patrol to straffe balloons in vicinity of Consenvoye and Sivry, I attacked with two others a formation of vie (5) Fokkers. After firing several short bursts, observed the Hun go down out of control. While at 100 meters I was attacked by two (2) E.A, so I did not see the first E.A. crash. I turned on the other two who were on my tail, getting on the tail of one but guns jammed several times, and after fixing both could only shoot short bursts on account of the several stoppages. (1) One confirmation requested. The last I saw of Lt. Roberts, who was on this patrol with me, was in combat with several Fokkers in the vicinity of Consenveye and Sirvy.

Lt. W.J. Hoover reports:

Stated towards a rendezvous at Forges with a protection patrol. As I approached I observed several bursts of allied archie at an altitude a little below me. I attacked a Rumpler but only got a few rounds into him as 4 Fokkers were diving on me. I dove for home and they did not continue the attack. Having missed the patrol I climbed to 1500 meters and was making a patrol of the sector, when I saw several bursts of archie in the region of Melancourt. Sighted another E.A. (Single seater) and when I attacked he started diving for Germany, I followed him and got in some good bursts. He went down in a straight nose dive to 300 meters, when I pulled out. Was archied on the way home. Once confirmation requested.

Lt. H.W. Nicholson reports:

I was to meet a patrol with Lt. Dawson. This patrol was from the 94th and we were to meet at 1500 meters of Forges at 17 h 50. Patrol arrived about 17 h 58 just as I observed some Huns coming out of Germany. I dove on one of the bi-plane Rumplers, opening fire when about 600 meters from the ground, at about 18 h 00. I fought the machine down to 150 meters were it appeared to down out of control near Forges. I had to turn in order to maneuver with the second bi-plane which was attacking me. After a few bursts I turned away to rejoin the formation. One confirmation requested.

Lt. S.W. White reports:

I fired four (4) good bursts at a balloon N.E. of Verdun and it was pulled down about 6 H 10. North of Verdun I attacked a second balloon. It went down and I did not see it again, as I was driven away by two Hun planes.

[10] NARA. Prussian 5th Army Records. Kommandeur of the fliers 5. Army Ia No. 15471. A.H. Qu., the 26.9.1918. Mittangsmeldung.

[11] The Lafayette Foundation. Letter to Royal Frey from Bernard Mangels. August 11, 1963.

[12] NARA Records Group 92, Burial Records, Ivan A. Roberts.

[13] Hartney. *Up and at 'Em.* p. 268. Note: Hartney claims that if he knew Luke was back early from his leave in Paris he would have not let him fly. Realistically, however, this is revisionist history on the part of Hartney. He had to have known that the Ace of Aces was back—Grant would certainly have said something.

Chapter Fifteen

Note: Opening quotation courtesy of the Marie Jackson Collection. Sausage Hunting Has Thrills for Group of Birdmen, *by George Seldes*

[1] Kosek, John. "The Search for Frank Luke." *Over the Front.* p. 339.

[2] Marie Jackson Collection. Reprint of letter from Alfred Grant to the Luke family.

[3] NARA. Gorrell's. Operations Reports for September 28, 1918.

[4] NARA. Prussian 5th Army Records. Kommandeur of the fliers 5. Qu., the 28.9.1918.

[5] NARA. Gorrell's. Combat Report, Frank Luke, September 28, 1918.

Lt. Frank Luke reports:
I few north to Verdun, crossed the lines at about five hundred meters and found a balloon in its nest in the region of Bantheville. I dove on it firing both guns. After I pulled away it burst into flames. As I could not find any others I returned to the airdrome. One confirmation requested.

[6] The Lafayette Foundation. The Royal Frey Collection. Letter from Bernard Mangels to Royal Frey. This was further substantiated by the Library of Congress, the William Mitchell Collection, Billy Mitchell's War Diary, which corroborates this account.

[7] The Lafayette Foundation. Letter from C.S. Daniel, Adjunct to Captain Grant, to Royal Frey, August 26, 1963.

Chapter Sixteen

Note: Opening quotation is taken from Jon Guttman's article "Balloon Buster," American Heritage Magazine.

[1] Williams Diary. This is taken from the summary portion written after the war by Walter Williams detailing, from his perspective, the death of Frank Luke.

[2] Lafayette Foundation. The Wartime Diary of Russell Godine Pruden, Captain, Air Service, U.S. Army, July 16, 1917–March 31, 1919. Adjutant, 27th Squadron, AEF.

[3] Hartney. *Up and at 'Em.* p. 271.

[4] Ibid.

[5] The Lafayette Foundation. Letter from C.S. Daniel, Adjunct to Captain Grant, to Royal Frey, August 26, 1963.

[6] The Lafayette Foundation. The Royal Frey Collection. There are numerous accounts and variants of this line that appear in a wide range of books. Some say that Grant was going to put Frank up for the Legion of Merit (a French medal) and others have him saying the Congressional Medal of Honor. It is most appropriate that he would have said the DSC. Frank had been put in for his DSC on September 17 by Grant already but it was not an uncommon practice to put someone in for it again, adding Oak Leaf Clusters.

[7] Hartney's description is from *The Arizona Gazette*. "Aces Up!" February 19, 1928.

[8] Hartney. *Up and at 'Em.* p. 272.

[9] The Lafayette Foundation. Letter from C.S. Daniel, Adjunct to Captain Grant, to Royal Frey, August 26, 1963.

[10] Note: Hartney's accounts over the years seem to gloss over the fact that Harold Hartney let Frank into the air on his final flight.

[11] The Lafayette Foundation. The Royal Frey Collection. Letter from the American Balloon Corps Veterans by Craig Herbert, to Royal Frey, June 27, 1962.

[12] The Lafayette Foundation. The Royal Frey Collection. Letter from Karl Axater to Royal Frey December 5, 1963. Numerous variations of this message and how it was delivered have surfaced over the years. While Axater admits his memory is weak, this is probably the best remembrance of the line on the note.

[13] NARA. Prussian 5th Army Records. Kommandeur of the fliers 5. Field Orders. 9.29.1918.

[14] The Lafayette Foundation. POW Report of Granville Woodard.

[15] The Museum of Flight, Dahlberg Center for Military Aviation. Letter written July 22, 1981, from Georges Reguier.

Chapter Seventeen

[1] The Lafayette Foundation. Bernard Mangels' Account from a Letter to Royal Frey on August 11, 1963.

[2] NARA. Prussian 5th Army Record. German Field Orders 29 September 1918.

[3] *The Arizona Republican*. "Waiting for Luke During the Night the Famous Boy Aviator Did Not Return." November 1, 1918.

[4] Rickenbacker and Driggs. *Fighting the Flying Circus.* p. 319.

[5] The Lafayette Foundation. The Royal Frey Collection. Grant's diary entries regarding Luke were provided in letter form to Royal Frey.

6 The Lafayette Foundation. This comes from Jerry Vasconcells' flight log on file with the Foundation. Also this is substantiated by the entries in The Wartime Diary of Russell Godine Pruden, Captain, Air Service, U.S. Army, July 16, 1917–March 31, 1919. Adjutant, 27th Squadron, A.E.F. Vasconcells' binoculars are in the holdings of the Foundation as well.

7 The Lafayette Foundation. Bernard Mangels' Account from a Letter to Royal Frey on August 11, 1963.

8 Ibid.

9 The Lafayette Foundation. Bernard Mangels' Account from a Letter to Royal Frey on September 20, 1963.

10 Brown. "A Grand Old House." *Phoenix* (April 1977): 56.

Chapter Eighteen

1 Williams Diary. October 1, 1918.

2 Marie Jackson Collection.

3 The Lafayette Foundation. Letter from C.S. Daniel, Adjunct to Captain Grant, to Royal Frey, August 26, 1963.

4 Marie Jackson Collection. Letter from Nelson Cliff to Marie Rapson.

5 Archibald. *Heaven High, Hell Deep.* pp. 314–316.

6 *The Arizona Republican.* "Frank Luke Killed in Action." November 26, 1918.

7 NARA. Gorrell's. Also the Library of Congress, *Stars and Stripes.* "Officer Who Sent Aviators to Front Now Seeks Missing. Graves of 70 Fliers Who Failed to Return Found by Captain Zinn." March 28, 1919.

8 Marie Jackson Collection. *The Arizona Republican.* "Hero Medal Has Been Awarded to Frank Luke." April 14, 1919. This article features an interview/letter from Frederick Zinn.

9 NARA Records Group 92, Burial Records, Frank Luke Jr.

10 Microfilm B0036 Alford, James S. Major. *The History of the 1st Fighter Group, Volume 1—The 1st Pursuit Group in World War I. Chronology of the First Pursuit Group, 1918.* Air University Archives.

11 Marie Jackson Collection. *The Arizona Republican.* "Hero Medal Has Been Awarded to Frank Luke." April 14, 1919.

Chapter Nineteen

1 NARA Records Group 92, Burial Records, Frank Luke Jr.

2 Treadwell *America's First Air War.* p. 121.

3 The airfield retained that name until the Navy took it over in 1939.

[4] Microfilm B0036 Alford, James S. Major. *The History of the 1st Fighter Group, Volume 1—The 1st Pursuit Group in World War I. Chronology of the First Pursuit Group, 1918.* Air University Archives.
[5] Marie Jackson Collection.
[6] Separate interview with Charme Kirby and John Luke.
[7] Information on Red Jackson comes from the U.S. Naval Academy, Nimitz Library, Special Collections and Archives Division, William W. Jeffries Memorial Archives, *Lucky Bag* (1919). Marie's life was pieced together from a wide range of source material, including interviews with family members, the Oklahoma Historical Society, interviews with Douglas Jackson and Charme Kirby, and a wealth of genealogical research conducted by Jean Armstrong.
[8] Kloss "Joe Wehner, the Other Half of the Famous Balloon Busters." *Over the Front.* p. 136.
[9] The Lafayette Foundation. Program for burial for Joe Wehner. Program for dedication of the VFW Hall.
[10] NARA Records Group 92, Burial Records, Ivan A. Roberts. The letters of the Roberts family to the Army regarding their son, his dental records, and the search are preserved in this file.

Chapter Twenty

[1] Graham. *The Gold Star Mother Pilgrimages of the 1930's.* The specific information on the Luke and Roberts family trips as part of this program were found in NARA Records Group 92.
[2] *The Arizona Republic.* "Ex-Phoenix Clerk Dies in Coast City." April 15, 1953. Additional information on the life of Bill Elder has been obtained through genealogical research, city directories, etc.
[3] Death certificate, Frank Luke, Arizona State Board of Health. Also information was gathered on this from an interview with John Luke.
[4] *The Arizona Republic.* "A.C. 'Pidge' Pinney, Prominent Sportsman and Merchant Dies." June 26, 1931.
[5] "Interview with Charles R. D'Olive. Formerly Lt. Charles R. D'Olive, 94th Pursuit Squadron, U.S. Air Service." *The Cross and Cockade Journal.* p. 8.
[6] The Lafayette Foundation. The Royal Frey Collection. This serves as the source of the original copies of the material and the supporting correspondence. The public version is referenced via Frey. "A.E.F Combat Airfields and Monuments in France." *Journal of the American Aviation Historical Society.* pp. 195–200.

The following is the text of the 1962 affidavit.
Murvaux Affidavit—1962
At approximately 2:00 P.M. on Sunday, 29 September 1918, an Allied pursuit
plane made a strafing attack on a group of German soldiers in the area of La
Maisonette, a large building on a hillside about two kilometers south-west of
Murvaux, Meuse, France. This attack consisted of several firing passes. During the
attack eleven German soldiers were killed. Although there were Frenchmen in the
area surrounding the building, none were harmed by the attack. These Frenchmen,
engaged in cutting down trees for lumber, were working under the supervision of
German military personnel. La Maisonette still exists of this date, and may be seen
on the hillside in the south-easterly direction about one half kilometer from the
road between Dun-sur-Meuse and Murvaux.
At approximately 3:30 P.M. to 4 P.M. on the same day about three or four Allied
pursuit airplanes engaged and shot down two German airplanes. This aerial battle
took place south-west of Murvaux, in the direction of the town of Liny. Although
we did not see the German aircraft after the crashed to earth, we did see them
go down out-of-control. We believe the aerial battle took place as far away from
Murveaux as Liny, which is approximately six kilometers from Murvaux.
Shortly after sunset on this same day, at approximately 6:30 P.M. to 7:00 P.M., we
saw an Allied pursuit airplane shot down three German observation balloons in
the space of just a few minutes.
The first balloon was destroyed at Villers-devant-Dun, the second at Sassey, the
third near the western edge of Cote St. Germain, about two kilometers west of
Murvaux. During these attacks the airplane was fired upon heavily but did not
appear to have been hit . The airplane then flew eastward from the direction of
Dun-sur-Meuse toward Murvaux at not over 50 meters altitude. As it began to
approach the southern edge of Murvaux, German troops began firing at it with
revolver cannon of approximately 20 mm to 37 mm caliber. One gun was located
on the hillside south of the church at Murvaux, and the other two were situated
on the hillside south of the Cote St. Germain at a spot north of Murvaux. However the aircraft was so low that it appeared difficult to hit it with this cannon fire.
It passed by the church at al altitude which was not much higher than the church
steeple, and then it made a turn to the left around the eastern side of Murvaux and
began flying in the direction form which it had just come. At no time did it fire
it's machineguns at the village. About the time the airplane rolled out of its turn
over the northern edge of the village, the pilot was apparently struck by the enemy
gunfire, for the airplane suddenly went into a glade toward the ground, its engine
still running. It banked slightly to the right, and then landed straight ahead at a

point one kilometer west of Murvaux. When the plane landed, its engine stopped. The terrain where it stopped sloped slightly downhill to the south to a small creek which paralleled the road to the north at about 200 meters distance.

German soldiers immediately headed for the airplane from both Murvaux and Cote St Germain. Since they believed the pilot of the airplane to be the same one who had attacked them so often in the past and who had caused so much damage and destruction to them, they wished to capture him before escaped.

The Germans were very afraid of this man and had previously vowed to shoot him down, if given the opportunity. When they reached the plane about ten minutes after shooting it down, the pilot was gone.

Although it had begun to get dusk, the German soldiers noticed a trail of blood leading from the aircraft southward toward the creek. The wounded pilot had crawled on his hands and knees approximately 75 meters to the creek. We did not know whether it was to get a drink of water because of his pain, to wash his wound, or to hid in the bushes lining the creek. As the German soldiers came down the slope and approached the creek while following the trail of blood, the pilot raised himself from the ground where he had lain wounded, drew his gun and fired it at the German soldiers. He immediately fell to the ground dead. We do not know whether the German soldiers actually called upon him to surrender, but we are definitely certain, beyond any doubt, that they did not fire their guns at the pilot. His last act was one of defiance, and he died as a result of his wound in the air and not as a result of any wounds he received on the ground.

The German solders immediately searched the body and found a notebook in which were notations, apparently made by the pilot, which indicated that he had shot down 24 enemy airplanes and observation balloons. The German commandant of the garrison in Murvaux took the notebook as well as the pilots flying helmet and goggles, and other items in the pockets of the pilot's clothing. A German soldier started to remove the watch from the pilot's wrist, but a German officer told him to leave it on the body. It was about this time that the German commandant made a remark to the effect, "Well, it was about time we got him."

The Germans decided to leave the body lie where it was for the night. They announced, however, that they would shoot any of us Frenchmen who attempted to get to the body or the airplane.

The next morning the Germans ordered one of the men of our village, Monsieur Nicholas Vohner, to take his horse and two-wheeled cart to the spot where the body had lain all night by the creek and bring it back to the village for burial. Mr. Vohner was accompanied by his four year old nephew, Charles Hervieux and Monsieur Delbart Cortine. Five to seven German soldiers accompanied them.

During the time that the body as Murvaux to its grave, both the pilot's features and the wound in his body were clearly seen my many of us in the village . The body had been placed on the wagon on its back in such a manner that we could easily see the face and the opened eyes. The pilot had blue eyes and short-cropped blond hair. His size appeared to have been about average size and height and stock build.

According to what we could see and what Monsieur Vohner told us later that there was only one wound in the body. A large caliber shell had penetrated the chest near the right breast and came out under the left shoulder blade. The wound was a little over an inch in diameter where the projectile had entered the right breast and about two inches in diameter where it had come out of the back.

The body was transported in the wagon eastward along the mains street of the village past the church, around the church on the rear (east) side, and southward up a slope outside of the east wall of the village cemetery. This cemetery was located along the south side of the church on a slight rise which gradually sloped upward to the south. The body was not conducted through the entrance of the cemetery.

The spot chosen for the pilot's burial place was outside of the south wall of the cemetery about 50 feet up the slope and ten feet east of the path. Approximately six months before, the body of a German Army Captain had been removed from the ground where it had been buried in order to return it to Germany, and the ground had not been filled with dirt. So as not to have to dig another grave, the Germans decided to bury the pilot's body in the hole that remained.

One of the French women of the village requested permission to wrap the body in a sheet, but the Germans would not permit her to do so. Nor would they permit any of us French people to conduct any kind of burial service or to get near the scene during the actual burial.

The body was buried sometime between 9:00 A.M. and 10:00 A.M. No casket of any time was used, nor were there any Christian funeral services or rites performed by the Germans for the dead airman. His body was simply placed in the open grave, bare-headed and clothed in the same boots, trousers, and flying jacket as when the pilot died. The grave in which the body was buried was only approximately eighteen inches deep.

After the funeral and on the same day, two allied pursuit airplanes appeared over Murvaux but were driven away by German gunfire from the same weapons used to down the buried flyer. We, French people and the German soldiers in the area, believed that the pilots of these two airplanes were searching for the downed airplane and its pilot.

The next day, Tuesday, 1 October 1918, all the inhabitants of Murvaux were evacuated from the village to Belgium on the orders of the German authorities. At the time we left Murvaux, the downed airplane had already been removed. The mother of Charles Hervieux remembered seeing the Germans hauling the airplane away on a truck.

Two days after the Armistice, on 13 November, we returned to our village. No trace of the airplane could be found, nor did we ever learn what happened to it after the Germans took it form Murvaux. Other than the body in the grave nothing connected with the incident remained.

Early in 1919, some colored men from the United States arrived in Murvaux to remove the body. At the time it was removed from the grave, it was in almost perfect condition except for a small pot on the right cheek where the skin had started to come off. The body appeared about the same as it did on the day that the Germans buried it.

An American lady arrived at the time. She announced herself as the fiancée of an American aviator who had been shot down in the area. She viewed the body and said that it was not her fiancé. Since two other pilots had been shot down and killed in the area of Murvaux, and since the lady did not mention the name of her fiancé we have always believed that her fiancé possible had been one of the two other pilots.

After being removed from the grave, the body was taken away from Murvaux, by the Americans. It was subsequently buried in the US Military Cemetery at Romagne, about 12 kilometers to the southwest of our village. One of the Americans who removed the body is believed to be Sergeant Minot. He was white and from Pennsylvania.

During the time the Americans were here some of them questioned us in what French they could speak and what had happened to the dead pilot, and they asked us for our names. We related to them the same details that appear in this statement.

To the best of our knowledge, none of the people of Murvaux signed any kind of statement as to what happened, or were we requested to sign any statement. If Cortine and Monsieur Vohner ever signed such a statement, we certainly never knew it, nor did we hear them mention it.

The undersigned, who were residents of Murvaux in September, 1918; Leon Henry 28 years of age at the time; Auguste Cuny, 21 years of age at the time; Gabriel Didier, 20 years of age at the time; and Charles Hervieux, 4 years of age at the time, give the above statement of our own free will and swear it true and correct with reference to the details surrounding the death of the Allied airman, later identified as Lieutenant Frank Luke Jr., 27th Aero Squadron, Air Service, AEF.

Leon Henry	August Cuny
Didier Gabriel	Charles Hervieux

Witnesses to the Signatures:

Larue Danielle	Cot Jerte ESC K H: 10 Verdun
2nd Lt. Howard R. Brehme	1406 Broadview (Apt. B) Columbus, Ohio
2nd Lt. Gerald H. Swedlow	162 South Remington Rd., Columbus, Ohio
Major Royal D. Frey	22235 Yellow Springs, Springfield, Ohio

7 *The Arizona Gazette.* "Aces Up!" February 22, 1928.

8 *The Arizona Republic.* "Frank Luke's Buddies to Hold Reunion Here." September 18, 1970. Also the Williams Diary.

9 Wyngarden. *Jagdgeschwader Nr. II Geschwader 'Berhold'.* p. 119.

10 Musciano. *Eagles of the Black Cross.* p. 188.

11 Interview with Walter Kloss.

12 The Lafayette Foundation. The Royal Frey Collection. Correspondence with Bernard Mangels.

13 The Lafayette Foundation.

14 Musciano. *Eagles of the Black Cross.* p. 188.

15 Willard Library Battle Creek, holdings on Frederick Zinn.

16 Hartney. *Up and at 'Em.* p. 276.

17 *The Denver Post—Empire Magazine.* "Colorado's Lone World War Ace: The Jerry Vasconcells Story." p. 6.

18 NARA Records Group 92, Burial Records, Ivan A. Roberts.

19 John Luke Interview.

Author's Afterword

1 Hall. *The Balloon Buster.* pp. 105–106.

2 The Lafayette Foundation.

3 The Lafayette Foundation.

4 Williams Diary.

5 The Lafayette Foundation. Letter to Cliff Nelson.

About the Author

BLAINE L. PARDOE is the author of numerous science-fiction novels and the bestselling office politics book *Cubicle Warfare*. He has appeared on numerous television and radio programs and networks, including *The O'Reilly Report*, *The G. Gordon Liddy Show*, *Good Day New York*, CBS News, and NPR promoting his writing. He has been a guest speaker at the U.S. National Archives, the New York Military Affairs Symposium, and the U.S. Naval Museum. His works have been published in five different languages around the world.

Mr. Pardoe is a graduate of Central Michigan University. He is currently a doctoral student at Argosy University. In his "day job," he works as an associate director in technology at Ernst & Young.

He has spent years researching the life of Frank Luke, Jr. He is currently working on several books, including one on the life and adventures of Frederick Zinn, and another on Bert Hall. He can be reached at bpardoe870@aol.com.